AF619588

HISTORY OF
DELHI SULTANATE

FARHAN FAROOQUI

Published by

Hawk Press
4836/24, Ansari Road, Daryaganj
New Delhi – 110 002
Phones : 9643330713, 91-11-23278618, 91-11-35676207
E-mail: thehawkpress@gmail.com
www.thehawkpress.com

ISBN : 978-93-95034-37-1

Contents

Preface

The Delhi Sultanate was an Islamic empire based in Delhi that stretched over large parts of the Indian subcontinent for 320 years (1206–1526). Five dynasties ruled over the Delhi Sultanate sequentially: the Mamluk dynasty (1206–1290), the Khalji dynasty (1290–1320), the Tughlaq dynasty (1320–1414), the Sayyid dynasty (1414–1451), and the Lodi dynasty (1451–1526). It covered large swathes of territory in modern-day India, Pakistan, Bangladesh as well as some parts of southern Nepal.

The establishment of Delhi Sultanate began with the invasion of Muhammad Ghori. He had brought a large number of slaves and appointment them as officers. When he died in AD 1206 resulted in a scramble for supremacy among his three generals- Qutub-ud-din Aibek (Commander of his army), Tajuddin Yalduz (ruled Karman and Sankuran between Afghanistan and Sind) and Nasiruddin Qubacha (held). Here, we are giving a timeline of Delhi Sultanate in chronological order and causes of decline of Delhi Sultanate.

Under the sultans of the Khalji dynasty (1290–1320), the Delhi sultanate became an imperial power. Ala-al-Din (reigned 1296–1316) conquered Gujarat (c. 1297) and the principal fortified places in Rajasthan (1301–12) and reduced to vassalage the principal Hindu kingdoms of southern India (1307–12). His forces also defeated serious Mongol onslaughts by the Chagatais of Transoxania (1297–1306).

Muhammad ibn Tughluq (reigned 1325–51) attempted to set up a Muslim military, administrative, and cultural elite in the Deccan, with a second capital at Daulatabad, but the Deccan Muslim aristocracy threw off the overlordship of Delhi and set up (1347) the Bahmani sultanate. Muhammad's successor, Firuz Shah Tughluq (reigned 1351–88), made no attempt to reconquer the Deccan.

The emergence of Delhi Sultanate, for the first time, marked the development of an autonomous Muslim power in India. The Delhi Sultanate or the 'Sultanat-e-Dilli' reigned India from 1290 to 1526 AD. Till this time, Delhi has served just as a base for the Muslim powers to rule while, in truest sense, Lahore remained the capital. The Slave dynasty, undoubtedly, made Delhi their capital but it was the rulers of Delhi Sultanate that strengthened the base. The first ruling empire that was part of the Delhi Sultanate was the Khilji dynasty. However, it would be wrong to assume that the Khilji dynasty did not exist in India before 1290. They had captured Bengal whilst Muhammad Ghori had Delhi in the list of his conquests.

The Delhi sultanate administration was governed as per the Muslim laws that were based on the Quran and Sharia. About the Delhi sultanate, there are primary duties of the Sultan and nobles to observe the Islamic laws in the matters of the state. The planned administration has various departments with different ministers appointed to carry specific responsibilities.

—Author

1

Beginning of the Sultanate

Muhammad Ghori established the first real Muslim state in North India. Upon Sultan Ghori's death in 1206, Qutubuddin Aybak, after a brief power struggle, succeeded in establishing himself as ruler of the empire in Afghanistan, Pakistan, and northern India; Ghori's Central Asian possessions had been captured by none other than the Mongol warlord, Genghis Khan.

The areas over which Qutubuddin established his rule were those over which he already exercised power as Sultan Ghori's local receiver-general of periodic exactions and levies. Therefore, although his formal tenure as ruler was only four years, Qutubuddin managed to consolidate the administrative system that was established by his predecessor Sultan Ghori. This was achieved despite his having to quell rebellions by nobles like Taj- ud-din Ildiz and Nasiruddin Qubachah. Qutubuddin ruled initially from Lahore and later moved the capital to Delhi; he is hence considered the first Muslim ruler of South Asia. Qutubuddin Aybak initiated the construction of Delhi's earliest Muslim monuments, the Quwwat-ul-Islam mosque and the Qutub Minar. Historical records compiled by Muslim historian Maulana Hakim Saiyid Abdul Hai attest to the iconoclasm of Qutubuddin Aybak. The first mosque built in Delhi. These were completed by his successor, Iltutmish. Aibak, was otherwise known as "Lakh Baksh" or "giver of hundred thousands" because of his generosity. He was thus a pious Muslim, praised by contemporary Muslim clerics. He also patronized Nizami and Fakhr-i-Mudabbir, both of whom dedicated their works to Aibak. Tazul Maasir is a work primarily dealing with Aybak.

Death and Succession

Qutubuddin died accidentally in 1210. While he was playing a game of polo on horseback (polo aka chougan in India), his horse fell and Qutubuddin was impaled on the pommel of his saddle. He was buried near the Anarkali bazaar in Lahore. Qutubuddin Aybak's son Aram, died in 1211 CE, so Shams-ud-din Iltutmish, another ex-slave of Turkic ancestry who was married to Qutb-ud-din's daughter, succeeded him as Sultan of Delhi.

INDIAN CAMPAIGNS OF MUHAMMAD GHORI AND HIS OBJECTIVES

After consolidating his hold over the kingdom of Ghazni, Muhammad Ghori directed his attention towards the conquest of India. Like Mahmud of Ghzni, he also led several expeditions over a long period of thirty years. He was an ambitious and capable military general, though not a genius like Mahmud, his main objectives was to establish an empire in India.

The expansion of Islam and his ambition to glorify his name through his military exploits could be said to be his secondary aims. Loot and plunder was definitely not his aim Albeit he took care to acquire enough gold and silver as booty or tribute from the vanquished chiefs. It helped him in raising a strong army for the defence of his Afghan dominions against the onslaught of Khwarizm Shahs.

As a shrewd empire-builder. Muhammad Ghori did not purse his campaigns ruthlessly nor in quick succession. Instead, He launched every expedition with a set plan to serve his imperial interest and after every conquest, took pains to establish firm military and civil hold over the acquired territories before taking the next step forward. A couple of times, he received crushing defeats at the hands of his enemies; nevertheless, his personal failures and shortcomings in resources did not waver him in his faith as an empire-builder. He displayed an extraordinary patience, courage of conviction and fixity of purpose in the face of difficulties. He fully exploited the weaknesses as well as virtues of his Rajput adversaries and laid the foundations of a powerful Muslim state in Northern India.

AN ESTIMATE OF MUHAMMAD GHORI

Muhammad Ghori was undoubtedly a great ruler of his time. By virtue of his military genius he built up his empire which extended from

Iraq and the Caspian Sea to the Ganga. He was a brave warrior and an able general who knew how to lead and an army ti vivtory against heavy odds. He was fearless and was a born leader, though his army was made up of diverse racial and religious elements such as Arabs, Afghans, Turks and even Hindus, he was able to weld them into a homogeneous force under his bale command. Sultan Ghori appeared in India as a ruthless invader whose only interest was to rob the country of its wealth. Many flourishing cities of India were razed to the ground. So were the temples which were great works of art. Death and desolation marked the trail of Muhammad and his army.

He is still remembered as a breaker of idols and a conqueror with an unbounded lust for wealth. According to Professor Muhammad Habib, "Muhammad was not a fanatic and his expeditions against India were not motivated by religion but love of plunder/" Professor Habib further adds that 'Islam does not sanction plundering raids and vandalism and that Muhammad rendered a disservice to his religion by his acts of barbarism in India." It cannot be denied, however, the Mahmud's expeditions to Indian were promoted both by his lust for plunder as well as his zeal to spread Islam.

His genuine belief in this regard is supported. By the fact that he insisted on breaking the idol of Somnath and refused to listen to the pleadings of Brahmin priests who offered him large amounts of money instead. He took pride in being known as an idol breaker. Mahmud's expeditions to India were considered as Jihad by his court historian Utbi. A strict Sunni himself, he insisted on his Muslim subjects observing the tenets of Islam. Though he was not a nation builder, he certainly deserve a high place in history for paving the way for the establishment of the Sultanate of Delhi which was to rule over Indian for over four centuries.

EXPEDITION OF MUHAMMAD GHORI TO INDIA

Muhammad of Ghori launched expeditions into India, first capturing Multan from a fellow Muslim chief in 1175-76. Three years later he invaded Gujarat and was roundly defeated by the Hindu King. Another three years later, and Shahabuddin Ghori was back to take Peshawar and Sialkot in 1181. Now in alliance with the Hindu Raja of Jammu Vijaya Dev, he attacked Lahore in 1187, which was held by his ancestral enemy, the descendent of Mahmud of Ghazni, and made him prisoner. Mahmud of Ghazni's line of Sultans and Governors became extinguished.

EFFECT AND IMPACT OF MUHAMMAD GHORI'S INVASION ON INDIA

Muhammad Ghori who came as an invader in India had been discussed by many scholars from time to time .The impact of Ghori's invasion on India was immense as his invasions for the first time proved the weakness of Hindu rulers in securing their territories from foreign invasion.

Also for the first time his invasion paved the way for a new dynasty known as the Slave Dynasty.

The third impact which is often associated with Ghori's invasion is that it carried the germs of communalism and anti religious feelings towards the non-Islamic religions. Thus, Muhammad Ghori who came to India in 1175 through Multan, left India after the Battle of Tarain but continued to rule till 1206 till he was assassinated in an upsurge in the western regions of Ghorid Dynasty near Jhelum now located in Pakistan. His incessant invasions opened the doors of India to all foreign rulers in future.

INVASION OF MUHAMMAD GHORI

Several invasions were carried out by Muhammad Ghori, who was an ambitious ruler and the brother of Ghiyas-ud-din Muhammad. Muhammad Ghori wanted to expand his empire for power and glory. He was the governor and general under the Ghori dynasty.

Unlike his elder brother, who tried to extend the empire towards the west, Muhammad Ghori, wanted to expand his empire towards the east.

There are a series of invasion by Muhammad Ghori which led to the establishment of Turkish rule in India. Muhammad Ghori first conquered part of Khorasan from the Seljuks and then began a series of campaigns in India.

His first Indian expeditions were the foundations of Mohammedan rule in India. He reduced Sindh and Multan in the course of two expeditions and even made an unsuccessful attack on Bhima Deva Chalukya of Gujarat.

He had already got possession of Peshawar and Punjab and the whole of Sindh down to the seacoast. Thereafter, he acquired and strengthened the fort of Sialkot and lastly he defeated and captured Khushru Malik, the last member of the house of Ghazni. Thus, Ghori dynasty became the lords of the Punjab. Muhammad Ghori now possessed the whole line of the Indus River down to the sea. Then he started strengthening his Indian base and prepared his eastern frontier town of Sirhind. He had got rid himself of all Muslim rivals, had reorganised his forces and could now face the Rajputs of Hindustan. Muhammad Ghori's preparations alarmed the great Prithviraj Chauhan, the ruler of Delhi and Ajmer.

At that time, the most powerful of Rajputanas were Jai Chandra of Kanauj and Prithviraj of Delhi but their jealousy and mutual hatred prevented them from offering a united resistance to the invader. Muhammad Ghori had his first battle with Prithviraj in 1191 AD. In this first invasion, Ghori confronted Prithviraj at Tarain near Thaneswar. In this battle, the Hindu chief was assisted by his Rajputs brothers his rival of Kanauj.

Ghori himself was wounded in this battle and had to be carried away from the field. The Muslim army broke away in a panic and was pursued for forty miles by the winners.

The Rajputs besieged Sirhind and, after a long blockade, got favourable terms from the garrison. Muhammad Ghori returned with even a larger army in the next year in 1992 AD. He met with the opposition Prithviraj as the head of a large Rajput alliance and with numerous horses and elephants. But Prithviraj was defeated in this battle.

The fall of Prithviraj was adopted as a tactics by the Mohammedans and made the Hindus feel suddenly assaulted and they started to think that they were fleeing from the field. Samarsi of Chitor, the brother-in-law of Prithviraj and known for his wisdom and bravery, and Govind Rai, his brother, were both slain.

Prithviraj himself fled from the field, but was taken back and miserably executed. The victory was followed by the quick reduction of Samana, Hansi and other places in the neighbourhood. Muhammad Ghori then captured Ajmer which was the chief capital of the enemy and gave it to the charge of a natural son of Prithvi Raj on condition of his paying tribute.

He returned to Ghazni leaving his favourite slave, Qutub-Ud-Din Aibak, in charge of the Conquest of Ajmer. The latter quickly captured Meerut, Aligarh and Delhi, the last of which he made his head-quarters. Shortly afterwards he extinguished Hindu rule in Ajmer and annexed it permanently to the Muslim dominion.

The next target of Muhammad Ghori became Kanauj. He attacked Kanauj in 1193 and perished the Ganges. The king Jai Chandra was defeated near Chandwar. Then Ghori advanced to Varanasi which was the second capital of the Gaharwars and destroyed its temples. According to the

Mohammedan chroniclers, all the country up to Varanasi was captured and all the Hindu coins were re struck with the name of the conqueror. Muhammad Ghori made Qutub-ud-Din the viceroy of his all his conquests in Hindustan as he was a very capable ruler. In the meantime, a Turkish-Afghan adventurer in the service of Muhammad Ghori, by name Muhammad Bin Bakhtiyar Khilji, who had gained fame under Qutub-Ud-Din, attacked Bihar in 1197 A.D. He rooted out easily the Pala dynasty and collapsed the Buddhism that had its stronghold there. This expedition continued up to Bengal and attacked the aged Rai Lakshmana Sena of Gaur at his capital, Nuddea (Navadwipa).

Muhammad destroyed Nuddea, the home of Sanskrit learning, and made Lakhnauti his capital in 1199 AD. Muhammad Ghori thought of extending his arms to the region of the Himalayas but his attempt proved futile and he had to return after great loss. Muhammad Ghori desired to expand his kingdom in the west and invaded Khwarizm with a huge force but he sustained a disastrous defeat and had to escape with his life.

Tajuddin Eldoz, a slave of Ghori who was in charge of Ghazni, shut its gates against his master. The defeat of Muhammad Ghori assumed independence. Qutub-Ud-Din remained steadfast and loyal and helped his master in recovering the leftovers. Muhammad Ghori was deceitfully murdered during his journey from Lahore to Afghanistan by a party of Khokhars in 1206 A.D. His dynasty could not survive long after him. The Turkish slaves who had served as generals under him assumed independence.

Muhammad Ghori was less fanatical than Sultan Mahmud. From the beginning he aimed at the building up of a permanent dominion and tried to consolidate his conquests under regular rule. He brought the fairest part of Hindustan under Muslim control and was the real creator of the Muslim rule in India. His work in India turned out to be solid and bore good fruit in the hands of Qutub-ud-Din and his successors. Muhammad Ghori charged Qutub-ud-Din with the duty of extending the dominion of Islam in India and succeeded in founding a dynasty of rulers in Delhi. Muhammad Ghori had planned a permanent settlement and his scheme was successful in the hands of his general and successor, Qutub-ud-Din.

CAUSES OF THE SUCCESS OF MUHAMMAD GHORI AGAINST THE RAJPUT

The success of Muhammad was largely due to his own strength of character. He possessed a higher ideal from which he refused to deviate even after his initial failures in India and his defeat by Khwarizm Shah. Muhammad planned his attacks and conquests beforehand, changed them whenever necessary, removed his weaknesses when known and did not take unnecessary risks in battles and politics. As a military commander, he kept his eyes upon all his campaigns.

When engaged in fighting the Khokars in India, he had not lost touch with his campaigns in Central Asia and was equally interested in the building work of a frontier fortress at the bunks of the river Oxus. This is the reasons for why he was ultimately successful in his military campaigns.

Muhammad was the real founder of Turkish rule in India and therein lay his greatest accomplishment and prominence. Muhammad had a keen eye in the cultural progress of his subjects. He patronised scholars like Fakhr-ud-din Razi and Nizami Uruzi. However, his greatest success was the establishment of the Turkish Empire in India which added a fresh chapter in the Indian history.

BATTLES WITH PRITHVIRAJ CHAUHAN

It was in 1191 AD when Ghori's army of 120,000 men was proceeding towards Punjab through Khyber Pass, was confronted by the army of Hindu rulers under the commandership of Prithviraj Chauhan and other Hindu allied rulers comprising of 200,000 men.

Prithvi's army under the command of his general Govind Raj rushed to defend the boundaries of their territories and restricted the invader on the land of Tarain near Thanesar in the present Haryana approximately 150km north of Delhi.

The Battle of Tarain was mainly regarded as a strategic warfare in which Ghori's army was mainly divided into three flanks–left, right and center, while Prithviraj's army mainly fought with elephant cavalry which was totally unknown to Ghori's army. This brought a sudden jerk to Ghori's army.

Although Ghori's army faced severe defeat yet it did not get demoralised and came back to win more vigorously in the simultaneous years. Muhammad Ghori's ambitions to conquer and defeat Hindu rulers came more vigorously in the second Battle of Tarain in which he now reorganised himself more strongly and strategically. This time his army was divided into five flanks in which one strip of soldiers were kept hidden to attack later. This defeated the Indian army very badly bringing an end to the Hindu rule forever.

DEATH OF MUHAMMAD OF GHORI

There is a literary story about the death of Muhammad of Ghor, which has considerable appeal, but which is not borne out by historical documents. It first appears in an epic poem by Chand Bardai about his friend Prithviraj which is called the Prithviraj Raso. Over time, the Prithviraj Raso has been embellished with the interpolations and additions of many other authors.

As a prisoner in Ghor, Prithviraj was brought in chains before Muhammad Ghori.He haughtily looked Ghori straight into the eye. Ghori ordered him to lower his eyes, where upon a Prithviraj scornfully reminded him that the "eyes of a rajput is lowered only when a rajput dies".On hearing this, Ghori ordered that his eyes to be burnt with red hot iron rods.

Prithviraj's former court poet Chand Bardai, came to Ghori to be near Prithviraj in his misery. Chand Bardai came in disguise and paens. On the one hand, he earned Mahmud's regard; on the other, he took every opportunity to meet with Prithviraj and urge him to avenge Ghori. The two got an opportunity to kill Muhammad Ghori when Ghori announced an archery competition.

Chand Bardai told Ghori that Prithviraj was so skilled an archer, that he could take aim based only on sound, and did not even need to look at his target. Ghori disdained to believe this; the courtiers guffawed and taunted Chand Bardai, asking how a blind man could possibly shoot arrows.

In the spirit of their usual barbaric mockery, they brought the blind and hapless Prithviraj out to the field. Pressing a bow and arrows into his hand, they taunted him to take aim. Chand Bardai told Ghori that this taunting would avail nothing, for Prithviraj would never do as some sundry courtiers bade him do. He said that Prithviraj, as an anointed king, would not accept orders from anyone other than another king. His ego thus massaged, and in the spirit of the occasion, Mahmud Ghori agreed to personally give Prithviraj the order to shoot. Some iron plates were hung and Prithiviraj was asked to aim at them. A man was to strike the plate with a hammer and Prithviraj was supposed to hit that plate.

Thus, Chand Bardai provided Prithviraj with an oral indication of where Ghori was seated by composing a couplet on the spot and reciting the same in Prithviraj's hearing. The couplet, composed in a language understood only by Prithviraj went thus:"Char bans, chaubis gaj, angul ashta praman, Ta upar sultan hai, Chuke mat Chauhan." (Four measures ahead of you and twenty four yards away as measured with eight finger measurement, is seated the Sultan. Do not miss him now, Chauhan).

Ghori then ordered Prithviraj to shoot. Prithviraj thus came to know the location of Ghori and started shooting at the plates.When he hit the target courtiers said "vah" "vah" and Ghori said "Shabash", recognising Ghori's voice and turning in the direction from where he heard Ghori speak. Prithviraj took aim based only on the voice and on Chand Bardai's couplet, he sent an arrow racing to Ghori's throat. Ghori was thus stuck dead instantly by Prithviraj.

2

Delhi Sultanate Early Phase

During the Delhi Sultanate, several Turkic and Afghan dynasties ruled from Delhi, including the Mamluk dynasty (1206-90), the Khilji dynasty (1290-1320), the Tughlaq dynasty (1320-1413), the Sayyid dynasty (1414-51), and the Lodi dynasty (1451-1526). In 1526 the Delhi Sultanate was absorbed by the emerging Mughal Empire.

MAMLUK DYNASTY

The Mamluk Dynasty or Ghulam Dynasty, directed into India by Qutubuddin Aybak, a Turkic general of Central Asian birth, was the first of five unrelated dynasties to rule India's Delhi Sultanate from 1206 to 1290. Aibak's tenure as a Ghorid administrator ranged between 1192 to 1206, a period during which he led invasions into the Gangetic heartland of India and established control over some of the new areas.

Aibak rose to power when a Ghorid superior was assassinated. However, his reign as the sultan of Delhi was short lived as he expired in 1210 and his son Aram Shah rose to the throne, only to be assassinated by Iltutmish in 1211. The Sultanate under Iltutmish established cordial diplomatic contact with the Abbasid Caliphate between 1228–29 and had managed to keep India unaffected by the invasions of Genghis Khan and his successors.

Following the death of Iltutmish in 1236 a series of weak rulers remained in power and a number of the noblemen gained autonomy over the provinces of the Sultanate. Power shifted hands from Rukn ud din Firuz to Razia Sultana till Ghiyas ud din Balban rose to the throne and successfully repelled both external and internal threats to the Sultanate.

The Khalji dynasty came into being when Jalaluddin Firuz Khilji overthrew the last of the Slave dynasty rulers, Muizuddin Qaiqabad, the grandson of Balban, and assumed the throne at Delhi.

ARCHITECTURE

The architectural legacy of the dynasty includes the Qutb Minar, Mehrauli by Qutubuddin Aybak, *Sultan Ghari* near Vasant Kunj, the first Islamic Mausoleum (tomb) built in 1231 AD for Prince Nasir ud din Mahmud, eldest son of Iltumish, and Balban's tomb, also in Mehrauli Archaeological Park.

LIST OF SULTANS

- Qutubuddin Aybak (1206–1210).
- Aram Shah (1210–1211).
- Shams ud din Iltutmish (1211–1236), son-in-law of Qutubuddin Aybak.
- Rukn ud din Firuz (1236), son of Iltutmish.
- Raziyyatuddin Sultana (1236–1240), daughter of Iltutmish.
- Muizuddin Bahram (1240–1242), son of Iltutmish.
- Alauddin Masud (1242–1246), son of Ruknuddin.
- Nasiruddin Mahmud (1246–1266), son of Iltutmish.
- Ghiyasuddin Balban (1266–1286), ex-slave, son-in-law of Iltutmish.
- Muizuddin Qaiqabad (1286–1290), grandson of Balban and Nasiruddin.

IKHTIYAR UDDIN MOHAMMED BIN BAKHTIYAR KHALJI

Ikhtiyar Uddin Mohammed bin Bakhtiyar Khilji also known as *Malik Ghazi Ikhtiyaru 'l-Din Mohammed Bakhtiyar Khilji*. He was an afghan military general of Qutubuddin Aybak.

EARLY LIFE

IIkhtiyaruddin Mohammed bin Bakhtiyar Khilji also known as *Malik Ghazi IIkhtiyaruddin Mohammed Bakhtiyar Khilji*, a member of the Muslim Pashtun Khilji or as it is known in Afghanistan Ghilzai tribe, who was head of the armies that conquered much of northeastern India. He was one of the military generals of Qutubuddin Aybak. Mohammed Khilji conquered Bihar in 1193. His troops destroyed the famous Buddhist university at Nalanda (in modern Bihar State) in the year 1193. Later, he also brought Bengal's ruler Lakshman Sen under his authority, and captured his capital in 1205. He is the founder of the Khilji dynasty and is considered to be the first muslim ruler of Bengal.

Khalji came from the town of Garamsir in northern Afghanistan. Tradition has it that Khalji's conquest of Bengal at the head of 18 horsemen was foretold. It is held that he was of common birth, had long arms extending below his knees, a short physical stature and an un-favourable countenance. He was first appointed as the Dewan-i-ard at Ghor. But later he lost the job for irregularities in work. Then he approached India in about the year 1193 CE and tried to enter in the army of Qutb al-Din but failed. Then he went further eastward and took a job under Maklik Hizbar al-Din who was then the commander of the army of Badayun in northern India. After a short period he went to Oudh where Malik Husam al-Din, the governor, recognized him for his worth. Husam gave a landed estate in the south-eastern corner of modern Mirzapur District. He gathered some brave and adventurous Turks under his banner and soon consolidated his position, carrying out raids into neighboring territories.

CONQUESTS

Khalji's career took flight with a campaign which subjugated Bihar in 1203 CE. This effort earned him political clout in the court at Delhi. Bihar (Hindi:, Urdu:) is a state of the Indian union situated in the eastern part of the country....

The next year he took his forces into Bengal. As he came upon the city of Nadia it is said that he advanced so rapidly that only 18 horsemen from his army could keep up.

Khalji went on to capture the capital Gaur and conquer much of Bengal. Rather than consolidating Bengal, however, he led a disastrous campaign into Tibet and died in 1206 CE on the retreat.

ARAM SHAH

Aram Shah (1210-1211) was a Muslim Turkic ruler of medieval India during the Slave Dynasty (or Mameluk dynasty) and the second Sultan of Delhi. The relationship of Aram with Qutubuddin Aibak (1206-1210) is a subject of controversy. According to some, he was Aibak's son, but Minhaj-us-Siraj distinctly writes that Qutubuddin only had three daughters. Abul Fazl has made the "astonishing statement" that he was the Sultan's brother. A modern writer has hazarded the opinion that "he was no relation of Qutubuddin" but was selected as his successor as he was available on the spot. In fact, there were no fixed rules governing the succession to the Crown in the Turkish State. It was determined largely by the exigencies of the moment and the influence of the Chihalgani or 'Corp of Forty'. The Chihalgani, who were the administrative and military elite of the Ilbari tribe, crowned him king thinking that he would be able to deal with the problems facing the Sultanate. Aram was ill-qualified to govern a kingdom. The Chihalgani soon conspired against him and invited Shams-ud-din Iltutmish, then Governor of Badaun, to replace Aram. Iltutmish responded to their call, and, advancing with all his army, defeated Aram in the plain of Jud near Delhi in 1211.What became of Aram is not quite certain.

JALAL AL-DIN MANGBURNI

Jalal al-Din Mangburni also known as Jalal al-Din Mangburni or Minkburny in the east was the last ruler of the Khwarezmid Empire. Following the defeat of his father, Ala al-Din Mohammed II by Genghis Khan in 1220, Jalal al-Din Mangburni came to power but he rejected the title shah that his father had assumed and called himself simply sultan. Due to the Mongol invasion and sacking of Samarkand, he was forced to flee to India with an escort of only five thousand men. At the river Indus however, the Mongols caught up with him and killed his forces and thousands of refugees at the Battle of Indus. He escaped and sought asylum in the Sultanate of Delhi. Iltumish however denied this to him in deference to the relationship with the Abassid caliphs.

Jalal al-Din Mangburni spent three years in exile in India before returning to Persia. He gathered an army and re-established a kingdom. He never consolidated his power however, and he spent the rest of his days struggling against Mongols, pretenders to the throne and the Seljuk Turks of Rum. He lost his power over Persia in a battle against the Mongols in the Alborz Mountains and fled to the Caucasus, to capture Azerbaijan in 1225, setting up their capital at Tabriz. In 1226 he attacked Georgia and sacked Tbilisi, destroying all the churches.

Jalal had a brief victory over the Seljuks and captured the town Akhlat from Ayyubids.

However, he was later defeated by Sultan Kayqubad I at Erzincan on the Upper Euphrates at the Battle of Yassi Chemen in 1230, from where he escaped to Diyarbakir while the Mongols captured Azerbaijan in the ensuing confusion. He was murdered in 1231 in Diyarbakir by a Kurdish assassin hired by the Seljuks or possibly by Kurdish highwaymen.

Jalal al-Din Mangburni's followers remained loyal to him even after his death and raided the Seljuk lands of Jazira and Syria for the next several years, calling themselves the *Khwarezmiyyas*. Ayyubid sultan Salih Ayyub later hired them as mercenaries against his uncle Salih Ismail and they captured Jerusalem in 1244. The *Khwarezmiyyas* served under Mameluks of Egypt before they were finally beaten by Mansur Ibrahim some years later.

CONSOLIDATION OF POWER

Southern Bihar was captured by Iltutmish in 1225-26. Lakhnauti was captured in 1226. Revolts continued until the Khalji Maliks of Bengal were reduced to complete submission in the winter of 1231. Alauddin Jani was appointed Governor of Lakhnauti.

With the death of Genghis Khan in 1227, Iltutmish attacked Qabacha. Multan and Ucch were captured. Qabacha was surrounded on all sides in the fort of Bhakkar, on the banks of Indus. He drowned while attempting to escape. Sindh and Multan were incorporated into the Delhi Sultanate and placed under separate governors.

Due to his problems first with Turkish nobles and then with the Mongols, Iltutmish had ignored the Rajputs, who had regained territory lost earlier to the Turks, for the first fifteen years of his reign. Starting in 1226, however, Iltutmish began a series of campaigns against the Rajputs. Ranthambore, Mandsaur, Bayana, Ajmer and Sambhar were captured. Nagaur was captured in 1230 and Gwalior in 1231. Iltutmish's army was forced to retreat with heavy losses from Gujarat by the ruling Chalukyas.

Iltutmish's son Nasiruddin Mahmud captured the Gangetic valley territories of Budaun, Benaras, and Kanauj, which had fallen into the hands of local Hindu chieftains. Rohilkhand was taken with heavy losses.

In 1235, Iltutmish sacked Ujjain and destroyed its temples including the Mahakala Temple.. He built, *Gandhak-ki-Baoli*, a stepwell for Sufi saint, Qutbuddin Bakhtiar Kaki, who moved to Delhi during his reign.

DEATH AND SUCCESSION

Iltutmish's eldest son, Nasiruddin Mahmud, had died in 1229 while governing Bengal as his father's deputy. The surviving sons of the Sultan were incapable of the task of administration. In A.D. 1236 Iltutmish, on his death-bed, nominated his daughter Raziya as his heiress. But the nobles of the court were too proud to bow their heads before a woman, and disregarding the deceased Sultan's wishes, raised to the throne his eldest surviving son, Ruknuddin Firuz.

The death of Iltutmish was followed by years of political instability at Delhi. During this period, four descendants of Iltutmish were put on the throne and murdered. Order was re-established only after Balban became the Naib or Deputy Sultan and later on Sultan in A.D. 1265.

KHALJI

The Khalji or Khilji dynasty, who had established themselves as rulers of Bengal in the time of Mohammed Ghori, took control of the empire in a coup which eliminated the last of the Mamluks.

The Khaljis conquered Gujarat and Malwa, and sent the first expeditions south of the Narmada River, as far south as Tamil Nadu.

The Delhi Sultanate rule continued to extend into southern India, first by the Delhi Sultans, then by the breakaway Bahmani Sultanate of Gulbarga, and, after the breakup of the Bahmani state in 1518, by the five independent Deccan Sultanates. The kingdom of Vijayanagar united southern India and arrested the Delhi Sultanate's expansion for a time, until its eventual fall to the Deccan Sultanates in 1565.

TUGHLUQ

SAYYID

The Sayyid dynasty ruled the Delhi Sultanate from 1414 to 1451, succeeding the Tughlaq dynasty. The dynasty was established by Khizr Khan, who was deputised by Timur to be the governor of Multan (Punjab). Khizr Khan took Delhi from Daulat Khan Lodi on May 28, 1414 and founded the Sayyid dynasty.

LODI

Lodi Dynasty was a Ghilzai (Khilji) Afghan dynasty, who ruled over the Delhi Sultanate during its last phase, displacing the Sayyid dynasty. Founded by Bahlul Lodi, it ruled from 1451 to 1526. The last ruler of this dynasty, Ibrahim Lodi, was defeated and killed by Babur in the first Battle of Panipat on April 20, 1526. Sikander Lodi is considered the greatest rule of the dynasty.

MONETARY SYSTEM

In the first half of the 14th century, the Sultanate introduced a monetary economy in the provinces (*sarkars*) and districts (*parganas*) that had been established and founded a network of market centres through which the traditional village economies were both exploited and stimulated and drawn into the wider culture. State revenues remained based on successful agriculture, which induced Sultan Mohammed bin Tughluq (1325-51) to have village wells dug, to offer seed to the peasants, and to encourage cash crops like sugarcane.

MONGOL INVASION

Perhaps the greatest contribution of the Sultanate was its temporary success in insulating the subcontinent from the potential devastation of the Mongol invasion from Central Asia in the thirteenth century. However, the invasion of Timur in 1398 significantly weakened the Delhi Sultanate. The Delhi Sultanate revived briefly under the Lodis before it was conquered by the Mughal emperor Babur in 1526.

FALL OF SULTANATE

The last Lodi ruler, Ibrahim Lodi was greatly disliked in his court and subjects alike, being considered overly ambitious. Daulat Khan, the governor of Punjab and Alam Khan, his uncle, sent an invitation to conquer Delhi to Babur, the ruler of Kabul.

The first Battle of Panipat (April 1526) was fought between the forces of Babur and the Delhi Sultanate. Ibrahim Lodi was killed on the battleground. By way of superior generalship, vast experience in warfare, effective strategy, and appropriate use of artillery, Babur won the First battle of Panipat and subsequently occupied Agra and Delhi. The new Mughal dynasty was to rule India for another 300 years.

FEMALE SULTANA RAZIA SULTANA

The Delhi Sultanate is the only sultanate of India to be ruled by a female, Princess Razia Sultana (1236-1240). While her reign was short, she is regarded well in the eyes of historians. Princess Razia Sultana was very popular and considered more intelligent than her brothers.

She ruled from Delhi in the east, to Peshawar in the west, and from Kashmir in the north to Multan in the south. Rebels including Malik Altunia, forced her into battle. Forced to marry Altunia to save her life, both she and Altunia were was killed during a battle to reclaim the sultanate from her brother.

CULTURAL ASPECTS

The Sultans of Delhi enjoyed cordial, if superficial, relations with other Muslim rulers in the Near East but owed them no allegiance.

The Sultans based their laws on the Qur'an and the sharia, and permitted non-Muslim subjects to practice their own religion if they paid jizya, or head tax. The Sultans ruled from urban centre, while military camps and trading posts provided the nuclei for towns that sprang up in the countryside.

LEGACY

The Sultanate ushered in a period of cultural renaissance. The resulting "Indo-Muslim" fusion left lasting monuments in architecture, music, literature, and religion. Due to the sacking of Delhi in 1398 by Timur (*Tamerlane*), other independent Sultanates were established in Awadh, Bengal, Jaunpur, Gujarat and Malwa.

RUKN UD DIN FIRUZ

Rukn ud din Firuz (1236) was a Muslim Turkic ruler and the fourth Sultan of Delhi of medieval India who ruled for just seven months during the Slave Dynasty (or Mameluk dynasty). He was the son of Shams ud din Iltutmish (1211-1236) and was raised to become Iltutmish's heir.

However after Iltutmish's death in April, 1236 he was viewed as being unfit to rule and was murdered in November 1236. Raziyyat ud din Sultana, Iltumish's daughter, succeeded him as ruler.

GHIYAS UD DIN BALBAN

Ghiyasuddin Balban (1200 - 1287) was a Turkic ruler of the Delhi Sultanate during the Mamluk dynasty (or Slave dynasty) from 1266 to 1287.

BIOGRAPHY

He was son of a Turkish noble of the Ilbari tribe, but as a child was captured by Mongols and sold as a slave at Ghazni. Khwaja, Jamaluddin Basri of Baghdad Later, he was bought by Sultan Iltutmish in 1232 CE, who at the orders of his own master, Qutubuddin Aibak, released him from slavery and brought him up in a manner befitting a prince. He was liberally educated. He was first appointed as Khasdar (king's personal attendant)by the Sultan. He became the head of the 'Chalissa', a group of forty Turkish nobles of the state. After the overthrow of Razia Sultana he made rapid strides in the subsequent reigns.

He was initially the Prime Minister of Sultan Nasir ud din Mahmud from 1246 to 1266 and married his daughter, but Balban declared himself the Sultan of Delhi after the previous sultan Nasir ud din Mahmud's death because Sultan Nasir ud din Mahmud had no male issue. Sultan Balban ascended the throne in 1266 at the age of sixty with the title of Ghyas ud din Balban.

During his reign, Balban ruled with an iron fist. He broke up the 'Chihalgani', a group of the forty most important nobles in the court.

He tried to establish peace and order in the country of India. He built many outposts in areas where there was crime and garrisoned them with soldiers.

Balban wanted to make sure everyone was loyal to the crown by establishing an efficient espionage system. Sultan Balban had a strong and well-organized spy system.

Balban placed secret reporters and news-writers in every department. The spies were independent authority only answerable to Sultan. Balban was strict administrator of justice. He did not show any partiality even to his own kith and kin.

About his justice Dr. Ishwari Prasad remarked "So great was the dread of Sultan's inexorable justice that no one dared to ill-treat his servant and slaves."

When a complaint was made that Malik Barbaq, a powerful landlord of Badaun killed one of his own servant. Balban ordered his death sentence. The news-writer (spy), who was responsible for Badaun reporting was also executed because he failed to report this act of injustice to Sultan.

He ruled as the Sultan from 1266 until his death in 1287, and was succeeded by his grandson, Muizuddin Qaiqabad, who reign (1287-1290). His successors were weak and incompetent and the throne was eventually captured by Jalaluddin Firuz Khilji in 1290, bringing an end to the Slave dynasty.

Balban's tomb is today, situated in the Mehrauli Archaeological Park, beyond the Qutb complex.

MUIZUDDIN BAHRAM

Muizuddin Bahram (1236) was a Muslim Turkic ruler and the sixth Sultan of Delhi in medieval India during the Mamluk dynasty (or Slave dynasty). He was the son of Shams ud din Iltutmish (1211-1236) and brother of Razia Sultan (1236-1240). While his sister was in Bathinda, he declared himself king with the support of forty chiefs.

His sister tried to regain the throne with the aid of her husband Altunia, a chief of Bathinda, though they were eventually arrested and executed.

Even so, during Muizuddin Bahram's two years as king, the chiefs that had originally supported him became disordered and constantly bickered among each other. It was during this period of unrest that he was murdered by his own army in 1242. After his death, he was succeeded by Ala ud din Masud, a son of Rukn ud din Firuz.

ALA UD DIN MASUD

Ala ud din Masud (1242-1246) was a Muslim Turkic ruler and the seventh Sultan of Delhi in medieval India during the Mamluk dynasty (or Slave dynasty). He was the son of Rukn ud din Firuz (1236) and the nephew of Razia Sultan (1236-1240).

After his predecessor, Muizuddin Bahram, was murdered by the army in 1242 after years of disorder, the chiefs chose for him to become the next ruler.

However, he was more of a puppet for the chiefs and did not actually have much power or influence in the government. Instead, he became infamous for his fondness of entertainment and wine. By 1246, the chiefs became upset with Ala ud din Masud's increasing hunger for more power in the government, and replaced him with Nasir ud din Mahmud (1246-1266), another son of Iltutmish.

NASIR UD DIN MAHMUD

Nasir ud din Mahmud, Nasir ud din Firuz Shah (1246-1266) was a Muslim Turkic ruler and the eighth Sultan of Delhi of medieval India during the Mamluk (or Slave dynasty).

He was the youngest son of Shams ud din Iltutmish (1211-1236), and he succeeded Ala ud din Masud after the chiefs replaced Masud when they felt that he began to behave as a tyrant. As a ruler, Mahmud was known to be very religious, spending most of his time in prayer and renown for aiding the poor and the distressed. However, it was actually his Deputy Sultan or Naib, Ghiyas ud din Balban, who primarily dealt with the state affairs. After Mahmud's death in 1266, Balban (1266-1287) rose to power as Mahmud had no children to be his heir. His fortified tomb built by Iltutmish in 1231, known as Sultan Ghari, lies in the Vasant Kunj area, close to Mehrauli, in New Delhi. The octagonal tomb chamber, is one of finest examples of Mamluk dynasty architecture, which also include the Qutub Minar.

3

Alauddin Khalji

Alauddin Khalji (real name Ali Gurshasp; died 1316) was the second ruler of the Turko-Afghan Khalji dynasty in India. He is considered the most powerful ruler of the dynasty, reigning from 1296 to 1316. His historic attack on Chittor in 1303 AD, after hearing of the beauty of queen of Chittor, Rani Padmini, the wife of King Rawal Ratan Singh and the subsequent story has been immortalized in the epic poem Padmavat, written by Malik Muhammad Jayasi in the Awadhi language in the year 1540. Alauddin is also noted in history for being one of the few rulers to repeatedly defeat the warring Mongols and thereby saving India from plundering raids and attacks.

Alauddin Khalji was known for his market and revenue reforms. He sought to introduce measurement of land and assessment on the basis of measurment and collected ½ of the poduce as land revenue from the peasants. He also appointed officers to collect the land revenue from these areas; these were not assigned to anybody as Iqta. He collected the land revenue in cash, made the peasants sell the grain to banjaras who took the grain to towns and sold it at prices fixed by the state. He sought to control the prices of horses as well. These measures were adopted only in Delhi and surrounding regions. The fixing of prices benefited the army as they were paid a fixed salary. He was harsh towards the elites - khuts and muqaddarns who, prior to Alauddin had enjoyed the power to collect extra taxes from the peasants. It is believed that one of the objectives of introducing revenue and market reforms by Alauddin Khalji was to eliminate the Hindus. After his death his market reforms could not be continued.

Muhammad bin Tughlaq's bold measures included the transfer of capital to Deogir. This experiment ended in a failure. After transfer of capital ended in failure, he introduced the token currency, which was a bronze coin to be used in place of the silver tanka. Even though his measures were unique, he finally had to take back these measures. He even exchanged old coins for new but that did not save the token currency. Contemporary scholars have looked at him in different light. Zia Uddin Barani would look at the harmful effects while the Moroccan traveler, Ibn Battuta, who came to Delhi in 1333 could not see any harmful effects of these experiments.

Like Allauddin Khalji, Muhammad bin Tughlaq also tried to bring changes in the agrarian set up. Some historians point out that he made an over assessment because of which many peasants fled the region. But the states share remained half. A severe famine in this period worsened the situation. Muhammad bin Tughlaq tried to provide relief to those affected and made efforts to improve and extend cultivation. The sultan left Delhi and rendered in a camp called swargadwari near kanauj. He also set up a separate department called diwan-i amir-i kohi whose function was to extend cultivation by providing loans. During Muhammad- bin Tughluq's reign lot of changes were brought about. He gave high official positions to low born too.

Firuz Shah Tughlaq's steps have been viewed as an attempt to prevent the breakup of Delhi Sultanate. He gave concessions to the nobles in order to please them. The tenor of his policy was very different from that of Muhammad- bin Tughluq. He made the iqtas hereditary. The land assigned to an official could be taken back along with his official position prior to Firuz Shah Tughlaq but now they functioned like hereditary holders. The principles of heredity extended to the army as well. His control over the administration diminished gradually. He took certain steps to project himself as a true Muslim. Firuz Shah Tughluq imposed Jaziyah, a religious tax on non-Muslims. By imposing this he claimed to be ruling according to shariat. The rulers of Delhi Sultanate were caught up between the ulama, demanding strict implementation of Shariat but the majority of the population could not have been dealt in this manner. Moreover, Delhi sultans were dependent on their collection of land revenue from the people.

Large canals were dug and repaired under Firuz Shah Tughluq. One of them flowed from Sutlej to Hansi. He also built a canal from Jamuna. These were to be used for irrigation and for consumption in new towns

- Hissar Furuzah (in Haryana), Firuzabad (in U. P.). He kept 180,000 slaves to produce various handicrafts in the royal karkhanas. Firuz ShahTughluq died in 1388. But the nobles and rajas did not let his successor Nasiruddin Mahmud who ruled from 1394-1412 to fight the problems. The sultan only controlled the region from Delhi to Palam.

Delhi Sultans were responsible for centralization of administration. These changes were seen for the first time under Balban, but by the time of Firuz Shah Tughluq, disintegration of Delhi Sultanate had started. Government under Delhi Sultanate consisted of the King and various departments taking care of administration at the central level. The revenue department looked into the assessment and collection of revenue.

Wazir was in-charge of revenue department and looked into income and expenditure of the state. Muhammad-bin-Tughluq appointed an Auditor for inspecting the accounts maintained by the wazir. Firuz Shah Tughluq took back cetain stringent measures introduced by Muhammad bin Tughluq. Next in importance was the military department headed by ariz-i-mumalik. Major changes in the revenue and military set up took place under Alauddin Khalji. He introduced branding of horses [dagh] and maintaining of a descriptive roll [chera] of each soldier.

Other departments included diwan-i-risalat and diwan–i-insha. Diwan-i-insha dealt with religious matters. It was presided over by the chief qazi. Intelligence agents or barids were appointed across the empire. There was a household department consisting of royal Karkhanas, responsible for manufacture and storage of goods required by the King and the royal household. Firuz ShahTughluq appointed a large number of slaves to work in these royal karkhanas. Wakil–i-dar was in-charge of this department.

The officers at the Pargana level [shiqs] were appointed by the state. An important officer at Pargana level was amil. Khut and Muqaddam were important people at village level. Khuts were landowners and Muqaddams were the village headman. The officers at different provinces were paid through iqtas. In the formative stage iqtas were territories given to an officer called muqtis or walis. They were responsible for maintenance of law and order within the area of their jurisdiction. They were also responsible for collection of land revenue according to state demand. They paid themselves, maintained the required contingent out of this collection. As Delhi Sultanate grew more centralized the actual income of the muqti was ascertained and salaries to the muqtis were paid in cash. After meeting his expenses, muqti was to remit the income to the state.

Major changes in the administration appeared to have taken place under Alauddin Khalji. He crushed the rich landed elements at the village level. Prior to him Balban curbed the rais and ranas, the rulers of the indigenous regions, which were still not a part of the Delhi Sultanate. Historians have also traced the changes that took place in technology with the arrival of Turks. Notable innovations were the rahat (miscalled the Persian wheel). By the use of this device, water could be lifted from deeper levels (wells). Another significant technological innovation could be seen in the buildings constructed during this period. The buildings were erected by the use of mortar and the use of arch and dome. Alauddin Khalji's price regulations were equally innovative. Through these measures he was able to provide the army with all the amenities. The Turkish state expanded under Alauddin Khalji and Muhammud-bin-Tughlaq, but it declined in its effectiveness under Firuz Shah Tughlaq. Under the Delhi Sultans the official class emerged as an elite stratum, which was competing with the rais and ranas, the local elements for more surplus. Firuz Shah Tughlaq imposed Jaziyah, a separate tax to be collected by the state from non- muslims. This measure was taken to please the religious class [ulama].

BIOGRAPHY OF ALAUDDIN KHALJI

Alauddin Khalji was the nephew and son in law of Jalal-ud-din. His surname is Khalji in Persian and Arabic documents, but the original Pashto is Ghiljai. The obvious difference in spelling and pronunciation arises in lack of letters between Arabic/Dari and Pashto. At first, Jalal-ud-din appointed Alauddin as the governor of Kara near the city of Allahabad. In 1296 Alauddin killed his uncle. But Malika Jahan, the widow of Jalal-ud-din, put her younger son Ruknuddin Khalji on the throne. Alauddin quickly marched on Delhi from Kara. He entered Delhi with his uncle's head on a pike and on October 3, 1296, proclaimed himself the King of Delhi. Arkali Khan, Jalal-ud-din's older son, and Ruknuddin were blinded. Malika Jahan was imprisoned.

Very soon he went about despoiling the wealth of nobles, frequently blinding, imprisoning or killing them. In 1297, Alauddin sent an army to plunder Gujarat, under the generalship of Ulugh Khan and Nusrat Khan. This army looted the temple of Somnath and the Shivalinga was broken into pieces and was being carried back to Delhi. Kanhad Dev Songara, the ruler of Jalore in Rajasthan attacked and defeated Ulugh Khan and captured the broken Shivalinga which was washed in the Ganges River, and the fragments were established in various temples in Jalore. Muhammad Shah helped Kanhad Dev Songara. Muhammad was a general in Khalji's army.

After the war, Muhammad Shah went and stayed with Hammir Dev Chauhan at Ranthambore. Ulugh Khan apprised Alauddin who ordered him and Nusrat Khan to conquer Ranthambore. In 1299 they started out with 80,000 cavalry and a large infantry to attack Hammir Dev Chauhan. Hammir's army repulsed the attack and killed Nusrat Khan. Ulugh Khan escaped and reached Delhi. Khalji was taken aback by this defeat and wanted revenge. He finally came himself in 1301, and there was a long siege.

Hammir was very well prepared. When the fort would not fall after repeated bloody skirmishes, Khalji resorted to diplomacy. Hammir was very suspicious but he heeded to his councilors who told him that the sword is not always the best recourse. Ratipal and Ranmal, who were close confidants of Hammir, were sent to the Khalji camp. Ranmal's father was hung by Hammir for treachery and his property was confiscated. Ranmal earned the trust of Hammir by being brave in battles that Hammir fought but perfidy was in his blood. Khalji bribed these two generals of Hammir's army and consequently Ranthambore fell. After the annexation of Gujarat, he took to the practice of making the innocent families of rebels against the government suffer.

CONQUEST OF ALAUDDIN KHALJI

Alauddin was a very ambitious and a shrewd warrior. To materialize his vision to rule most territories of the country, he set out a conquest. During his conquest he looted many states in the north. His strong support during his conquest were his brother Ulugh Khan, Nusrat Khan, Zafar Khan and his brother-in-law, Alp Khan. In 1297, Alauddin sent a huge army under the command of Ulugh Khan and Nusrat Khan to conquer Gujarat. Rai Karan Dev second was the ruler of Gujarat. He fought for sometimes and then ran away. Alauddin's army captured the capital Anhilwara.

The beautiful queen of Karan Dev second was made prisoner. She was taken away to Delhi. Alauddin married her. Alauddin's army plundered Gujarat and took away a large amount of booty. But, the greatest prize of all bagged in 'Hazar Dinari' slave, Malik Kafur, who became the prime minister of the King later. Alauddin's second conquest was Ranthambhor a very famous fort of Rajputana. Qutb-ud-Din and Iltutmish conquered it, but now it was being ruled by a Rajput king, Hamir Dev. In 1299, Alauddin sent an army under Ulugh Khan and Nusrat Khan to capture the fort of Ranthambhor, but the Rajputs defeated them. Even Nusrat Khan was killed in the battlefield. When Alauddin heard of this, he personally proceeded against Ranthambhor in 1301. The Rajputs fought bravely.

It took a few months to capture Ranthambhor. The most famous conquest in the Khilijian history was the conquest of Chittor by Alauddin. The King of Chittor,Rana Bhim Singh was captivated on Monday, Aug. 26, 1303 and Chittor fell. Thousands of Rajput women with Rani Padmini inside had entered a cellar and burnt themselves to ashes preferring a fiery death and unsullied honour to the lecherous hell of Islamic torture and venery. Discomfited Alauddin in impotent anger massacred thousands of children and old men found in the fort. In 1305 Alauddin Khalji captured Malwa and annexed Ujjain, Mandu, Dhar and Chanderi. Alauddin Khalji's expedition to Bengal was not successful and it remained independent. The next in line for Alauddin's conquest was Malwa which was under the rule of Rai Mahlak Dev. In 1305, Alauddin Khalji sent an army to Malwa under Ain-ul-Mulk Multani. The Rajput King Rai Mahlak Dev opposed the invaders, but he was killed in the battlefield. This victory helped the Delhi Army to occupy Ujjain, Mandu, Dhar and Chanderi. By the end of 1306 A.D. practically the whole of Northern India came into the hands of Alauddin. Now, Alauddin directed his attention towards the conquest of the South. He was the first Muslim king, who tried to invade the South. After the North had been brought under his control, it was natural for Alauddin to try for the extension of his influence over the South. Ram Chandra Deva was the king of Devgiri.

He gave refuge to Rai Karan Dev second, the fugitive ruler of Gujarat. Rai Karan Dev second made arrangements to marry Deval Devi, his daughter, to a Prince named Shankar. Shankar was the eldest son of Ram Chandra Deva, the King of Devgiri. At that time, there were four main kingdoms in the South, Devgir, Telangana, Hoysala and Pandya kingdom. In 1307, Alauddin sent an expedition against Devgiri under Malik Kafur, a slave. The King Ram Chandra Deva was defeated and was brought to Delhi. Alauddin treated Ram Chandra Deva with all honours. He even gave him a royal canopy and the style of King of kings.

Ram Chandra Deva continued to rule Devgiri As a vassal of Alauddin Khalji. The daughter of Kamla Devi, Deval Devi also was sent to Delhi, where she was married to Khizar Khan, son of Alauddin. Kamla Devi already was a wife of Alauddin. In 1310, Alauddin's army under Malik Kafur besieged Warangal, the capital of Telangana. Ram Chandra Deva of Devgiri gave all assistance to Malik Kafur. The King of Telangana, Pratap Rudra Deva was sued for peace. He gave Kafur 100 elephants, 7,000 horses and large quantities of jewels and coined money. He also agreed to send tribute to Delhi every year. Then Malik Kafur was sent to Dwarsamudra, the capital of King Vir Vallabh, the Hoysala ruler. Vir Vallabh was defeated and made prisoner. The rich temples of the city were plundered and Malik Kafur got a lot of gold, silver, jewel and pearls from these temples. Vir Vallabh was brought to Delhi. Later, he could rule over Dwarsamudra only as a vassal of Delhi. From Dwarsamudra, Malik Kafur marched towards Madura. Madura was the capital of Pandya Kingdom. Vir Pandya, the King of Madura abandoned his capital and ran away with his queens. Malik Kafur plundered the city. The main temple was destroyed and a mosque was built there. He got many elephants, 20,000 horses, 2,750 pounds of gold and lots of jewels. No such treasure had been brought to Delhi ever before. In 1312, Malik Kafur attacked Devgiri again, because Shankar Deva, the successor of Ram Chandra, withheld the tribute promised by his father and tried to regain his independence. Shankar Deva was killed. His kingdom was captured.

EMPIRE OF ALAUDDIN KHALJI

Alauddin Khalji succeeded in conquering most parts of India. Larger portion of north India was annexed to his empire. He also defeated many rulers in south India except the Pandyas, who were forced to accept his suzerainty. The places in north India which were incorporated within his empire were Gujarat, Jaisalmer, Ranthambhor, Chittor, Malwa, Siwana, and Jalore. The kingdoms in south India that were under his dominion were the Hoysala kingdom and the kingdom of Devagari. Gujarat was a prosperous state and in the latter half of 1298 A.D. Alauddin Khalji sent an expedition under Ulugh Khan and Nusrat Khan to Gujarat. On the way, Jaisalmer was also conquered.

At that time Karna was the ruler of Gujarat who was defeated by the army of Alauddin. Ranthambhor was a stronghold of Chauhana Rajputs. Alauddin wanted to conquer it because of its strategical importance. He dispatched Ulugh Khan and Nusrat Khan to attack Ranthambhor. Though the fort was besieged but Nusrat Khan was killed in the combat and the invaders were forced to retreat. Then Alauddin himself besieged the fort. It took one long year for Alauddin to successfully capture the fort. Chittor was another centre for the powers of the Rajputs. The fort of Chittor was constructed on a high hill and was regarded as unconquerable. Alauddin attacked Chittor in 1303 A.D. and besieged the fort. A part of Malwa was already in the hands of the Sultan but it was never completely conquered. Alauddin sent Ain-ul-mulk, governor of Multan, to attack Malwa, who besieged the fort of Mandu. Siwana was attacked in 1308 A.D. by Alauddin and was eventually captured.

The conquest of Jalor completed the conquest of Rajasthan by Alauddin Khalji. Bundi, Mandor, Tonk and probably Jodhpur also surrendered to Alauddin. All the strong forts of Rajasthan were captured by him and that provided safety to the passages towards Gujarat and South India. In the beginning of the 14th century Alauddin decided to conquer the south India. The purpose of Alauddin in attacking the kingdoms of south India was two fold. The south was not plundered so far by Muslim invaders and therefore possessed vast wealth and therefore he wanted to plunder the resources of south India.

His other aim was to force them to accept his suzerainty and get annual tribute from them which would be a regular source of wealth for him and would also increase his prestige in India. Alauddin sent Malik Kafur to attack Telangana in 1309 A.D. He conquered Sirbar on the way and reached the capital city of Warangal in 1310 A.D. The capital was well defended by two round walls, the outer one being that of earth and the inner one that of stone and also by two moats filled with water between the two walls. The ruler of Telengana accepted the suzerainty of Alauddin and agreed to pay annual tribute and gave one hundred elephants, seven hundred horses and all his accumulated treasure as gift. Vir Ballala of the Hoysala Empire also agreed for peace with Alauddin and agreed to pay annual tribute. Alauddin's policy towards the south was successful.

He succeeded in fulfilling his object. Alauddin was the first Muslim Sultan of Delhi who dared to attack south India and was successful. Most of the kingdoms of the south were forced to accept his suzerainty and pat annual tribute to him. Thus Alauddin Khalji succeeded in establishing a vast empire in India. Towards the North West it extended up to the Indus River and after 1306 A.D. even Kabul and Ghazni came under his sphere of influence. Towards the east it extended up to Avadh and Orissa. Punjab in the north to the Vindhyas in the south, all territories formed part of his empire. In the south except the Pandya ruler, all of them accepted his supremacy. The empire of Alauddin Khalji was certainly more extensive as compared to all other previous Muslim rulers of Delhi.

COINS OF KHALJI

When the kingdom of Delhi was passed on to another dynasty of the Khaljis in the 1290 A.D, a new change was made in the currency by the Khalji rulers. The Khalji rulers reigned between 1290 and 1320 A.D. The five rulers of this dynasty introduced new patterns in the system of currency. The first two rulers of the Khalji dynasty, Jalaluddin Firoz and Ruknuddin Ibrahim followed the coins of Balban in almost all respects. The third ruler of this dynasty, Alauddin Khalji had enriched his treasury by conquests in South India. He issued voluminous coins during his time.

He and his successor, Qutbuddin Mubarak Shah, issued gold and silver 'tankah' and coins of heavy weight. Alauddin had issued gold coins weighing 5, 10, 50 and 100 tolas (unit). His son Qutbuddin Mubarak issued gigantic coins of both gold and silver coins in no less than fourteen denominations in two shapes, round and square. These coins were also issued in 5, 10, 20, 30, 40, 50, 60, 70, 80, 90, 100, 150 and 200 tolas. Though these coins were issued by the ruler of Khalji dynasty, no specimens had been found. Only the mint master of the Delhi mint, Thakkur Pheru, had referred to them in his accounts of the working of the mint, of which he was in charge during the reign of these rulers.

These coins belonged to a Sultan of Malwa and the Mughal emperors. According to the scholars, these coins were the massive blocks of metal of artistically stamped bullion which were hoarded as stores of value. These coins were occasionally given to ambassadors, diplomatic agents and other distinguished persons as complimentary gifts or souvenirs of imperial favour and magnanimity. As per the historical evidences, Alauddin Khalji changed the pattern of the inscriptions of the coins. He dropped the name of the Khalifa from the obverse side of his gold and silver coins. He introduced the self laudatory title 'Sikandar-us-sant Yamin-ul-khilafat' which was the connotation of the second Alexander, the right hand of the 'Khilafat'.

Qutbuddin Mubarak used an even more arrogant title, 'Al-imam al-azam Khalifa rub al-almin', which defined the supreme head of Islam, the Khalifa, the lord of the heaven and the earth. The gold and silver coins, from the very beginning of their issue by the Sultans of Delhi, including Muhammad bin Sam, were identical in their content *i.e.* inscription, fabric and weight. Firoz Khalji and Alauddin Khalji retained on their billon coins the bilingual reverse introduced by Balban. Meanwhile,

Alauddin Khalji introduced another type of coin where his name and title were divided on the two sides of the coins.

This type was followed by his successors. Qutbuddin Mubarak added a few more types of coins to it. All the billon coins were known by the name of 'Kani' or 'gani' and carried a number of denominations. The denominations of the coins were named typically like 'eggani' for one, 'dugani' for two, 'chaugani' for four, 'chhagani' for six, 'athagani' for eight, 'baragani' for twelve, 'chaubisagani' for twenty four and 'arhtalis-gani' for forty eight.

Above them was the silver 'tankah' which was valued at sixty 'ganis'. Thus 'gani' was the unit coin and was known as 'jital' in the pre-Khalji period and 'dam' in the Khalji and later eras. The values of the 'ganis' were dependent on the proportions of the copper and silver metals mixed on them. According to the historical evidences, an 'eggani' coin contained 95 per cent of copper and 5 per cent of silver; 'dugani' contained 9.75 per cent of silver; a 'chaugani' contained 16.4 per cent of the white metal. Likewise the percentage of silver in the other coins increased. The other three bigger denominations had a higher weight in proportion to their value, determined by the weight of the 'athagani' coins and they contained silver in the same proportion.

Even, Alauddin Khalji issued coins from Deogir, when he led his expedition there and occupied it. He also issued coins from Ranthambhor after its conquest under the name of Darul-Islam, which he gave to it. After him, his successor, Qutbuddin Mubarak changed the name of Deogir to Qutbabad and issued coins containing this name. The names of some other places were also found on the coins and it had been said that these coins were issued during military campaigns. Thus, these coins were noteworthy phenomenon in the numismatic history of India. The coins of Khalji dynasty brought a change in the then economical stature of the society.

REVENUE SYSTEM OF ALAUDDIN KHALJI

Alauddin Khalji implemented a number of revenue and taxation measures which aimed at establishing an authoritative and despotic state. In order to manifest his desire to extend his empire, it was necessary to increase the income of the state. Other factors were also responsible for bringing about a change in the existing financial and revenue structure of the state. Alauddin Khalji's position was threatened by the revolts of the Hindus while the Mongols were posing danger to his empire. Thus a requirement of a well equipped large army was necessary. There are also other reasons which determined the financial policy, for instance, the class which worked as middleman between the state and the peasants enjoyed best advantages.

This class had increased its landed property without the consent of the State and, while it collected maximum revenue from the peasants, it paid the minimum to the state. Thus this class enjoyed best advantages at the cost of the state. By implementing various financial policy Alauddin wanted to break up their power and influences on people. Alauddin Khalji ordered confiscation of all those lands which were given to the people by previous rulers as milk (state srant), inam (state gift), waqf (charitable endowment) and pension in return of state service.

He confiscated lands of those people who were not serving the state in any form and again redistributed it among those who were doing helpful service to the state. A complete record was maintained regarding who was assigned how much land and of what quality. This measure of Ala-ud-din Khalji increased the Khalisa-land (state land), left the possession of land in the hands of competent and useful persons and diminished authority of the old nobility. One of the revenue measures of Alauddin attacked the privileged position of hereditary revenue officers like Khuts, Chaudhris and Muqaddams who were all Hindus. It was alleged that they collected maximum revenue from the peasants but appropriated to themselves as much of it as they could. They escaped payment of taxes like Khiraj, Jizya, Ghari and Charai. Therefore, they had become rich and affluent. Alauddin abolished their privileges and snatched away their right to collect revenues.

They were asked to pay revenue and all other taxes and thus, there remained no distinction between the Khuts (zamindars) and the Balahars (ordinary peasants). By this policy Alauddin broke up the power of the Hindus to rise in revolt. Alauddin raised the revenue demand to one-half of the gross produce. The land revenue was to be assessed by the technique of measurement on the basis of standard yields. Alauddin was the first Muslim ruler who introduced this system which certainly marked a progress upon the customary sharing system. The Sultan preferred to collect the revenue in kind instead of cash. Alauddin also imposed two new taxes. The one was grazing tax on all milch cattle and the other was the house-tax. Taxes like jizya and irrigation tax and import and export duties remained as usual.

The system of Alauddin imposed heavy burden on the peasantry. The peasants had to pay seventy five per cent of their income to the state as taxes. While Muslim merchants paid only five per cent of the value of their merchandise as tax, Hindu merchants were asked to pay ten per cent. This revenue system of Alauddin could not be implemented universally within the entire imperial territory. The collection of revenue by state officers after measurement of land was done only in Delhi and its nearby territories. This system was not introduced in lower Doab, Awadh, Gorakhpt, Bihar, Bengal, Malwa, West Punjab, Gujarat and Sindh. Alauddin established a new department known as Diwani–i–Mustakhraj to look after his revenue administration. He also engaged a large number of junior and senior officers for the same purpose.

He raised the salaries of revenue officers so that they might become free from temptation of bribery. Though, it was not possible to root out corruption and dishonesty from the revenue department, yet Alauddin succeeded in bringing about fair improvement in it by terrorising both his officers and the subjects by his severe punishments given to them in case of non-fulfillment of their responsibility. Primary objectives of Alauddin were to increase the income of the state and root out possibilities of revolts. By implementing the revenue policy, he succeeded in fulfilling his objectives.

MILITARY ADMINISTRATION OF ALAUDDIN KHALJI

Alauddin Khalji realised the importance of a strong military administrative system in order to establish a highly centralised and despotic government and an extensive empire in India. He fulfilled the necessity by keeping a permanent standing army at the capital. The army of Alauddin Khalji was recruited, equipped, trained and paid by the center. The army minister directly recruited the soldiers of the sultan's army.

The soldiers were supplied with horses, arms etc. by the state and were paid in cash by the royal treasury. The soldier with one horse was paid two hundred thirty four Tankas for a year while a soldier with two horses was paid seventy eight Tankas more. The sultan's army consisted of 4,75,000 cavalrymen. War elephants also constituted an important part of the army.

Swords, bows and arrows, mace, battle axe, dagger were important arms used by the soldiers. Stone-throwing machines were also used in wars. Alauddin Khalji's army was based on the Turkish model and divisions of units rested on the decimal system. Alauddin also took measures to stop the corrupt practices by the soldiers which were reducing the effective strength of the army. He instituted the practice of recording the huliya (descriptive roll) of individual soldiers and that of Dagh (branding of horses).

The Diwan-i-Arz kept the record of all of them. Besides a strict review of the army was occasionally made and horses and arms of soldiers were thoroughly examined. Alauddin repaired the forts constructed by Sultan Balban on the north-west frontiers. He also constructed new forts there and other places also like Kampil, Patiali and Bhojpur.

Soldiers were permanently in these forts and arrangements were made for regular supply of arms to them. Grain and fodder always remained stored in these forts. Thus, all forts were always kept prepared for all eventualities in case of any invasion. During his reign, larger part of northern India was conquered, all rulers of south India were defeated and all Mongol invasions were successfully repulsed. This proves that had Alauddin Khalji succeeded in building up a strong army.

ECONOMIC POLICY OF ALAUDDIN KHALJI

Alauddin Khalji adopted several economic policies to maintain a steady market system. Though the treasury of the Sultan was full but it was necessary to regulate the prices of the goods for the interests of the subjects. Alauddin kept a large standing army at the centre and paid it in cash.

Therefore, his expenses on the army were enormous. Alauddin had distributed wealth lavishly among his subjects which reduced the value of the currency in the market. Thus, it became necessary for Alauddin to reduce the salary of his soldiers and also to reduce the cost of the articles in the market. Alauddin's motive was to check the rising prices which were due to manipulation of the business community and not to reduce the prices to a lower level than the normal.

The necessity of his market-policy arose also because of the necessity of keeping a huge standing army and paying it in cash. Some historians have pointed out that the cause of this economic policy was humanitarian. Alauddin desired that all his subjects should get necessary articles in sufficient quantity and at proper prices. While according to many scholars, the primary object of Alauddin in enforcing these measures was purely political. He kept a permanent standing army at the centre and paid it in cash but desired that the soldiers remain comfortable with reasonable amount of salary. Therefore, he tried to check the inflationary prices, and the exploitation of merchants to raise the prices falsely and, thereby, was forced to fix the prices of articles and impose them sternly. Alauddin fixed up the prices of nearly all articles.

The prices were fixed not only of all varieties of grain, pulses, cloth, slaves, cattle and horses only but even those of essential articles of every day use as that of meat, fish, dry fruits, sugarcane, vegetable, needles, colours, betel-leaves etc. Separate markets were fixed up for different articles.

Alauddin established go downs where grain was stored in reserve to be released in times of scarcity. In times of need everything was rationed *i.e.* everybody was allowed to purchase only that much which was just adequate for his need. Thus, arrangements were so made that the people might not feel insufficiency of anything anytime. That is why revenue was collected in kind both from Khalisa land and the lands of feudatory chiefs. Only those traders who were registered with the state were allowed to purchase grain from the peasants.

All merchants were required to register themselves at the office of Shahna-i-mandi. All merchants were forced to bring at least some fixed minimum quantity of different articles to capital so that there was no scarcity of anything. Everything was sold at fixed rates and even the highest officer of the Sultan was not allowed to alter the rate or price of any article without prior permission of the Sultan. Nobody could dare to sell any commodity underweight as the same amount flesh was cut off from his body.

No peasant or merchant could hoard any commodity. Speculation and black-marketing was totally stopped. All these regulations were strictly enforced and the guilty ones were harshly punished. The economic policy of Alauddin was enforced only in Delhi and its nearby areas. Alauddin was successful in fulfilling his object during his lifetime.

He wanted to keep an enormous permanent standing army at the centre and for that purpose he fixed the prices of all commodities. He succeeded in his effort. He maintained a strong army at the centre which successfully repulsed invasions of the Mongols and successfully conquered practically the whole of India for him and his enforcement of price fixation of all commodities was also fully successful.

CONQUEST OF CHITTORE BY ALAUDDIN KHILIJI

Alauddin Khalji was the first to sack Chittaur on 1303 A.D., overpowered by a passionate desire to possess the regal beauty, queen

Padmini. Legend has it, that he saw her face in the reflection of a mirror and was struck by her mesmerizing beauty. But the noble queen preferred death to dishonour and committed 'Jauhar'.

While his expedition to Chittor the Rajputs inflicted heavy losses on Alauddin's army. While Alauddin was at Chittor, the Mongals invaded Delhi. Alauddin had to lift the siege of Chittor within a month of commencing it and rush to Delhi to face the Mongals. Turgha Khan headed the Mongals army. The two armies met at Siri, a suburb of Delhi. Alauddin's army was in a bad shape, as the Rajputs in Chittor had decimated half of his army. The Mongals won but for some reason did not capture Delhi and retreated.

A few months later, Alauddin again attacked Chittor. The King of Chittor,Rana Bhim Singh was captivated on Monday, Aug. 26, 1303 and Chittor fell. Thousands of Rajput women with Rani Padmini inside had entered a cellar and burnt themselves to ashes preferring a fiery death and unsullied honour to the lecherous hell of Islamic torture and venery. Discomfited Alauddin in impotent anger massacred thousands of children and old men found in the fort. In 1305 Alauddin Khalji captured Malwa and annexed Ujjain, Mandu, Dhar and Chanderi. Alauddin Khalji's expedition to Bengal was not successful and it remained independent.

NORTH INDIAN EXPEDITIONS

GUJARAT

Karnadev Vaghela II of the VaghelaVaghela dynasty was the king of Gujarat. Alauddin Khalji sent two of his great generals Ulugh Khan and Nusrat Khan. Nusrat Khan starterd for Gujarat from Delhi on February 24, 1299 A.D., Ulugh Khan started from Sindh and joined Nusrat Khan near Chittorgarh.The army crossed Vanasa river and captured the Ravosa fort. Karnadev was defeated and fled to the kingdom of Devagiri with his daughter Devaladevi and Gujarat was captured by Alauddin Khalji.

RANATHAMBOR

Alauddin Khalji once again sent two of his celebrated generals Ulugh Khan and Nusrat Khan to Ranathambor. Hamir Dev Chauhan of the Chauhan dynasty was the king of Ranathambor. In a counter attack from the Rajputs Nusrat Khan was killed and Ulugh Khan returned to Delhi. Alauddin Khalji then himself led the expedition to Ranathambor in 1301 A.D. After one year of siege he was able to conquer Ranathambor due to the treachery of the Rajput general Ranamal. Ironically, later Ranamal was killed by Alauddin Khalji.

MEWAR

Mewar was the most powerful kingdom of all the Rajput kingdoms. On 28 January 1303 Alauddin Khalji started for Mewar. First Alauddin Khalji captured the city of Chittorgarh and besieged the Chitor fort, this event is known as first sack of chittor. Rana Ratan Singh fought valiantly with his Rajput army. The Rajputs were able to hold their fort for seven months.

But, due to the long siege, there grew a severe shortage of food, drinking water and other rations. The Rajputs performed Jauhar and were all killed in the ensuing battle. Alauddin Khalji appointed Khidr Khan as the governor of Chitor. But Khidr Khan was forced to retreat due to repeated counter attacks of the Rajputs. Alauddin Khalji then appointed Maldeo, a Rajput, as the governor of Chitor. But Mewar was able to regain her independence immediately after the death of Alauddin Khalji.

MALWA

Alauddin Khalji's conquest of Mewar, Ranathambor and Gujarat stuck fear in the mind of the remaining Rajput Kingdoms. But Mahlak Dev refused to give in to Alauddin Khalji so easily. He gathered 20,000 horsemen and 90,000 infantry to confront Alauddin's army. Harnanda Koka was the general of his army. On the other hand Ain-ul-Mulk Multani was on the head of a 160,000 Muslim army. After a bloody war Harnana Koka was killed and the Rajput forces retreated. Malwa along with Mandu,Dhara and Chanderi fell to Alauddin Khalji. Ain-ul-Mulk Multani was appointed the governor of Malwa. It was in year 1294 A.D. when he acquired koh-i-noor Koh-i-Noor from Malwa and brought it to Delhi.

MARWAR

Alauddin Khalji invaded Marwar in 1308. Satal Dev was the king of Marwar and the owner of the famous Siwana fort. Alauddin Khalji sent Malik Kamaluddin as the general of his army. After a fierce battle the Marwari army was defeated. Satal dev was captured and was executed.

JALORE

Alauddin Khalji invaded Jalore next. The first expedition was a failure, Khalji's army was defeated by Kanhad Dev Songara. Alauddin

Khalji then sent Malik Kamaluddin. The Rajput's were no match for this army and succumbed to the superior skill and valor of Malik Kamaluddin's forces.

EXPEDITIONS IN SOUTHERN INDIA

DEVAGIRI

Alauddin Khalji invaded Devagiri once when he was the crown prince. Alauddin Khalji once again invaded Devagiri in 1306. The invincible Malik Kafur was on the spearhead of the army. He was accompanied with Khwaja Haji. The governors of Malwa and Gujarat were ordered to help Malik Kafur. The huge army conquered Devagiri almost without a battle. Alauddin Khalji appointed Raja Ramchandra the governor of Devagiri. He was given the title "Rai Rayan" (king of kings).

WARANGAL

After conquering Devagiri Alauddin Khalji invaded Warangal with Malik Kafur as the General of the Muslim army. Ramchandra helped Malik Kafur in this battle. After a fierce battle Malik Kafur was able to occupy the Warangal fort.King Prataprudradev of the Kakatiya dynasty signed a treaty with Alauddin Khalji. Alauddin Khalji got the famous Kohinoor diamond from Warangal.

DWARASAMUDRA/HALEBEEDU

After conquering Devagiri and Warngal Alauddin Khalji sent Malik Kafur against king Veera Ballala of the Hoysala dynasty. Veera Ballala surrendered without a fight. Malik Kafur returned to Delhi with immense booty.

PRICE CONTROL SYSTEM

Alauddin Khalji Introduced Price control system in order to maintain a large scale army because he was in danger from Mongols like every ruler of India. He fixed the price of every commodities by himself and make it sure that there should be a balance between demand and supply. He reduced the pay of the soldiers and enhanced the size of his army. His army did not suffer of low salary because the things were cheap.

4

Delhi Sultanate, 1204–1342

The only near-contemporary account of Muhammad Bakhtiyar's 1204 capture of the Sena capital is that of the chronicler Minhaj al-Siraj, who visited Bengal forty years after the event and personally collected oral traditions concerning it. "After Muhammad Bakhtiyar possessed himself of that territory," wrote Minhaj, he left the city of Nudiah in desolation, and the place which is (now) Lakhnauti he made the seat of government. He brought the different parts of the territory under his sway, and instituted therein, in every part, the reading of the *khutbah*, and the coining of money; and, through his praiseworthy endeavours, and those of his Amirs, *masjids* [mosques], colleges, and monasteries (for Dervishes), were founded in those parts.

The passage clearly reveals the conquerors' notion of the proper instruments of political legitimacy: reciting the Friday sermon, striking coins, and raising monuments for the informal intelligentsia of Sufis and the formal intelligentsia of scholars, or *'ulama*.

Both their coins and their monuments reveal how the rulers viewed themselves and wished to be viewed by others. Both, moreover, were directed at several different audiences simultaneously. One of these consisted of the conquered Hindus of Bengal, who, having never heard a *Khutbat*, seen a Muslim coin, or set foot in a mosque, were initially in no position to accord legitimate authority either to these symbols or to their sponsors. But for a second audience—the Muslim world generally, and more immediately, the rulers of the Delhi sultanate, the parent kingdom from which Bengal's new ruling class sprang—the *Khutbat*, the coins, and the building projects possessed great meaning. It is important to bear in mind these different audiences when "reading" the political propaganda of Bengal's Muslim rulers.

Militarily, Muhammad Bakhtiyar's conquest was a blitzkrieg; his cavalry of some ten thousand horsemen had utterly overwhelmed a local population unaccustomed to mounted warfare. After the conquest, Bakhtiyar and his successors continued to hold a constant and vivid symbol of their power—their heavy cavalry—before the defeated Bengalis.

In the year 1204–5 (601 A.H.), Bakhtiyar himself struck a gold coin in the name of his overlord in Delhi, Sultan Muhammad Ghuri, with one side depicting a Turkish cavalryman charging at full gallop and holding a mace in hand. Beneath this bold emblem appeared the phrase *Gauda vijaye*, "On the conquest of Gaur" (i.e., Bengal), inscribed not in Arabic but in Sanskrit. On the death of the Delhi sultan six years later, the governor of Bengal, 'Ali Mardan, declared his independence from North India and began issuing silver coins that also bore a horseman image. And when Delhi reestablished its sway over Bengal, coins minted there in the name of Sultan Iltutmish (1210–35) continued to bear the image of the horseman. For neither Muhammad Bakhtiyar, 'Ali Mardan, nor Sultan Iltutmish was there any question of seeking legitimacy within the framework of Bengali Hindu culture or of establishing any sense of continuity with the defeated Sena kingdom. Instead, the new rulers aimed at communicating a message of brute force. As Peter Hardy aptly puts it, referring to the imposition of early Indo-Turkish rule generally, "Muslim rulers were there in northern India as rulers because they were there—and they were there because they had won."

Such reliance on naked power, or at least on its image, is also seen in the earliest surviving Muslim Bengali monuments. Notable in this respect is the tower (*minar*) of Chhota Pandua, in southwestern Bengal near Calcutta.

Built toward the end of the thirteenth century, when Turkish power was still being consolidated in that part of the delta, the tower of Chhota Pandua doubtless served the usual ritual purpose of calling the faithful to prayer, inasmuch as it is situated near a mosque. But its height and form suggest that it also served the political purpose of announcing victory over a conquered people. Precedents for such a monument, moreover, already existed in the Turkish architectural tradition. Bengal's earliest surviving mosques also convey the spirit of an alien ruling class simply transplanted to the delta from elsewhere. Constructed (or restored) in 1298 in Tribeni, a formerly important center of Hindu civilization in southwest Bengal, the mosque of Zafar Khan appears to replicate the aesthetic vision of early Indo-Turkish architecture as represented, for example, in the Begumpur mosque in Delhi (ca. 1343). Clues to the circumstances surrounding the construction (or restoration) of the mosque are found in its dedicatory inscription:

> *Zafar Khan, the lion of lions, has appeared*
>
> *By conquering the towns of India in every expedition, and by restoring the decayed charitable institutions.*
>
> *And he has destroyed the obdurate among infidels with his sword and spear, and lavished the treasures of his wealth in (helping) the miserable.*

Zafar Khan's claims to have destroyed "the obdurate among infidels" gains some credence from the mosque's inscription tablet, itself carved from materials of old ruined Hindu temples, while the mutilated figures of Hindu deities are found in the stone used in the monument proper. Near Zafar Khan's mosque stands another structure, built in 1313, which is said to be his tomb; its doorways were similarly reused from an earlier pre-Islamic monument, and embedded randomly on its exterior base are sculpted panels bearing Vaishnava subject matter.

How was the articulation of these political symbols received by the several "audiences" to whom they were directed? As late as thirty years after the conquest, pockets of Sena authority continued to survive in the forests beyond the reach of Turkish garrisons. Whenever Turkish forces were out of sight, petty chieftains with miniature, mobile courts would appear before the people in their full sovereign garb—riding elephants in ivory-adorned canopies, wearing bejeweled turbans of white silk, and surrounded by armed retainers—in an apparent effort to continue receiving tribute and administering justice as they had done before. In 1236 a Tibetan Buddhist pilgrim recorded being accosted by two Turkish soldiers on a ferryboat while crossing the Ganges in Bihar. When the soldiers demanded gold of him, the pilgrim audaciously replied that he would report them to the local raja, a threat that so provoked the Turks' wrath as nearly to cost him his life. Clearly, after three decades of alien rule, people continued to view the Hindu raja as the legitimate dispenser of justice.

If Muslim coins and the architecture of this period projected to the subject Bengali population an image of unbridled power, they projected very different messages to the parent Delhi sultanate, and beyond that, the larger Muslim world. Throughout the thirteenth century, governors of Bengal tried whenever possible to assert their independence from the parent dynasty in Delhi, and each such attempt was accompanied by bold attempts to situate themselves within the larger political cosmology of Islam. For example, when the self-declared sultan Ghiyath al-Din 'Iwaz asserted his independence from Delhi in 1213, he attempted to legitimize his position by going over the head of the Delhi sultan and proclaiming himself the right-hand defender (*Nasir*) of the supreme Islamic authority on earth, the caliph in Baghdad. This marked the first time any ruler in India had asserted a direct claim to association with the wellspring of Islamic legitimacy, and it prompted Iltutmish, the Delhi sultan, not only to invade and reannex Bengal but to upstage the Bengal ruler in the matter of caliphal support. After his armies defeated Ghiyath al-Din in 1227, Iltutmish arranged to receive robes of honour from Caliph al-Nasir in Baghdad, one of which he sent to Bengal with a red canopy of state. There it was formally bestowed upon Iltutmish's own son, who was still in Lakhnauti, having just had the erstwhile independent king of Bengal beheaded. By having the investiture ceremony enacted in the capital city of the defeated sultan of Bengal, Iltutmish vividly dramatized his own prior claims to caliphal legitimacy. For the time being, the delta was politically reunitedwith North India, and for the next thirty years Delhi appointed to Bengal governors who styled themselves merely "king of the kings of the East" (*malik-i muluk al-sharq*).

But Delhi was distant, and throughout the thirteenth century the temptation to throw off this allegiance proved irresistible, especially as the imperial rulers were chronically preoccupied with repelling Mongol threats from the Iranian Plateau. So governors rebelled, and each brief assertion of independence was followed by their adoption of ever more exalted titles on their coins and public monuments. In 1281 Sultan Ghiyath al-Din Balban, the powerful sovereign of Delhi, ruthlessly stamped out one revolt by hunting down his rebel governor and publicly executing him. Yet within a week of Balban's death in 1287, his own son, Bughra Khan, whom the father had left behind as his new governor, declared his independence. Bughra's son, who ascended the Bengal throne as Rukn al-Din Kaikaus (1291–1300), then boldly styled himself on one mosque "the great Sultan, master of the necks of nations, the king of the kings of Turks and Persians, the lord of the crown, and the seal," as well as "the right hand of the viceregent of God"—that is, "helper of the caliph." On another mosque he even styled himself the "shadow of God" (*zill Allah*), an exalted title derived from ancient Persian imperial usage.

Exasperated with the wayward province, Delhi for several decades ceased mounting the massive military offensives necessary to keep it within its grip. In fact, the actions of Sultan Jalal al-Din Khalaji (r. 1290–96) betray something more than mere indifference toward the delta. A contemporary historian recorded that on one occasion the sultan rounded up about a thousand criminals ("thugs") and "gave orders for them to be put into boats and to be conveyed into the Lower country to the neighbourhood of Lakhnauti, where they were to be set free. The *thags* would thus have to dwell about Lakhnauti, and would not trouble the neighbourhood (of Dehli) any more." Within a century of its conquest, then, Bengal had passed from being the crown jewel of the empire, whose conquest had occasioned the minting of gold commemorative coins, to a dumping ground for Delhi's social undesirables. Already we discern here the seeds of a North Indian chauvinism toward the delta that would become more manifest in the aftermath of the Mughal conquest in the late sixteenth century.

KHILJI DYNASTY

With the death of Muhammad Ghori, the Mamluk dynasty gradually became weak and finally Jalal-ud-din Khilji captured Delhi, the centre of power and established the Khilji dynasty and set onto expand the empire. Ala-ud-din Khalji inherited the throne and the dynasty thrived under his able rule. His ruling period is marked by market control regulations, innovative administrative and revenue reforms. The period is considered as the golden era of Khilji rule. Ala-ud-din's most trusted noble Malik Kafur after him succeeded in making Shahab-ud-din Umar as the successor of Ala-ud-din. Qutub-ud-din Mubarik Shah, another son of Ala-ud-din Khalji removed his younger brother Umar after the death of Malik Kafur and became the sultan. With the rise of a Hindu slave, who was given the name Khusrav Khan by Mubarik, Khilji dynasty came to an end. The Khilji dynasty ruled for 30 years from 1290 to 1320.

TUGHLAQ DYNASTY

When Khusrav came into power, he replaced most of the Muslim officers by Hindu officers in the key positions. These Hindu officers openly insulted Islam and this situation was very difficult for the Muslim to tolerate. They gathered around a Tughlaq noble, Ghazi Malik. He killed Khusrav and wanted to give the power back to the Khilji Dynasty. But there were no survivor amongst the decedents of Ala-ud-din. In this situation, he ascended the throne and took the title of Ghias-ud-din

Tughlaq. Thus he became the founder of the Tughlaq dynasty. After killing Ghias-ud-din, his son Muhammad bin Tughlaq succeeded him. He tried to implement a number of his own schemes. Unfortunately for him, most of his schemes failed and he became unpopular amongst the masses. After him his cousin, Firoz Shah's long rule of 37 years is known for his marvellous administrative reforms. It was Amir Timur's that acted as the final nail in putting an end to the Tughlaq dynasty.

SAYYID DYNASTY

Tughlaq dynasty eventually came to an end in 1414 when Khizar Khan founded the Sayyid dynasty in Delhi. In 1414, Khizar won the battle against Mahmud Shah, the last Tughlaq ruler and established Sayyid Dynasty. It was during his reign that a number of states and provinces of Delhi Sultanate declared their independence. Kaizar tried to reintegrate them but failed. The Sultanate was, thus, reduced to Sind, Western Punjab, and western Uttar Pradesh. Rule of Mubarik Shah, the successor of Kaizar, was full of internal and external revolts. The next successors also faced political instability. The era of Sayyid Dynasty came to an end when Buhlul Lodhi occupied Delhi and established the Lodi Dynasty.

LODI DYNASTY

Buhlul Lodi occupied the province of Punjab and then captured Delhi. After him, his son Nizam Khan established himself as the most capable ruler of the Lodi Dynasty. He took the title of Sikandar Shah. The death of Sikandar Lodi created a disharmony between his two sons: Ibrahim Lodi and Jalal Lodi. A war of succession followed and resulted in the gradual downfall of the Lodi Dynasty. Ibrahim Lodi was the last sultan of the dynasty. He was defeated in the hands of Babur in the battle of Panipat on 1526. This battle brought an end of 320 years rule of the Sultans in Delhi.

QUTUBUDDIN AYBAK

Qutubuddin Aybak was a Turkic ruler of medieval India, the first Sultan of Delhi and founder of the Slave dynasty (also known as the *Ghulam* dynasty). He served as sultan for only four years, from 1206 to 1210.

EARLY YEARS

Qutubuddin was born somewhere in Central Asia; he was of Turkic descent. While still a child he was captured and sold as a slave (*ghulam*). He was purchased by the chief Qazi of Nishapur, a town in the province of Khorasan in northeastern Iran. The Qazi treated him like one of his own sons, and Aibak received a good education, including fluency in Persian and Arabic and training in archery and horsemanship. When his master died, his master's sons, who were jealous of Aibak, sold him to a slave merchant. Qutubuddin was purchased by General Mohammed Ghori governor of Ghazni.

CAREER

Starting with his native Ghor, an Aimak principality, Mohammed Ghori managed to establish control over most of present-day Afghanistan, Pakistan and northern India. Under his command, Qutubuddin Aybak sacked Delhi in 1193. As governor of northern India Qutubuddin Aybak established the first verifiable Muslim administration through collection of state taxes, establishing the rule of law, equitable distribution of land and revenues to the nobles under his charge, and governance based on a mixture of locally elected representation through Mashura courts and nominated administrators.

Qutubuddin rose through the ranks to become Sultan Ghori's most trusted general. His greatest military successes occurred while he was directly under Sultan Ghori's guidance and leadership. Qutubuddin was responsible for executing and consolidating Sultan Ghori's conquests in northern India. He was left in increasingly independent charge of the Indian campaigns and the exaction of levies from the areas in India that were under Sultan Ghori's conquests, as after 1192 Sultan Ghori concentrated on Central Asia.

QUTB-UD-DIN AIBAK IN SLAVE DYNASTY

Qutb-ud-din Aibak exercised his rule over the provisions where he was the Ghori's local receiver-general during the periodic expeditions. He initially ruled from Lahore to Delhi later developed as capital. Aybak During his period took initiative to construct Delhi's Earliest monuments, the 'Qutub Minar' and the 'Quwwat-ul-Islam mosque' (the first mosque in Delhi). But these monuments remained incomplete as Aybak died accidentally in 1210. Aram shah, the successor of Aybak turned to be an incapable ruler. The Sultanate of Delhi was facing some internal problems that time. The 'Chihalgani' or the 'Corp of Forty' invited Shams-ud-din Iltutmish to replace Aram Shah.

ACHIEVEMENTS OF AIBAK AS A COMMANDER

After the second battle of "I'arain, Aibak was appointed Viceroy of the conquered provinces of Ghori in India. He did yeoman service to the infant Muslim empire, liven during absence ol his master he continued the series of victories and crushed t he revolts of the Rajputs from A. D. 1192 to 1205. He not only organized the provinces conquered by Ghori but also extended his territory. Prominent historian Lanepoole has written about him, "Aibak's chief exploits were achieved during his Viceroyalty."

The credit for the conquest of Ajmer, Kannauj and Kalinjar from A. D.1193 to 1203 goes to him. First of all Aibak invaded the fort of Hansi and established his sway over it. Later on, he defeated the Tomar ruler in A. D. 1193 and occupied Delhi. In the same year he achieved victory against Meerut and Bulandshahar. In A. D. 1194, Ghori again invaded India in order to punish Jaichand, King of Kannauj. During this invasion Aibak greatly helped his master. Ghori after achieving victory against Kannauj handed over the province to Aibak for its administration.

Among the early achievements of Aibak the suppression of the revolt of Ajmer is a significant event in the history of Medieval India. Between A. D. 1192 to 1197, the Rajputs of Delhi and Ajmer revolted against the supremacy of Ghori from time to time. Aibak crushed these revolts successfully and saved the infant Muslim empire from decline. In A. D. il92 Hari Raj, King of Ajmer, was the first to revolt against the Muslim rule. Aibak crushed the revolt but in A. D. 1195 Hari Raj again revolted with the support of the Tomar King of Delhi. The army of Aibak could not succeed in crushing this revolt, hence Aibak himself went on this campaign and besieged the fort of Ajmer. After defeat, Hari Raj committed suicide due to remorse and the reign of Muslims was established over Ajmer. In the same year Aibak got success against the Jats and conquered the fort of Ranthambhor. Qutbuddin Aibak retaliated by invading Anhilwara and sacked the kingdom of Bhimdeo. In A. D. 1202, he invaded the fort of Kalinjar and compelled the Chandela ruler Parmardi Deva to be confined in his fort for some months. Ultimately, the Turks became victorious and the same story of plunder and slaughter was repeated. Aibak also gained victory in his expeditions against Mahoba, Kalpi and Badaun. When he was busy in attaining victories in southern and western campaigns, his able commander Ikhtiyaruddin Muhammad-bin-Bakhtiyar Khalji penetrated into Bihar and Bengal and achieved success. The credit of these victories achieved in the reign of Ghori goes to Aibak, therefore, after the death of Ghori in A. D. 1206, he could become Sultan in India without much opposition.

QUTUBUDDIN AIBAK CAME INTO POWER

With Aibak declaring himself king after Muhammad Ghuri's death, the Sultanate came to be regarded as an Indian state and not as an extension of the Afghan kingdom. This was an important development and, of course, came with complications. To begin with, the Turks in India felt threatened by the Rajputs and with reason too. But strangely enough (or, as some would say, predictably) the threat never materialized. However the Turks had no such luck with the other clouds looming over their horizons.

The tricky thing about declaring independence is that the ruler back home is not quite philosophical about letting go of a part of his empire, however small. Taj-ud-din Yaldoz, king of Ghazni, was ready to fight it out if it took all summer.

He made his wish to annex Punjab so apparent that Qutub-ud-din felt compelled to move his capital from Delhi to Lahore, which was closer to Afghanistan. What made tackling Ghazni easier for Aibak was that Muhammad Ghuri had himself invested viceregal powers and the title of Malik upon him (Aibak). and what made Yaldoz's job trickier was that the people of Lahore were overwhelmingly pro-Aibak. Taj-ud-din Yaldoz was actually the ex-governor of Kirman (in Afghanistan) and a usurper himself, so in the rise of Aibak he perceived a threat to his own newly-acquired throne. However, by 1208, Qutub-ud-din was so successful in neutralizing Yaldoz that he was able to secure from him the right to rule over not only Hindustan, but also Ghazni. But not for long. Aibak was soon driven out of Ghazni by Yaldoz and had to return to Lahore.

ACHIEVEMENTS OF QUTUB-UD-DIN AIBAK

There are several achievements of Qutub-Ud-Din Aibak, who is regarded as the real founder of the Turkish rule in India. Qutub-Ud-Din is regarded as the real founder of the Turkish rule in India. He is also regarded as the founder of Slave Dynasty in India. After ascending the throne at Delhi, Qutub-Ud-Din Aibak decided to keep himself independent and keep his kingdom free from the politics of Central Asia. He first strengthened his position in Delhi and Lahore.

He influenced most of the Turkish nobles in India to accept his subordination and married his sister to Qabacha and his daughter to

Iltutmish. Qutub-Ud-Din was troubled by the instable affairs of Bengal and Bihar. Ali Mardan, who had set himself as an independent ruler, was dethroned and imprisoned by the Khilji nobles and Muhammad Sheran was offered the throne on the condition that he too would maintain the independence of Bengal. On the request of Ali Mardan to interfere in the affairs of Bengal, Qutub-Ud-Din handed over the task to his noble Qaiwaz Rumi Khan. He used both force and diplomacy and ultimately succeeded in convincing the Khalji nobles of Bengal that they should accept Ali Mardan as the governor of Bengal under the suzerainty of Delhi. Finally, Ali Mardan became the governor of Bengal and agreed to pay an annual tribute to Qutub-Ud-Din.

Qutub-Ud-Din could not practice the policy of extension of his kingdom. He could not even divert his attention towards the Rajputs who were successful in recovering few of their places from the Turks. He was mostly pre occupied in defending his independent position and therefore, the affairs in the North West and Bengal in the east remained his basic concerns. This is the reasons why he mostly remained at Lahore instead of Delhi. Qutub-Ud-Din got a very little time as an independent ruler.

AN ASSESSMENT OF QUTUB-UD-DIN AIBAK

Qutubuddin Aibak was the first Turkish ruler of Delhi Sultanate. He founded the Slave dynasty in medieval age. He ruled for four years, *i.e.* from 1206 to 1210. He was made slave and was sold to the chief Qazi of Nishapur. He was well educated and well treated by Qazi but after his death Qutubuddin Aibak was sold to Sultan Muhammad Ghori. The conquests of northern India were executed mainly by Qutb-ud-din Aibak, which helped Ghori to spread his tentacles there. Qutubuddin Aibak was crowned the Sultan of Delhi in 1206 after the death of Muhammad Ghori. It was at the time of Qutb-ud-din Aibak the construction of Quwwat-ul-Islam mosque and the Qutub Minar had started which were later completed by his successor Iltutmish.

ACCESSION OF QUTBUDDIN AIBAK

In A. D. 1206 on his way to Ghazni Ghori breathed his last. His empire was inherited by his slaves as he had no son to succeed him. Aibak who was a Viceroy of his Indian empire was invited by the Amirs of Lahore to assume the powers for Ghori wanted it and already bestowed the title of Malik and Subedar on Aibak. Dr. A. L. Srivastava supports this on the basis of the writings of Fakhr-i-Mudabbir who refers to the appointment of Qutbuddin Aibak as Wali Ahd (heir apparent) after the victory against Khokhars in A. D. 1205. Professor Habibullah also writes that powers of commanding the vanquished territory were given to Qutbuddin after the second battle of Tarain but K. A. Nizami does not agree and holds a different view.

He writes, "The actual position seems to have been that Muizuddin's death left Yaldoz, Aibak and Qubacha to struggle for supremacy and decide the issue on the basis of the survival of the fittest. Aibak had, therefore, to press hard to get his position recognized." Ghori's nephew Ghiasuddin who succeeded him at Ghazni was not a competent ruler. However, Aibak did not assume the title of Sultan, nor did he issue currency in his name. It was because he had not received formal manumission from Muhammad Ghori and as a shrewd politician, he did not want to become a prey of the jealousies of Turkish nobles; rather he wanted to consolidate his position and power through diplomatic measures.

To achieve his mission he adopted the policy of matrimonial alliances. He gave away his daughter to Iltutmish and his sister to Nasiruddin Qubacha in marriage. He himself married the daughter of Yaldoz. Thus he tried to establish sweet relations with all the powerful persons of his times so that his position could be strong. He also requested Ghiasuddin, the nephew of Ghori to recognize him as an independent ruler of India and assured him all help against the ruler of Khwarizm, Ghiasuddin accepted his request and sent him the royal insignia and standard and also bestowed on him the title of Sultan. Thus the formal manumission was granted to Aibak in A. D. 1206.

DIFFICULTIES OF AIBAK

Qutub-Ud-Din faced all difficulties with determination. He decided to keep himself independent and keep his kingdom free from the politics of Central Asia. However, he moved with caution. He first strengthened his position in Delhi and Lahore. He persuaded most of the Turkish nobles in India to accept his subordination and married his sister to Qabacha and his daughter to Iltutmish. Qutub-Ud-Din was troubled by instable affairs of Bengal and Bihar as well. Qutub-Ud-Din could not pursue the policy of extension of his kingdom. He could not pay attention even towards the Rajputs who succeeded in recovering few of their places from the Turks. Mostly he remained busy in defending his independent position and, therefore, the affairs in the north-west and

Bengal in the east remained his primary concerns. That is why mostly he remained at, Lahore instead of Delhi.

DEATH OF QUTUB-UD-DIN

Following Qutub-ud-din's sudden death, the Amirs and Maliks (the Turkish nobles) at Delhi put Aram Shah on the throne as a stopgap arrangement. Just who this Aram Shah was and why was he selected to succeed Aibak remains a mystery. He has been variously portrayed as Aibak's son, brother, just the convenient man available and many such things, but the truth is not known.

What is better known is that Aram Shah was a weak and unpopular king and the people of Delhi flatly refused to accept him as their ruler. Following their excellent example, powerful governors like Nasir-ud-din Qabacha of Multan and Ali Mardan of Bengal also rejected his overlordship. Were the nobles in Delhi attempting to put a puppet king on the throne? Or was this simply a move to make Altamash's ascendancy to the throne unquestioned?

ILTUTMISH

Shamsuddin Iltutmish, or Altamash was the third Muslim Turkic sultan of the Sultanate of Delhi and the third ruler of the Mamluk dynasty (or Slave dynasty) (died 1236). He was a slave of Qutub-ud-din-Aybak and later became his son-in-law and close lieutenant. He was the Governor of Badaun when he deposed Qutubuddin's successor Aram Shah and acceded to the throne of the Delhi Sultanate in 1211.

He remained the ruler until his death in May 1, 1236. He built the Hauz-i-Shamsi reservoir in Mehrauli in 1230 AD, which also has Jahaz Mahal standing on its edge, used by later Mughal Emperors. In 1231, he built Sultan Ghari, he built the mausoleum of his eldest son, Prince Nasiruddin Mahmud, which was the first Islamic Mausoleum in Delhi. His own tomb exists, within the Qutb complex in Mehrauli, Delhi.

EARLY LIFE AND CAREER

Shamsuddin belonged to the tribe of Ilbari in Turkestan. He was remarkably handsome in appearance and showed signs of intelligence and sagacity from his early days, which excited the jealousy of his brothers, who sold him into slavery. His accomplishments attracted the notice of Qutubuddin-Aybak, then Viceroy of Delhi, who purchased him at a high price. He rose quickly in Qutubuddin's service, married his daughter, and served in succession as the Governor of Gwalior and Baran. He later served as Governor of Badaun between 1206 and 1211 until his accession to the throne in Delhi. In recognition of his services during the campaign of Mohammed of Ghur against the Khokhars in 1205-06, he was, by the Sultan's order, manumitted.

SULTAN OF DELHI

Rider bearing lance on caparisoned horse facing right. Devnagari Legends: Sri/hamirah'. Rev:Arabic Legends: 'Shams al- dunya wa'l din Abul Muzaffar Iltutmish al-Sultan'.

RISE TO POWER

In A.D. 1210 Qutubuddin Aibak died. Aram Shah, the new Sultan alienated the Turkish nobility with his incompetence. The nobles invited Shamsuddin to overthrow Aram Shah. In 1211, Shamsuddin defeated Aram Shah and assumed the throne was given the title "Altmush or Iltmash [and also Iltutmish]" when he was throned. Altmush (pronounced ahlt-MUSH) in the Turkish language translates into 60, which was the age of Shamsuddin at the time he was made king.

EARLY CHALLENGES

On his accession, Iltutmish faced a number of challenges to his rule. Nasir-ud-Din Qabacha, the Governor of Uchh and Multan, asserted his independence and occupied Lahore. The Sultan of Ghazni, Tajuddin Elduz, attempted to bring Delhi under his control. Ali Mardan, a Khalji noble, who had been appointed Governor of Bengal by Qutubuddin in 1206, had thrown off his allegiance to Delhi after his death and styled himself Sultan Alauddin. His successor, Ghiyasuddin, conquered Bihar. The Hindu princes and chiefs were discontented at their loss of independence and had recovered Kannauj, Benaras, Gwalior, and Kalinjar had been lost during Qutubuddin's reign while Ranthambore had been reconquered by the Chauhans during Aram Shah's rule. To add to Iltutmish's troubles, some of the Amirs of Delhi expressed resentment against his rule.

The new Sultan faced the situation boldly. He first effectively suppressed a rebellion of the Amirs in the plain of Jud near Delhi, and then brought under his control the different parts of the kingdom of Delhi with its dependencies like Badaun, Benaras and Sivalik.

In 1215-16, Elduz, who had been defeated and expelled from Ghazni by the forces of the Shah of Khwarezm, moved towards Punjab and laid claim to the throne of Delhi. Iltutmish defeated him at Tarain. Elduz was later executed.

In 1217, Iltutmish moved towards Qabacha at the head of a large army. Qabacha attempted to retreat from Lahore towards Multan but was defeated at Mansura. Iltutmish refrained from attacking Sindh due to the presence of Mongols on his north-west frontier. Iltutmish was preoccupied with the Mongol threat and did not threaten Qabacha until 1227.

MONGOL THREAT

In 1221, the Mongols, under Genghis Khan appeared for the first time on the banks of the Indus. They had overrun the countries of Central and Western Asia with lightning rapidity. The Mongols captured Khiva and forced its ruler, Jalaluddin Mangabarni to flee to the Punjab.

He sought asylum in the dominions of Iltutmish. The Sultan of Delhi refused to comply with the request. Mangabarni entered into an alliance with the Khokhars, and after defeating Qabacha of Multan, plundered Sindh and northern Gujarat and went away to Persia. The Mongols also retired. India was thus saved from a terrible calamity, but the menace of the Mongol raids disturbed the Sultans of Delhi in subsequent times.

RAZIA SULTANA

Razia al-Din (1205-1240), throne name *Jalalat ud-Din Raziya,* usually referred to in history as *Razia Sultan* or *Razia Sultana,* was the Sultana of Delhi in India from 1236 to 1240. She was of Turkish Seljuks ancestry and like some other Muslim princesses of the time, she was trained to lead armies and administer kingdoms if necessary. Razia Sultana, the fifth Mamluk Sultan, was the very first woman ruler in the Muslim and Turkish history.

RAZIA AS SULTAN

Razia succeeded her father Shamsuddin Iltutmish to the Sultanate of Delhi in 1236. Iltutmish became the first sultan to appoint a woman as his successor when he designated his daughter Razia as his heir apparent. (According to one source, Iltumish's eldest son had initially been groomed as his successor, but had died prematurely.)

But the Muslim nobility had no intention of acceding to Iltutmish's appointment of a woman as heir, and after the sultan died on April 29, 1236, Razia's brother, Ruknuddin Feroze Shah, was elevated to the throne instead. Ruknuddin's reign was short. With Iltutmish's widow Shah Turkaan for all practical purposes running the government, Ruknuddin abandoned himself to the pursuit of personal pleasure and debauchery, to the considerable outrage of the citizenry. On November 9, 1236, both Ruknuddin and his mother Shah Turkaan were assassinated after only six months in power.

With reluctance, the nobility agreed to allow Razia to reign as Sultan of Delhi. As a child and adolescent, Razia had had little contact with the women of the harem, so she had not learnt the customary behaviour of women in the Muslim society that she was born into. Even before she became Sultan, she was reportedly preoccupied with the affairs of state during her father's reign. As Sultan, Razia preferred a man's tunic and headdress; and contrary to custom, she would later show her face when she rode an elephant into battle at the head of her army.

A shrewd politician, Razia managed to keep the nobles in check, while enlisting the support of the army and the populace. Her greatest accomplishment on the political front was to manipulate rebel factions into opposing each other. At that point, Razia seemed destined to become one of the most powerful rulers of the Delhi Sultanate. But Razia miscounted the consequences that a relationship with one of her advisers, Jamal-ud-Din Yaqut, an Abyssinian Siddi (Habshi) slave, would have for her reign. According to some accounts, Razia and Yaqut were lovers; other sources simply identify them as close confidants. In any case, before long she had aroused the jealousy of the Turkish nobility by the favouritism she displayed toward Yaqut, who was not a Turk, when she appointed him to be Superintendent of the Stables. Eventually, a childhood friend named Malik Altunia, the governor of Bhatinda, joined a rebellion by other provincial governors who refused to accept Razia's authority.

A battle between Razia and Altunia ensued, with the result that Yaqut was killed and Razia taken prisoner. To escape death, Razia agreed to marry Altunia. Meanwhile, Razia's brother, Muizuddin Bahram Shah, had usurped the throne.

After Altunia and Razia undertook to take back the sultanate from Bahram through battle, both Razia and her husband were defeated on 24th of Rabi' al-awwal A.H. 638 (Oct. 1240), and fled Delhi and reached Kaithal the next day, where their remaining forces abandoned them, and they both fell into the hands of the enemy and were killed on 25th of Rabi' al-awwal A.H. 638, this date corresponds to October 14, 1240. Bahram, for his part, would later be dethroned for incompetence.

RAZIA'S LEGACY

As sultan, Razia reportedly sought to abolish the tax on non- Muslims but met opposition from the nobility. By way of response, Razia is said to have pointed out that the spirit of religion was more important than its parts, and that even the Islamic prophet Mohammed spoke against overburdening the non-Muslims. On another occasion, Razia reportedly tried to appoint an Indian Muslim convert from Hinduism to an official position but again ran into opposition from the nobles.

Razia was reportedly devoted to the cause of her empire and to her subjects. There is no record that she made any attempt to remain aloof from her subjects, rather it appears she preferred to mingle among them.

Her tolerance of Hinduism would later bring her criticism from Muslim historians. Razia established schools, academies, centres for research, and public libraries that included the works of ancient philosophers along with the Qur'an and the traditions of Mohammed. Hindu works in the sciences, philosophy, astronomy, and literature were reportedly studied in schools and colleges. Razia refused to be addressed as Sultana because it meant "wife or mistress of a sultan". She would answer only to the title "Sultan".

RAZIA'S GRAVE

Razia's grave lies among the narrow lanes of Old Delhi, in a courtyard in Bulbul-i-khana, Shahjahanabad, near the Turkman Gate entrance. Crumbling and covered by dust and grime, the grave has clearly suffered the ravages of time. The grave is surrounded on all sides by unattractive residential buildings. In the 13th century, the site of the tomb was a jungle, and no one knows how Razia's body ended up where it lies today. A second grave, believed to be that of her sister, Shazia, accompanies Razia's.

Some of the Muslim residents of the neighbourhood have turned a part of the tomb into a mosque, where prayers are conducted five times each day. However, there's also a claim that the tomb of Razia is situated in Kaithal city, Haryana state. The tomb lies in the north-western suburbs of the city where, a few years back, a jail was erected by the present administration.

ALAUDDIN KHILJI

Alauddin Khilji was the second ruler of the Khilji dynasty in India. He reigned from 1296 to 1316. His historic attack on Chittor in 1303 AD, after hearing of the beauty of queen of Chittor, Rani Padmini, the wife of King Rawal Ratan Singh and the subsequent story has been immortalized in the epic poem Padmavat, written by Malik Mohammed Jayasi in the Awadhi language in the year 1540.

BIOGRAPHY

Alauddin Khalji was the nephew and son in law of Jalaluddin. His surname is Khilji in Dari/Farsi and Arabic documents, but the original Pashtu is Ghilzai. The obvious difference in spelling and pronunciation arises in lack of letters between Arabic/Dari and Pashtu. At first, Jalaluddin appointed Ala-ud-Din as the governor of Kara near the city of Allahabad. In 1296 Ala-ud-Din killed his uncle. But Malika Jahan, the widow of Jalaluddin, put her younger son Ruknuddin Khilji on the throne. Alauddin quickly marched on Delhi from Kara. He entered Delhi with his uncle's head on a pike and on October 3, 1296, proclaimed himself the *King of Delhi*. Arkali Khan, Jalaluddin's older son, and Ruknuddin were blinded. Malika Jahan was imprisoned.

Very soon he went about despoiling the wealth of nobles, frequently blinding, imprisoning or killing them. In 1297, Alauddin sent an army to plunder Gujarat, under the generalship of Ulugh Khan and Nusrat Khan. This army looted the temple of Somnath and the Shivalinga was broken into pieces and was being carried back to Delhi. Kanhad Dev Songara, the ruler of Jalore in Rajasthan attacked and defeated Ulugh Khan and captured the broken Shivalinga which was washed in the Ganges River, and the fragments were established in various temples in Jalore. Mohammed Shah helped Kanhad Dev Songara. Mohammed was a general in Khilji's army. After the war, Mohammed Shah went and stayed with Hammir at Ranthambore. Ulugh Khan apprised Alauddin who ordered him and Nusrat Khan to conquer Ranthambore. In 1299 they started out with 80,000 cavalry and a large infantry to attack Hammir. Hammir 's army repulsed the attack and killed Nusrat Khan. Ulugh Khan escaped and reached Delhi. Khilji was taken aback by this defeat and wanted revenge. He finally came himself in 1301, and there was a long siege. Hammir was very well prepared. When the fort would not fall after repeated bloody skirmishes, Khilji resorted to diplomacy. Hammir was very suspicious but he heeded to his councilors who told him that the sword is not always the best recourse. Ratipal and Ranmal, who were close confidants of Hammir, were sent to the Khilji camp. Ranmal's father was hung by Hammir for treachery and his property was confiscated. Ranmal earned the trust of Hammir by being brave in battles that Hammir fought but perfidy was in his blood. Khilji bribed these two generals of Hammir's army and consequently Ranthambore fell. After the annexation of Gujarat, he took to the practice of making the innocent families of rebels against the government suffer.

QUTLUGH KHWAJA

But in 1299, the Mongols came back. It says much for the tenacious Mongol spirit that they were back so soon and in such strength that they took over the fort of Siri, just beyond Delhi, which Ala-ud-Din Khalji had built. This time they came under a leader who was a legend in his own right, Qutlugh Khwaja, the feared Central Asian warrior and son of Duwa Khan now commanding a force of 200,000 Mongols. Ala-ud-Din Khilji realized that the Mongols meant business. If Qutlugh Khwaja had come himself it meant war, not for gold but for the kingdom itself.

The situation was serious enough for the usually individualistic Sultan Ala-ud-Din Khilji to be forced into taking advice from others. Ala-ud-Din Khilji was urged to sue for peace by his advisors as Qutlugh was virtually wiping his feet at the doorsteps of Delhi. However Ala-ud-Din Khilji did not become the Sultan via cautious diplomacy. He rejected their advice and said,

If I were to follow your advice how could I show my face, how could I go into my harem? No, come what may tomorrow, I must march into the battlefield.

Ignoring their advice the young sultan attacked the Mongols. The advance guard of the army was led by Zafar Khan himself. He defeated the Mongols again and went off in hot pursuit of them as they withdrew. However, the wily Qutlugh tricked Zafar into a position where he was first surrounded and then killed by the Mongols. Ala-ud-Din Khilji took this loss calmly. Zafar Khan had been entirely too popular for his comfort anyway. However, the death of the general did not improve matters for the Mongols. In face of Ala-ud-Din Khilji's continued offensives, they had to retreat to the unconquerable heights from where they had come.

TARGHI

The Mongols took, what was for them, a long time to rally from this setback. They attacked at the worst time possible for Ala-ud-Din Khilji, when he was busy laying siege to Chittor. This time the Mongols travelled light. An army of 12,000 under Targhi's leadership trickled into India like a shadow and moved to Delhi at a pace that was astonishing even by Mongol standards. Such was the swiftness of the attack that many governors could not send their troops to Delhi in time.

Ala-ud-Din Khilji was forced to duck into Siri and stay put for about two months. The Mongols stomped through and pillaged not only the surrounding areas, but Delhi itself. However they could not get into Siri. Although minor skirmishes were fought, a decisive win eluded both parties. This deadlock dragged on for more than a couple of months. In the end when Ala-ud-Din Khilji was fervently hoping for a miracle to help him, his prayers were answered.

The Mongols were a nomadic restless lot, and Targhi was more impatient than most of them. When Ala-ud-Din Khilji dug in his heels and stayed put in his seemingly impregnable fortress for months, Targhi lost interest in the whole affair, washed his hands of it and ordered his army to withdraw. Barani, the contemporary historian at that time, attributed this marvel to the prayers of the Sufi mystic Shaikh Nizamuddin Auliya. Ala-ud-Din Khilji's defences were so strong and enduring that the whole situation had really become quite an impasse. He wisely realized that the Mongols could not hold out forever and had to go home to Central Asia some time. That was where the Mongol power was concentrated and they could not afford to be away for too long.

Targhi had to go back with the consolation that he was leaving behind a much disturbed and thoughtful Ala-ud-Din Khilji, The seriousness of the Qutlugh Khwaja and Targhi led Mongol invasions which had left Siri panting for breath, forced Ala-ud-Din Khilji to take stock of the situation. A defensive measure like hiding in Siri till the Mongol storm blew over must have gashed his proud spirit. He had the forts along the border strengthened and equipped with larger garrisons. New, more effective fortifications were built along this area. A whole new army, with its own special governor, was created whose portfolio was managing and guarding the border areas.

ALI BEG ET TARTAQ

A few months later the Mongols under the leadership of Ali Beg and Tartaq, suddenly appeared in the Punjab and the neighbourhood of Amroha. The Mongols plundered the Punjab and burnt everything to cinders along the way.

But this time Ala-ud-Din Khilji was ready for them. He sent a strong army led by two of his toughest generals Ghazi Malik and the famous Malik Kafur after them. They surprised the Mongols on their way back to Central Asia with their plunder. The two generals pooled in their immense talents and defeated the Mongols. The Mongol generals were captured and brought back to Siri, along with other prisoners. Ala-ud-Din Khilji had the generals trampled to death by elephants while the other prisoners were put to death and their heads hung from the walls of the fort.

KUBAK

Even after the gory treatment meted out to their last expedition, the Mongols came in again in 1306. They crossed the Indus near Multan and were moving towards the Himalayas, when Ghazi Malik (who was by then the governor of the Punjab) intercepted them. About 50,000 Mongols were made prisoners including Kubak, their leader. Ala-ud-Din Khilji put them all to death and sold their wives and children as slaves.

IQBALMAND KHAN

The last Mongol invasion took place in 1307-1308 under Iqbalmand. He had just about managed to cross the Indus when Ala-ud-Din Khilji's armies overtook them and put them all to the sword.

After 1308, the Mongols did not attack India again. There were a number of reasons for this. Principal among these was that during their earlier descent from the mountains into the Indus plains, the Mongols became aware of their handicap in an environment of higher temperatures, humidity and their lack of dexterity in riding horses at the speeds they were comfortable at in higher & drier areas. To a lesser extent, of course that Ala-ud-Din Khilji, by repeated ruthlessness, finally managed to drive home the point that he would deal firmly and mercilessly with invaders into his territory. This was one of the greatest achievements of Ala-ud-Din Khilji. He was an original thinker and brilliant as a strategist. If the Mongols had still been serious about an Indian empire, they could have kept sending armies to India. It is to Alauddin's credit that he drove the idea of an Indian empire from the heads of the Mongols.

But he did not stop there, Ala-ud-Din Khilji had to be sure that the Mongols would never come back. The only way to do that was to attack them, he sent plundering armies under the veteran general Ghazi Malik to Kandahar, Ghazni and Kabul. The Mongols were already so much in awe of him that they did not even bother to defend their own territories against him. These offensives effectively crippled the Mongol line of control leading to India until the arrival of Timur Lane.

MALIK KAFUR

Malik Kafur, was a eunuch slave who became a general in the army of Alauddin Khilji, ruler of the Delhi sultanate from 1296 to 1316 A.D. He was originally seized by Alauddin's army after the army conquered the city of Khambhat. Alauddin Khilji fell in love with the effeminate beauty of Malik Kafur, castrated and converted him to Islam. Kafur was also called "Thousand Dinar Kafur", probably the amount paid by sultan for his possession. The sultan had homosexual relation with Kafur.

Kafur rose quickly in the army. He was made *malik naib*, the senior commander of the army. In 1294 he led the sultan's army against the capital city of the Yadava kingdom, Devagiri. He led further invasions southward into the Kakatiya dynasty, winning immense riches for the sultanate and sacking many Hindu temples..

The booty from Warangal included the famous diamond Kohinoor. During the course of the attack he sacked and plundered many Hindu temples including the famous Hoyasaleshwara temple in Halebidu. Accordin to Muslim historian Jiauddin Barani, Kafur came back to Delhi with 241 tonnes of gold, 20,000 horses and 612 elephants laden with the looted treasure.

DUWA KHAN

Duwa (also known as Duad. 1307) was khan of the Chagatai Khanate (1282-1307). He was the second son of Baraq. He was the longest reigning monarch of the Chagatayid Khanate and accepted the Great Khan's supremacy. Under his rule, the Chagatai Khanate reached its peak.

HISTORY

In 1282 Kaidu appointed Duwa as head of the Chagatai Khanate, in an effort to gain peace between himself and the sons of Baraq, who had ravaged Central Asia for much of the past ten years. This promotion ensured the loyalty of the Chaghataids from that point to Kaidu's death. Several years earlier, in 1275, Duwa destroyed a force in Uighuria loyal to Kublai Khan, led by the Chaghataid Ajiki and Kublai's son Ayachi. He then laid siege to Kara Khoja (present Idikut shahri near Turpan) for six months with his brother Buzma by 120,000 troops.

They demanded the Uyghur commander Idikut Khochhar to surrender, having said to him: *We have just overcome the resistance of 300,000 troops, how you with only one city can to withstand us?* Khochhar replied to them: *I will follow my fate and destiny, this city is a place, where I was born and raised, its population has become my own family, if now I have to die, well, then let this city to have become my own grave*. Nevertheless, Mongol princes had failed to take the city by assaults and finally idikut Khochhar managed to have the siege lifted only by giving Duwa his daughter in marriage, and probably financial compensation as well. Soon afterwards, Idikut Khochhar died in the occasional combat with Kaidu forces near the border of Yuan China. Duwa also may have given assistance to an unsuccessful revolt of Brigung sect against Kublai's authority in Tibet. The following year, Kaidu and Duwa launched an expedition against Beshbalik, defeated the Yuan forces there and captured the city. In 1278 Duwa was reported to have led a raid into Yuan territory.

Kaidu's attempts to spread his power within the Ilkhanate gave Duwa an excuse to invade that Mongol kingdom in early 1295. Supported by Kaidu's son Sarban, he invaded Khurasan and Mazandaran while the Ilkhanid commanders were involved in a succession struggle far to the west. For eight months he stayed in Mazandaran; when he left, he pillaged many cities on the way back. Duwa attempted to convince the Kartids of Herat to defect to his side, but they refused. He attempted to plunder the cities of Kusui, which he failed to do; and Fushang, which he succeeded at, killing many of the inhabitants. A similar attempt on Herat never happened, since Duwa feared he would fail; he soon after was recalled by Kaidu back to Central Asia, and the campaign ended.

Stiffening resistance by the Yuan commanders forced Kaidu and Duwa to pull back several times in 1297. In 1298, Duwa avenged these defeats when he attacked the Yuan garrisons during the winter. Most of the Yuan commanders were eating and drinking and therefore incapable of fighting; the Great Khan Chancing's brother-in-law Korguz, who had been more ready, was unable to defeat him by himself. Duwa tried to convince him to abandon the Great Khan's side, but was unsuccessful in doing so.

Duwa then withdrew, only to be defeated in battle by the garrison troops in what is today known as Kebuduo. Duwa's brother-in-law was captured in the midst of the defeat. A prisoner exchange was agreed to, and his brother-in-law was returned, but Korguz died before returning to the Great Khan. In 1298 or 1299 Duwa appointed his son Kutluk Khoja as head of the Qaraunas, a Mongol group that controlled a large part of Khurasan.

In 1300 Yuan forces launched a large offensive against Kaidu. The latter called on Duwa for assistance, but the Chaghadaid refused, claiming his forces were exhausted. Surprised by the answer, Kaidu sent a command to him, but soon had to turn east to meet the Yuan. Still, Duwa and his men eventually came to help him, and during one battle in 1301 he himself was wounded and defeated. Shortly afterward, Kaidu died and the political situation changed. Duwa ignored Kaidu's choice of successor, Orus, and instead picked Kaidu's firstborn son Chapar to take his father's place. Chapar was enthroned in 1303, thanks to Duwa's effort. Duwa insisted Chapar "Let's we Mongols stop shedding blodd of each other. It is better to submit to the Great khan Temur".

Shortly afterward, Duwa sought to end conflict with Temur Khan (Chenzong), and around 1304 a general peace among the Mongol states was declared, bringing an end to the civil war of the Mongol Empire Asia that had lasted for the better part of a half century. Soon after, he proposed a joint Mongol attack on India, but the campaign did not materialize. The settlement favoured Duwa much more than Chapar, a fact which set a rift between the two. Duwa hoped to throw off the mastery of Kaidu's son; he therefore sought to improve relations with Chancing. He had the advantage of being a legitimate heir to Chagatai's realm, while Chapar did not.

Chapar refused to attend a meeting that Duwa arranged to celebrate the peace, and in 1305 or 1306 fighting broke out between the troops of both sides, probably due to Duwa's attempts to take control of parts of Chapar's lands granted to him by Chancing. The fighting lasted for a while but was inconclusive; while Chapar's brother Sarban gave up to the Ilkhanate and abandoned the Oxus region, but the region around Samarkand continued to be infested with supporters of Kaidu's family. Duwa proposed a peace; Chapar, believing that it was sincere and accepted, withdrawing his brothers. Duwa's forces then struck, defeating Chapar's supporter Baba, plundering Talas and overcoming Chapar's brother Shah. On the eastern front Duwa convinced the border commander of Yuan, Qaishan, to strike and defeat Chapar's brother Orus in June 1306.

Chapar then mobilized his own troops, but several of his commanders deserted him, and the Yuan sent a large force to Duwa's assistance. Surrounded by this army, Chapar surrendered. The northeast part of Duwa's realm was ceded to the Yuan Dynasty, and Duwa afterwards received gifts from Chancing, signifying the restored relations between the Chagatai Khanate and the Yuan Dynasty for the first time since the mid-thirteenth century.

Duwa at first gave Chapar a small domain and pension, but afterwards killed or captured many of his followers, and deposed Chapar in 1307 in place of his brother Yangichar, who had not fought Duwa previously. Part of Yangichar's realm was split off and given to Tugme, a grandson of Guyuk Khan. That same year, Duwa died, to be succeeded by his son Konchek.

Duwa's actions went a long way toward freeing the Chagatai Khanate from its subservience to Kaidu and his sons, a situation that had lasted since 1271. Nevertheless, Kaidu's sons continued to pose problems for the Chaghadaid state. Duwa's successes in recreating the Central Asian state also proved to be transitory; less than forty years later, the eastern part of the khanate would split off, and in the 1360s the western khans would be reduced to puppets by Timur.

SALDI

The Mongols attacked again under the command of Saldi and captured the fort of Siri. Zafar Khan holding the honour of being one of the few undefeated military commanders in history had no problem crushing this army, recaptured the fort and brought 2,000 Mongols prisoners before Sultan Alauddin Khilji. It was one of the worst defeats for the Mongols. Legend has it that Zafar Khan created such great terror in the minds of the Mongols that whenever their horses refused to drink water, the Mongols would ask them if they had seen Zafar Khan. The first invasion of the Mongols was an abysmal failure with Zafar Khan almost grinding them into the dust. The Mongols thereafter repeatedly invaded northern India. On at least two occasions, they came in strength. The second time around, they took Delhi but could not keep their hold on the Sultanate.

5

Slave Dynasty

Slave Dynasty ruled India for 84 years. The Muslim religion was introduced in India with the establishment of Turkish rule. Delhi became the first capital under Turkish rule. Muhammad Ghori used to raid in India and eventually conquered Delhi. Qutb-ud-din Aibak, slave cum lieutenant assisted him in those expeditions. With the introduction of 'Mamluks' scheme (Material slavery), Aybak became advantageous to rise up out of his birth status and achieved the right for higher position. This trusted slave of Muhammad Ghori became the in charge of North India. After the death of Ghur, Aybak became his successor. When Aybak, the slave raised to the status of sultan, the equality concept in Islam reached to its highest position. The Slave Dynasty served as the first Turkish Dynasty in India from 1206 to 1290. Qutub-ud-din Aibak, Shams-ud-din Iltutmish and Ghiyas-ud-din Balban were the rulers of this era.

SHAMS-UD-DIN ILTUTMISH IN SLAVE DYNASTY

Iltutmish, the successor of Aybak completed his unfinished works. The column was named after Khwaja Qutub-ud-din. A mosque was also built on Sultan's order. This Turkish slave turned Sultan, married to Aybak's daughter. After becoming the Sultan, Iltutmish faced a feeling of indignation from the Amirs of Delhi. But he managed the resentment strongly. During the reign of Iltutmish; the Mongols attacked India for the first time under the leadership of Genghis Khan. In 1236 Iltutmish died. He nominated his daughter Raziya as his heir ness on his death bed. Raziya Sultana and her husband Altunia were killed in their way to Delhi as the nobles of the court disagree to bow their hand in front of women. They offered the throne to Iltutmish's surviving son Rukh-ud-din Firuz. Bahram and Masad, next to successors were incompetent. The youngest son of Iltutmish, Nasiruddin Mahmud was raised as the sultan in 1246. Mahmud used to spend more of his time in prayers. So that state affairs were managed by his Prime Minister Ghiyas ud din Balban.

GHIYAS UD DIN BALBAN

Balban declared himself the sultan after the death of Nasiruddin. He paid more attention to the production of Weapons. He broke down the 'Chihalgani'. He ruled from 1266 till his death with a strong hand as he believed that the king should be very powerful. Balban adopted a blood and iron policy to maintain peace. He completed the task which was started by Iltutmish. He made the Muslim rule in India so strong that it lasted in one form or the other till 1857. Balban's two son, one died before he could succeed and one refused the throne as he was the governor of Bengal. Thus it made Balban to choose his grandson Kai Khusro to be the Successor. But when Balban died, the Muiz ud din Qaiqabad became the ruler. After four years of his reign, he suffered a paralystic stroke and was killed. His nobles replaced him by his three year old son Kaimus.

The most important institution that developed under the Slave Dynasty was the 'Chihalgani' or the Forty. Iltutmish recognized them as his personal supporter. To strengthen his rule, Balban crushed the power of these Forties, but actually this decision destroyed the real power of the Slave Dynasty. Jalal-ud-din Khilji overthrown the slave Dynasty and established the Khilji Dynasty.

INDIAN SLAVES WORKERS

Muslim regime in medieval times drafted slaves in every sphere of activity. Slaves were needed in thousands for any large enterprise which, in modern technological age, would be accomplished by a few machines or even gadgets. There was no dearth of slaves either. Muslim victories in India had provided kings and nobles with innumerable slaves. From government affairs to domestic errands slaves were employed on every work.

SLAVERY IN INDIA

The Arabs were the first invaders of India to capture and enslave large numbers of its inhabitants. In the 7th and 8th centuries, and later under the Ghaznavids (962-1187), huge numbers of Hindus became slaves. Many more were enslaved under the Delhi Sultanate (1206-1526), the Timurid *jihad* (1398), and the Mughals (1526-1857).

K.S. Lal claims that the slave-taking added significantly to the growth of the Muslim population in India: "... every slave captured in war or purchased in the market or sent in lieu of revenue or tribute was invariably converted to Islam, so that slave-taking in medieval India was the most flourishing and successful missionary endeavour."

The nobility owned huge numbers of slaves and maintained large slave armies. For example, a 14th century sultan kept 180,000 slaves of whom 40,000 were palace guards. In this situation of abundance the price of female slaves was very low. The large numbers of slaves captured in campaigns were either sold in local markets or sent to markets in central Asia.

SERVICES IN THE ARMY

Another cadre which absorbed the services of large number of slaves from the beginning of Muslim rule was the Army. Without a strong army there could be no conquest, no Muslim rule in India. Ziyauddin Barani declares that "Kingship is the army and the army kingship," that is, the one was concomitant to the other. Extension of Muslim rule in India was not possible without conquest and so the Sultanate was, by its very nature, committed to maintaining a large army.

Soldiers in permanent service and the king's bodyguards called Jandars, were largely drawn from his personal slaves *ghilman* and *mamalik*. Foreign slaves were purchased from all countries and nationalities. There were Turks, Persians, Seljuqs, Oghus (also called Iraqi Turkmen), Afghans, Khaljis etc., in the army of Ghaznavids and Ghaurids.

"To sustain the new principalities, slaves, imported as youths from peripheral regions were trained at the court of their masters to be a fighting and administrative elite loyal to them alone and thus comrades in arms." This tradition of obtaining slaves by all methods and from all regions, was continued by Delhi sultans. These foreign slaves may be called, for the sake of brevity, by the generic term Turks and Afghans.

Muhammad Ghauri in his last expedition brought ten thousand Afghan horsemen with him. In the time of Iltutmish, Jalaluddin Mangbarni of Khwarism, fleeing before Chingiz Khan, had brought contingents of Afghan soldiers. In course of time many of them took service under Iltutmish.

Balban appointed three thousand Afghan horse and foot in his campaigns against the Mewatis, and thousands of others for garrisoning difficult forts like Gopalgir, Kampil, Bhojpur, Patiali and Jalali. In his royal processions hundreds of Sistani, Ghauri, Samarqandi and Arab soldiers, with drawn swords, used to march by Balban's side. Like the Afghans, the Mongols (again a generic term ethnically), were enslaved or persuaded to join the forces of the Khaljis. They were called neo-Muslims under Alauddin Khalji. Persian element in the rank of officers and men was also prominent. Purchased Abyssinian slave-soldiers and officers became prominent under Raziyah. By the time of Firoz Shah Tughlaq indigenous slaves began to replace foreigners. As an example, "when the Sultan went out in state the slaves, accompanied him, in distinct corps-first the archers, fully armed, next the swordsmen, thousands in number (*hazar hazar*), the fighting men (*bandgan-i-aword*), the *bandgan-i-mahili* riding on male buffaloes, and slaves from the Hazara, mounted on Arab and Turki horses, bearing standards and axes. All these thousands upon thousands, accompanied the royal retinue. About 40,000 were everyday in readiness as his personal guards. Under Saiyyad and Lodi rulers, Afghans of all tribes and clans flocked into India like ants and locusts.

Indian slaves were obtained as presents, part of tribute from subordinate states, or enslaved during campaigns. Once broken and trained into loyalty and service they were easily drafted into the army. Most Hindus belonged to the infantry wing and were called Paiks. Some of these were poor persons who joined the army for the sake of securing employment. Others were slaves and war captives. In war small boys were preferred as captives and they were the easiest to capture. For instance, in his campaigns in Katehar, Balban massacred mercilessly, sparing boys only of the age of eight or nine. The age factor is significant. As these boys grew up, they could hardly remember their parentage or nativity, and remained loyal only to their master. In other cases also the situation was about the same. The slave was usually a prisoner of war, and according to Islamic usage his life was at the mercy of his captor. So when a conqueror or invader chose to spare the life of a slave and take him in his employment, it was an act of special benevolence for which the slave felt obliged to him. Many other Paiks were recruited from the open market. Prince Alauddin Khalji, as governor of Kara, recruited 2,000 Paiks with the revenue he was supposed to send to Delhi, and marched with them on an expedition to Devagiri (1296).

The Paiks were allotted sundry duties to perform. They fed, groomed, and looked after the horses of the cavalrymen who had a superior status. Alauddin Khalji had 70,000 cavalrymen besides other ranks. Thousands of slaves were needed to look after them. Similar was the case with elephant stables. These pilkhanas had thousands of elephants and *mahouts*, and *ghulams* and Paiks were on duty to feed and nourish them. The number of slaves for maintaining them and other animals can only be imagined.

During a campaign, the slaves cleared the jungles and prepared roads for the army on march. During halts and on arrival at the destination the slaves and Paiks set up the camp and fixed tents, sometimes on land the total circumference of which was twelve thousand five hundred and forty six yards (about ten kilometre square). They built Gargach and Sabat. Gargach was a covered platform on wheels for reaching the base of the fort under protection. Sabats were platforms raised from the ground to reach the top of the fort during assault. War drums and standards were placed in front of tents of load-carrying slaves who were kept under protective surveillance by mounted soldiers.

The Paiks were often so stationed as to bear the first brunt of the enemy's attack, but they could not leave their posts because "horses are on their right and left... and behind (them) the elephants so that not one of then can run away." But the Paiks were also great fighters. That is how Alauddin's army of invasion of Devagiri (1296) had 2000 Paiks. Most Persian chroniclers write about Paiks as being good soldiers lending strength to the Muslim army in Hindustan. Duarte Barbosa, a Portuguese official in India, writing in 1518 says this about them: "They carry swords and daggers, bows and arrows. They are right good archers and their bows are long like those of England... They are mostly Hindus." Their most important weapon was Dhanuk or Dhanush. During the time of the Khaljis (1290-1320), the Paik element had become prominent in Alauddin's army because he had wrested political power from the Turkish slave-rulers and could not entirely depend on Turkish soldiers. When Sultan Alauddin was about to encounter the Mongol invader Qutlugh Khwaja, Malik Alaulmulk, the Kotwal of Delhi, tried to dissuade him from taking any precipitate action and one of his arguments was that "our army is composed principally of the soldiery of Hindustan." Their presence in large number was disliked by the fanatical Alim and historian Ziyauddin Barani who was against the recruitment of non-Muslims in the army. Indeed among the Hindus there were sometimes such high officers as Malik Naik. According to Amir

Khusrau it was under Malik Naik, the Akhurbeg-i-Maisara (Master of Horse of the Left Flank), a 'Hindu *banda*', that thirty thousand horsemen were sent against the Mongols-All Beg, Tartaq, and Targhi. Alauddin's greatest general was Malik Kafur Hazardinari. Later in the day we come across names like Bahadur Nahar, Sarang Khan, Shaikha Khokhar and Mallu Khan, probably all converted Hindu warriors.

LOYALTY OF THE PAIKS IN TURKISH SLAVES

In an atmosphere of intrigue, suspicion and treachery, in which kings were overthrown and dynasties subverted by Turkish slaves or slaves turned nobles, the Paiks were known for their devotion and loyalty. Whether captured as small boys or grown ups in war or directly recruited as troopers, the Paiks in all situations remained mostly loyal to their masters. The foundation of this loyalty was the attachment of man to man, first by the relationship of the chief to his captive whose life had been spared, and if the warrior master succeeded in conquest and setting up a dominion, by the relation of suzerain to vassal. This adherence of loyalty to salt is a basic fact of Hindu tradition. There are many instances where the Paiks came to the rescue of their masters when danger threatened the latter's lives. For example, when Sultan Alauddin was marching to attack Ranthambhor (1301 C.E.), he halted at Tilpat for a few days during which Sulaiman, also known as Ikat Khan, planned to assassinate him. Ikat Khan had thought that just as Alauddin had obtained the throne by murdering his uncle Jalaluddin, so he could also kill his uncle and occupy the throne. That is why he had attacked the king. But the latter's loyal Paiks hedged around him from all sides and in their native shrewdness began to lament aloud that the Sultan was dead. The foolish and inexperienced Ikat Khan, partly because he was unable to lay hands on the Sultan and partly because he was in a hurry to seize the throne, readily believed the welcome wailings of the Paiks and dashed off towards the Camp and seated himself on Alauddin's throne. In the meantime, Alauddin's personal bodyguard Paiks dressed his wounds and he regained consciousness. He arrived in the Camp posthaste, ascended an eminence, and showed himself to the people. And Ikat Khan was beheaded.

After Alauddin's death, his favourite slave, General and Wazir, Malik Kafur, wished to gather all power in his own hands and towards that end began to order the execution of one prince after another. He sent four Paiks by the names of Mubshir, Bashir, Salih and Munir to blind the Sultan's son Mubarak Khan. But when the Paiks approached him in his prison cell Prince Mubarak reminded them of their loyalty and duty which they owed to the sons of the late king. Impressed by Mubarak's appeal they not only left him untouched, but also murdered Kafur and thus facilitated Mubarak Khan's ascension to the throne. Similarly, Rai Bhairon Bhatti, the personal attendant of Firoz Shah Tughlaq, came to his rescue when his own kith and kin made plans to murder the Sultan.

But there was no hard and fast behavioural pattern. The king was supreme but if the Paiks developed loyalty towards a nobleman who was inimical to the sultan, they could as well kill the king. That is how Sarwar-ul-Mulk, the Wazir of Sultan Mubarak Shah Saiyyad (1421-34), got the latter killed with the help of a group of Paiks. On the other hand, the loyalty of Hindu officers and soldiers has become legendary.

Indian slaves in the Muslim army performed all and sundry duties. They served as servants to cavalrymen. They cleared the jungles and laid roads during campaigns. They manufactured weapons, they fought in battles for their masters. Even so they were ever kept reminded of their inferior status so far as their remuneration was concerned.

And this was determined according to Islamic law. In the booty collected during war, the State's share was one-fifth, while four-fifth went to the combatants, but the share of a horseman was twice that of a footsoldier. As a Zimmi, the Hindu Paik had no share in the booty. Zimmi women and children cannot wage *jihad* and they too had no claim. But they were all to be paid something "in order to encourage them to fight and inferiority of their station be rendered manifest to them."

EMPLOYMENT IN LITERALLY WORKSHOP

Large numbers of slaves were drafted to work in the royal Karkhanas. The Karkhanas (literally workshops) of the Delhi sultans and Mughal emperors were both manufactories and storehouses where articles of delicacy were produced, sometimes in bulk, and imports from far off regions and foreign countries like China, Iraq and Alexandria, were received and stored. Shams Siraj Afif gives a detailed account of the Karkhanas of Firoz Shah Tughlaq although such workshops existed during the reigns of former as well as later sultans also. According to J.H. Krammers, "Industrial production in Muhammadan countries had developed in a particular way; it was chiefly characterized by being completely under the control of the rulers... and by its organization of the craftsmen in guilds. At the time of Islamic prosperity it had made possible a development of industrial skill which brought the artistic value of the products to an unequalled height.

In the first place should be mentioned the products of the textile industry..." Under Firoz Tughlaq (1351-88) there were thirty six Karkhanas *directly under the Sultan*. In these were manufactured and stored articles of gold and silver and brass and other metals, textiles, wines, perfumes, armours, weapons, horse and camel saddles and covers of elephants, leather goods and clothes. But the Karkhanas also looked after "the elephant, horse and camel stables, the kitchen, the butlery, the candle department, the dog-kennels, the water-cooling department and other establishments... the wardrobe, the '*Alam-khana* or insignia, the carpet stores, and the like... About two lakhs of tankahs were expended in the carpet department, and 80,000 *tankahs* on the 'Alam Khana." Each of these departments was under the charge of a senior Amir or Khan and lakhs of *tankahs* were sanctioned as recurring and non-recurring expenditure for each of the Karkhanas. Thus some sort of capital investment was there and the guilds were formed by slaves trained as artisans (*kasibs*) by expert mechanics and handicraftsmen. 12,000 slaves worked in the Karkhanas of Firoz Tughlaq and were given a salary from 100 to 10 *tankahs* according to each one's competence. These slaves formed some sort of guilds and produced excellent articles. "There was no occupation in which the slaves of Firoz Shah (or for that matter any other sultan) were not employed." We cannot and need not study about all the departments in detail. Here we will confine ourselves to a brief account of two departments, those of wardrobe and weapons. These will suffice to give an idea of the institution of Karkhanas which employed a very large number, if not the bulk, of the royal slaves.

TEXTILES, DRESSES AND ROBES

According to Shahabuddin Al Umri "every year the Sultan (Muhammad Tughlaq) distributes 200,000 complete dresses: 100,000 in spring and 100,000 in autumn (among nobles)... Dresses are also distributed to the monasteries and hermitages (*khanqahs* and*dargahs*). The Sultan keeps in his service 500 manufacturers of golden tissues, who weave the gold brocades worn by the wives of the Sultan, and given away as presents to the amirs and their wives." Ibn Battutah's list of the presents he carried from Muhammad bin Tughlaq to the Mongol emperor of Cathay also helps us appraise the development of textile industry in India manned by slaves. These presents comprised 100 pieces of cotton fabric called *bairami,* of matchless beauty priced at 100 *dinars*per piece; 100 pieces of silk called *juz* of variegated tints; 104 pieces of *Salahiya*, 100 pieces of *Shirinbaf*, 100 pieces of *Shanbaf*, 500 pieces of *muraz*, a kind of woollen fabric of various colours, 100 pieces of *Katan-i-Rumi*, 100 gowns without sleeves, a tent with six pavilions, four golden candlesticks and four embroidered with silver, four gold basins and six of silver, and ten dresses of honour embroidered. Also sent were ten quivers one of which was studded with pearls, and 10 swords the scabbard of one of which was inlaid with pearls and jewels. Ziyauddin Barani's list of such items of textiles also indicates their prices under Alauddin Khalji, that of Abul Fazl under the Mughals.

STAVES IN WEAPONS MANUFACTURE

Slaves also manufactured weapons and their accessories including armour for men and covering of gilded iron for elephants. As is well known, the most important element in the army was heavy cavalry. Mounted soldiers were armed with the bow for engaging in combat from a distance and with one or more weapons for hand to hand fighting, like the lance, the spear, the mace, the lasso. Fakhr-i-Mudabbir gives primacy to the bow and the sword as the most effective weapons of the horseman. Both these weapons were of different varieties. Among them all, the Hindu sword was the best and most lustrous (*gawhardartar*). Their export to such distant areas as Ummayad Spain and Seljuq Anatolia too is attested. He also declares that there is no better lance than the Indian. From the time of Iltutmish to that of Firoz Shah great development had taken place in the manufacture of weapons and engines of war like Arrada, Manjniq and Maghrabi. These were stone and missile throwing machines. Haqqaha were rockets. The *Sirat-i-Firoz Shahi* mentions some very interesting "equipments, outfits and instruments for waging war". In the midst of a hotchpotch of assortment of items like traps, nets, noose and snare, "we find a brief reference to such instruments as... Bandiqa (venetian crossbow for throwing stone balls); Faraqha Falakun (slings made of rope for throwing stones); Kaman Guruha (large mounted crossbow); Harf-i-Kilk (arrow with inverted sharp points); Julahiq (balls of stone thrown by balists); Zand-i-Atish (incendiary fire-steel) etc. All these weapons and equipments were manufactured by hundreds and hundreds of slaves, and were kept stored in the royal Karkhanas.

WORK IN PALACE AND COURT

For invaders and conquerors, the establishment of a regular

government takes some time. It is achieved through an evolutionary process. Its set up is completed in the course of decades. In medieval times this process was delayed by dynastic upheavals and arrival of fresh conquerors. But not too much. Most Muslim law-books and administrative manuals were ready when the Turks conquered Hindustan and stayed on to rule over it. And as in the case of construction of edifices and service in the army, slaves were required in large numbers for the working of the administrative machinery. Slaves were the hewers of wood and drawers of water in every sphere of life. The government departments which needed the largest number of slaves were the Diwan-i-Wazarat, Diwan-i-Arz, Diwan-i-Insha, the Diwan-i-Rasalat.

The detailed list of ministries, departments and offices is too large to mention. Thousands of slaves were required in the Revenue Department, thousands of others in the Postal Department as carriers of official communication and still others as spies. For shortage of space and paucity of detailed information about the employment of slaves in the households of nobles and other important Muslim elites, we shall confine our study of this aspect only to the Sultan's palaces for they "are exclusively occupied by the Sultan, his wives, concubines, eunuchs, male and female slaves and *mamaliks*". How many slaves were on duty in the King's palace?

It is difficult to surmise. One can only say-in thousands and thousands. At the gate there was the *nawbat* or the royal band played by a large number of instrument players in relay service-trumpets, drums, flagesletters, pipes etc. Hundreds were needed for carrying royal *alams* or standards, for wielding of fans to keep away flies from the royal person and wafting breeze, for carrying of *Chatr* (parasol) and *Durbash* (royal baton), and for attendance near the throne. The head of the Household staff, *Sarjandar* and *Sarsilahdar* or Commander of the Royal Bodyguard and head of the Royal Armour-bearer, required other hundreds of slaves to help them carry out their assignments.

Among other officials in charge of domestic attendance were *Sar-abdar* (or *Aftabchi* of the Mughals) who looked after the washing and toilet arrangements of the Sultan, the *Kharitadar* who looked after the royal writing case and *Tahwildar* who looked after the purse. Each of these officials had subordinate slaves and servants.

The *Chashnigir* (the predecessor of the *Bakawal* of the Mughals) supervised the royal kitchen with hundreds of subordinate slaves working under him. *Sar-Jamadar* was in charge of the royal wardrobe, the *Saqi-*

i-Khas of wines and other drinks. The *Mashaldar* supervised the lighting arrangements of the palace, and the provision of lamps, candlesticks, lamp-stands etc.

All these functionaries had a regular staff of subordinates comprising mainly of slaves. The scores of subordinates or slaves required to "run" the Muslim government in India ran into hundreds of thousands.

The Muqti and later the Subedar lived like a miniature king, the paraphernalia of his court and household was patterned on that of the King. The Iqtadars and subordinate officers tried to emulate the higher nobles and the number of slaves continued to, rise.

In the heyday of the Sultanate period, Shihabuddin Al Umari has this to say about the time of Muhammad bin Tughlaq. At the cost of this prince there are maintained 1,200 physicians; 10,000 falconers who ride on horseback and carry birds trained for hawking; 300 beaters go in front and put up the game; 3,000 dealers in articles required for hawking accompany him when he goes out hunting; 500 table companions dine with him.

He supports 1,200 musicians excluding his slave musicians to the number of 1,000 who are more especially charged with the teaching of music, and 1,000 poets of all the three languages, Arabic, Persian and Indian. According to one informant who based his account on the report of the royal cook, 2,500 oxen, 2,000 sheep, and other animals and birds were slaughtered daily for the supplies of the royal kitchen. How many slaves were required to cater to all these services and amusements can easily be conjectured. In the Mughal times the numbers of slaves as part of the ever-expanding paraphernalia went on growing.

Some numbers are available but details are not possible to give. The number of men employed in connection with sports and amusements was in aggregate very large. A numerous staff was employed specially for hunting and shooting, another for hawking, another for pigeon-flying.

All Muslim rulers and nobles had pigeon-boys-Alauddin Khalji alone had 50,000 of them. Provision was made for training the fighting instincts of a variety of animals "down to frogs and spiders." The stables swarmed with animals and men. The number of animals in the stables may be judged from the fact that Sher Shah employed 3,400 horses for royal postal communications in the Kingdom, and maintained about 5,000 elephants on an average. An elephants in the royal use had seven men to attend on it. Terry tells how Jehangir assigned four attendants to each of the dogs brought to him as presents from England.

SLAVES AND SERVANTS EMPLOYEE

The imperial camp employed between 2000 and 3000 servants in addition to a guard of cavalry; there was one tent in particular which required 1000 men for a week for its erection." As I have said elsewhere, in Akbar's time "each camp establishment required for its transport 100 elephants, 500 camels, 400 carts and a hundred bearers. It was escorted by 500 troopers. Besides, there were 100 *farrashes*, 500 pioneers, 100 water carriers, 50 carpenters, tent makers, and torch bearers, 30 workers in leather, and 150 sweepers." Akbar's "*zanana* contained more than 5000 ladies, each of whom had separate apartments; they were attended by an adequate staff of servants, and watched in successive circles by female guards, eunuchs... and porters". The Emperor set the standard in such matters, and everyone who occupied or aspired to a position at Court followed that example so far as his means allowed. Ten to twelve servants were attached to every lady of importance. Some princesses had as many slave-girls as a hundred.

Supplies for the Royal Household were obtained from distant sources, apparently regardless of the amount of labour expended. Wherever the Emperor might be, water for his use was brought from the river Ganga, a practice prevailing from the time of Muhammad Tughlaq if not earlier. Ice came daily by post carriages and by runners from snowy mountains. Fruit was supplied regularly from Kashmir and Kabul, and even from more distant places, such as Badakshan and Samarqand. Relay service on all these and many other such items required hundreds and thousands of slaves. The Emperor's personal officers modelled their establishments on similar lines, "one employing 500 torch-bearers, another having a daily service of thousand rich dishes, and so on". Each fighting man of any consequence in the Turki and Mughal army had in the field an average of two or three servants.

That the fashion was not confined to the entourage of the Emperor is shown by della Valle's statement that at Surat servants and slaves were so numerous and so cheap that "everybody, even of mean fortune, keeps a great family, and is splendidly attended". Pyrard says that the Zamorin of Calicut travelled with about 3000 men in his train, and that on the coast generally the prominent men had always a large following. He tells of the state maintained at Goa by the Bijapur envoy, who was accompanied about the town by a crowd of servants, pages, bearers, grooms, and musicians, and adds that all the great men of the Deccan indulged in similar display. Thevenot, writing of a later period (C. 1667) gives a corresponding description of the life in Golkunda. About North India in Jehangir's time, Pelsaert writes, "Peons or servants, are exceedingly numerous in this country, for everyone-be he mounted soldier, merchant or King's official-keeps as many as position and circumstances permit. Outside the house, they serve for display, running continually before their master's horse; inside, they do the work of the house," like the *bailwan*, the *farrash*, the *masalchi*, the*mahawat* etc. "it will be understood," writes W.H. Moreland, "that the profusion of servants, which attracts attention in India at the present day (early twentieth century), is no modern phenomenon, but is in fact an attenuated survival of the fashions prevailing in the time of Akbar and doubtless dating from a much earlier period," indeed from the time of Qutbuddin Aibak when every Muslim householder or soldier began to possess a number of slaves.

Such exploitation in the Mughal period provided droves of*khidmatgars* to British officers and men when they established and ran their Raj in this country." They found its impoverished people, ready to be used as Coolies to be sent abroad and exploited this nation as smartly as the Turks and Mughals had done in the medieval period.

SLAVE NOBLES: MUSLIM KINGS AND NOBLES IN HINDUSTAN

These Turkish slaves formed the ruling class of Muslim kings and nobles in Hindustan. A few became kings while most others remained nobles. The nobles were called Khans, Maliks and Amirs. The official status of a noble was determined by his *shughl* (office), *khitab* (title), *iqta* (land assignment) and *maratib* (status and position at the court). Each nobleman of any importance commanded his own army and held his own miniature court. Sometimes he gathered so much strength that the Sultan began to live in fear of him. Alauddin Ata Malik Juwaini in his *Tarikh-i-Jahan Gusha* writes that often the ruler of a Muslim country "talks with fear with his own purchased slave, if the latter possesses ten horses in his stable... If an army is placed under his command, and he attains to position of authority, he simply cannot be commanded. And often it happens that the officer himself rises in revolt (against the king)." This was precisely the situation during the period of the early sultans. When Sultan Muizzuddin was killed, the inheritance of his dominions was contested between his relatives and Amirs in the homeland and the Turkish slaves operating in India. "These slave Maliks and Amirs, deprived the Maliks and Amirs of Ghaur, by force, of the bier of the late Sultan, together with precious treasures, and took possession of them" while they sent his body to Ghazni. This conveys the idea of the clout of the Turkish slaves appointed in Hindustan. Aibak, Iltutmish, Yaldoz, Qubacha and Balban were all purchased slaves. They fought amongst themselves and faced opposition from their slave nobles. The nobles flouted the wishes and dictates of the rulers to make a show of strength. They formed pressure groups and rejected the king's nominee to the throne. Qutbuddin Aibak wanted his slave Iltutmish to succeed him, but the nobles raised Aram Shah to the throne of Delhi. Sultan Iltutmish made Raziyah his successor, but the Maliks raised Ruknuddin Firoz to the throne. Balban designated Kai Khusrau as his heir apparent, but the nobles placed Kaiqubad on the throne. As if this was not bad enough, in the thirteenth century, during the Slave Dynasty's rule in Hindustan, out of ten rulers they killed six-Aram Shah, Ruknuddin Firoz, Raziyah, Bahram, Alauddin Masaud and Nasiruddin Mahmud. These slave nobles extended Muslim dominions in India, collected huge treasures through loot, and made their constructive and destructive contribution in the various spheres of life. But they always posed a challenge to the king about how to control them.

No king could rule by himself; he had to govern through the nobles or Umara. They used to be appointed as Walis, Muqtis or Iqtadars to administer their assignments. W.H. Moreland enumerates the services rendered by some slave nobles like Tughan Khan, Saifuddin Aibak, Tughril Khan and Ulugh Khan Balban. But they had to be kept under control and there were many levers in the administrative machinery through which the Sultan kept a control over them. The lives of nobles, their titles and grants, were all dependent on the pleasure and mercy of the monarch. The absolute powers of the king regarding appointment and dismissal made the nobles completely dependent on him. The Sultan took extreme care in selecting them, and appointed to this cadre either his relatives or the most trusted persons. As a further safeguard some sort of a spoil system was resorted to. On accession a new monarch removed all nobles of his predecessor and appointed his own loyal slave supporters to important offices. Hence the Muizzi, Qutbi, Shamsi and Balbani slave Amirs (*Ghulams*) or nobles of Muizzudin bin Sam, Qutbuddin Aibak, Shamsuddin Iltutmish and Ghiyasuddin Balban.

Turkish nobles suffered from an inborn arrogance. Devoid of humanitarian learning and proud of military prowess, every one of them felt and said to the other: "What art thou and what shalt thou be, that I shalt not be?" Their continuous conflict born out of jealousy and intrigue, was a constant danger to the stability of the Muslim state and the monarch's position. To show them their place the Sultan used to inflict humiliating and barbarous punishments on those found guilty of some crime. Malik Baqbaq, the Governor of Badaon and holder of a Jagir of 4000 horse, got a servant beaten to death. Sultan Balban ordered Malik Baqbaq to be publicly flogged. Balban also publicly executed the spies who had failed to report the misconduct of Malik Baqbaq. Another great noble, Haibat Khan, was the Governor of Avadh. In a state of drunkenness, he got a man killed. Balban ordered Haibat Khan to be flogged with five hundred stripes. He was also made to pay a compensation of 20,000 *tankahs* to the widow of the victim. Haibat Khan felt so ashamed that after this incident he never came out of his house till the day of his death. Amin Khan, the Governor of Avadh, was hanged at the gate of the city of Ayodhya because he had failed to defeat in battle the rebel Tughril Beg of Bengal. Balban is said to have poisoned even his cousin, Sher Khan, the Governor of Bhatinda. A well-established espionage system helped in keeping the nobles terrorized. While terror tactics made individual nobles squirm, junior Turks were promoted to important positions and placed on par with the important. That is how the slave rulers tried to keep individual slave nobles under control.

Under the Khaljis and Tughlaqs (fourteenth century) the nobles lived under constant fear of the Sultan. "Nor did they do anything nor utter a single word which could subject them to reproof or punishment. " The Afghan nobles, who were considered to be difficult of control and therefore fairly independent, were no better. Whenever a *farman* was sent to a district officer by Sultan Sikandar Lodi (fifteenth century), the former received it with the utmost respect. Sikandar reduced the highest nobles to the position of slaves so that he could boast that "if I order one of my slaves to be seated in a palanquin, the entire body of nobility would carry him on their shoulders at my bidding." Badaoni gives an eye-witness account of the situation under Islam Shah Sur (sixteenth century). "In the year 955H (1548 A.D.), when he was of tender age (the chronicler Badaoni) went to the country of Bajwara, one of the dependencies of Baiana ... and witnessed the customs and rules in practice"-that the high nobles holding ranks of 500 to 20000 *sawars* were ordered to set up a lofty tent every Friday; a chair was placed in its centre on which were kept the shoes of Islam Shah (how could the shoes of the Sultan be procured? Were they sent along with the *farman*?). The nobles sat at their proper places with bowed heads in front of them to show their respect. Thereafter, the amin read out the *farman* containing new regulations and reforms to be carried out by the nobles. If any one disobeyed the royal orders, the officer concerned informed the Sultan and "the disobedient Amir would forthwith be visited with punishment together with his family and relations." The Sultan also took away the elephants and even *patars* (dancing girls) of the nobles at will.

Ghulams

Under the Mughals the nobles enjoyed a fair amount of respect but in principle their status was not changed. In fact, all nobles took pride in calling themselves *ghulams* of their superiors or the king. This indeed became a part of Muslim etiquette and culture. This explains how sometimes poets, physicians, musicians and scholars have all been bracketed together as slaves. In fact, they all were. It is true that some of them were not captured in war or purchased in slave markets. But there were certain conditions of slavery which were applicable to them as to the meanest of slaves.

They were prohibited from visiting one another or holding get-together parties without the permission or at least the knowledge of the king. Further, they were prohibited from contracting any matrimonial alliances without permission of the king or the master. The king was heir to the noble; on his death his property went to the king and not to his children, and the sons of the noble became slaves of the king in their turn. Most of the kings kept a strict watch on the activities of their greatest nobles. Hence there should be no misgivings about the status of nobles and slaves. They were all slaves, whether high or low. As pointed out by Pelsaert, their ranks, assignments, "wealth, position, confidence, everything hangs by a thread". The king could take away everything at any time. "A trifling mistake may bring a man to the depth of misery or to the scaffold." The position of the highest noble was as uncertain as that of any slave.

SUCCESS OF SLAVE KINGS

The success of slaves such as these has made many scholars praise the medieval Muslim slave system as being marvellous, asserting that it provided unlimited scope for rise so much so that a slave could even become a king. This is not a correct assessment. Slaves were not captured to be made kings; they were not purchased to be made kings. They were abducted, captured, or purchased to serve as domestics, guards, troopers etc. They were sold to make money. 'Slave' and 'king' are contradictory terms. If a few slaves could become kings, it was not because the system provided them with such opportunities but mainly because of their ability to indulge in unscupulous manipulations, muster armed band of followers, and strike for the throne at an appropriate moment. Isami puts the idea in suitable words in the mouth of the slave Sultan Shamsuddin Iltutmish who declared: "You cannot take the world through inheritance and boasting, you can take it only by wielding the sword in battle." Kingship was won through the sword, not by mere loyalty or service. Slave adventurists openly supplanted the forces of the reigning monarch to seize authority. The killings and blindings of Caliph Umar (644 C.E.), scions of Alauddin Khalji (1316), Mubarak Khalji (1320), Farrukhsiyar (1719) and Shah Alam (1788) by slave nobles clearly shows that treachery stalked every step of the reigning monarch, so that courtesy and conspiracy by slaves went hand in hand throughout the medieval period. In such an atmosphere, loyalty was a luxury only a few could indulge in. One thing is certain. In these 'favourable openings' for rise to the highest office no moral principles were involved. All this is seen in the careers of the Turkish slave rulers of India, who, just because they were successful, are called remarkable men by some modern historians. In all their cases applies the dictum: "Nothing succeeds like success." For if some slaves rose to become kings, myriads of others, equally ambitious and efficient, got nowhere.

Such an one was Ikhtiyaruddin Bakhtiyar Khalji. He had a hard time getting recognition. He belonged to the Khalji tribe of Ghaur in the province of Garmsir. He came to the court of Sultan Muizzuddin at Ghazni and applied for enrolment in the Diwan-i-Arz (Military Department), but he was rejected. Consequently, from Ghazni he proceeded towards Hindustan, but was again rejected by the Diwan-i-Arz at Delhi. He went to Badaon and later on to Avadh. The ruler of Avadh Malik Hisamuddin Aghilbek (Aghilbek is a Turkish word meaning Lord of the flock), gave him two fiefs for subsistence. He soon acquired all the requisites of power like arms, men and horses, and began to raid the territory of Bihar and Munghir. The fame of his bravery and news of his plundering raids spread abroad, attracting to his standard a body of Khalji warriors then found hanging about all over Hindustan. His exploits were reported to Qutbuddin Aibak, who sent him a robe of honour and appointed him to invade Bihar as the Sultan's general in 1202 C.E. Ikhtiyaruddin Bakhtiyar Khalji conquered extensively in Bihar and Bengal but then died unhonoured and unsung.

Yahiya concluded in the fifteenth century, "each and every noble wanted to become sultan", but of course only a few succeeded. Slave nobles who attained fame, position and crown, were feared, befriended and flattered; others were not given much attention. About the first set a few encomiums by Minhaj Siraj are worth reproducing. Qutbuddin Aibak was ugly and deformed, but because he ascended the throne, he was, according to our author, "endowed with all laudable qualities and admirable impressions... the beneficent Qutbuddin Aibak, the second Hatim, was a high spirited and open handed monarch, The Almighty God had endowed him with intrepidity and beneficence the like of which, in his day, no sovereign of the world, either in the east or west, possessed..." Nasiruddin Qubacha "was endowed with very great intellect, sagacity, discretion, skill, wisdom and experience...," while Bahauddin Tughril, the governor of Thangir or Bayana, "was a Malik of excellent disposition, scrupulously impartial, just, kind to the poor and strangers, and adorned with humility." Sultan Iltutmish was "just and munificent Sultan, upright, beneficent, zealous and steadfast warrior against infidels, the patronizer of the learned, the dispenser of justice... through his sovereignty... (and) valour the Ahmadi faith acquired pre-eminence. In intrepidity he turned out to be another impetuous Ali, and, in liberality, a second Hatim-i-Tai..." Even the belatedly recognized Ikhtiyaruddin Bakhtiyar Khalji was "a man impetuous, enterprising, intrepid, bold, sagacious, and expert." But when he lay dying of age and exhaustion after the Tibetan debacle, our author could say nothing more than that "Ali Mardan in some way went unto him, drew the sheet from his face, and with a dagger assassinated him", and add nothing more than that "these events and calamities happened in the year 602 H (1205-06 C.E.)."

Exaggerated praise was normal with the panegyrists for those slaves who succeeded in wresting the throne. In all cases the length of the sword and the strength of the supporters was more important than any claims on the basis of inheritance or even an investiture from the Caliph. The first four Caliphs were directly related to the Prophet. There was therefore very great respect for the Caliphs in the world of Islam. Conscious of the moral benefits accruing from Caliphal support, there developed a tradition with medieval Muslim rulers to request for and receive recognition of their sovereignty from the Caliph. But even this recognition was of no avail before the power of arms. As Prince Masud, son of Mahmud Ghaznavi, once declared, when his claims were being superseded by his brother Muhammad, "the sword is a truer authority than any writing" (or investiture from the Caliph).

In such a situation there was no sanctity of any letter of manumission either. Manumission was of great importance in law, polity and society of Islam. It is even asserted that "no slave could ascend the throne unless he had obtained a letter of manumission (*khatt-i-azadi*) from his master. ...because a slave is no longer slave when he is manumitted by his master." Sure enough, many of the slaves tried to obtain such letters; it provided legitimacy to their office. But many slaves whose star was in ascendance lived almost like kings without receiving or caring to receive any manumission letter. For example, as mentioned earlier, Alptigin in Khurasan had 500 villages of his own and an assemblage of 2000 slave troopers. As such as governor of Khurasan his position was not inferior to that of any sultan, although he had not been manumitted. But since the sword was the ultimate arbiter, even this moral prop was not that important. Most of the slave Maliks of Muizzuddin requested for letters of manumission from the Sultan's successor, Mahmud, and did receive them. Tajuddin Yaldoz and Nasiruddin Qubacha received their letters of manumission on request, but Qutbuddin Aibak received his letter of manumission more than one year after he had ascended the throne of Delhi. It is not clear when Balban received his letter of freedom. At one place the contemporary chronicler, Ziyauddin Barani, says that Balban used to maintain the paraphernalia of royalty even when he was a khan, at another that he ascended the throne after becoming free, and yet at another that all the Forty Amirs (*Chahlgani*) had obtained freedom (buzurgi) at one and the same time so that no one considered himself inferior to any other.

6

Tughlaq Dynasty

The Tughlaq Dynasty of north India started in 1321 in Delhi when Ghazi Tughlaq assumed the throne under the title of Ghiyath al-Din Tughluq. The Tughluqs were a Muslim family of Turkic origin. Their rule relied on their alliances with Turkic, Afghan, and other Muslim warriors from outside South Asia.

The empire grew under his son and successor Mohammed bin Tughlaq, but the latter became notorious for ill-advised policy experiments such as shifting the capital from Delhi to Daulatabad and introducing copper coins without effective regulation against forgery. Tughluqi has as a result become antonym for brilliant if stubborn eccentricity in the Hindustani language.

After Mohammed bin Tughlaq his cousin Feroz Shah Tughlaq assumed the throne. He was somewhat weak militarily mainly because of inept army. After Feroz died in 1388, the Tughlaq dynasty started to fade out and there were no able leaders; the dynasty was almost over within 10 years.

RULERS

- Ghiyas ud din Tughluq Shah I (1321-1325)
- Mohammed Shah II (1325-1351)
- Mahmud Ibn Mohammed (March 1351)
- Firuz Shah Tughluq (1351-1388)
- Ghiyas ud din Tughluq II (1388-1389)
- Abu Baker (1389-1390)
- Nasir ud din Mohammed Shah III (1390-1393)

- Sikander Shah I (March-April 1393)
- Mahmud Nasir ud din (Sultan Mahmud II) at Delhi (1393-1394)
- (1394-1398)

Nusrat Shah, grandson of Firuz Shah Tughluq, controlled the west from Firozabad

Nasiruddin Mahmud Shah, son of Mahmud Nasir ud din, controlled the east from Delhi.

GHIYATH AL-DIN TUGHLUQ

Ghiyath al-Din Tughluq was the founder and first ruler (1320 - 1325) of the Turkic Muslim Tughluq dynasty in India. He has been the founder of the third city of Delhi called Tughluqabad.

About the close of his reign Alauddin Khilji had prepared an expedition of 10,000 men under Ghazi Malik to go to Debalpur to fight with the Chagatai Khanate Mongols. Ghazi Malik was thus enabled to go and secure Multan, Uch and Sindh for himself, especially as Aláuddín's sons proved incapable and caused confusion in the affairs of the kingdom, which ultimately took away the kingdom, from the possession of the house of Khiljí. Alauddin Khilji's son Qutb ud din Mubarak Shah was a mad man and was soon removed from the throne of Delhi by the hand of a murderer. The nobles of the state then put Khusro Khan on the throne. The latter began to bestow undue favors on mischievous people and to waste public money. The Hindus began to join him in large number. Seeing this state of things, Ghazi Malik's son Fakhr Malik left Multan secretly and joined his father, informing him of what was happening at Delhi. Then, father and son, being both brave soldiers, collected the forces of Sindh and Multan and hastened to Delhi to help the Muslims against the Hindus. Arriving near Delhi with 3,000 veteran soldiers, they engaged in battle with the army of Khusro Khan, and defeated them. Then making their way into Delhi they again defeated Khusro Khan in battle and he fled away. About midnight the ministers and the headmen of the place came to Ghazi Malak and his son in their camp and gave up the keys of the fort. Early in the morning Ghazi Malik entered the city with all the pomp and glory of a King. Then he went into mourning for 3 days for the death of Alauddin Khilji and his son Qutb ud din Mubarak Shah. After these ceremonies were over he issued a proclamation with the view of finding out any member of the family of those princes in order that he might put him on the throne of Delhi. But as no such person could be found on search, the nobles, the troops, the learned men, the Syeds and other subjects united in selecting Ghazi Malik for the vacant post, as it was he who had removed all the cause of quarrel and disturbance in the country. Thus in 1320 (720 A.H.) Ghazi Malik was crowned as the Sultan of Delhi with the title of *Ghiyath al-Din Tughluq* and his son Fakhr Malik was given the title of *Mohammed Shah Tughluq*.

When, soon after this, Ghiyath al-Din Tughluq proceeded from Multan to Delhi, the tribe of Soomro revolted and took possession of Thatta. Ghiyath al-Din Tughluq appointed Tajuddin Malik as governor of Multan and Khwájah Khatír as governor of Bhakkar and he left 'Malik Ali Sher in charge of Sehwan. In 1323 he appointed his son Mohammed Shah his heir and successor and took a written promise or agreement to the arrangement from the ministers and nobles of the state. In 1324-1325 (720 A.H.) he died of heat apoplexy.

He had established himself as a great ruler. He removed corrupt officials from his administration. He reformed the judiciary and all existing police departments. He also reduced the land revenue to 1/10th of the produce. He was an efficient administrator and a capable military commander. He introduced a number of reforms for his welfare of his subjects and suppressed revolts in distant provinces. He restored peace and stability in the Delhi Sultanate. Ghiyath al-Din was succeeded by his son Mohammed bin Tughluq.

MOHAMMED BIN TUGHLUQ

Mohammed bin Tughluq (also Prince Fakhr Malik, Jauna Khan and Ulugh Khan) (c.1300 – 1351) was the Turkic Sultan of Delhi from 1325 to 1351. He was the eldest son of Ghiyath al-Din Tughluq. Ghiyath al-din sent the young Mohammed to the Deccan to campaign against king Prataparudra of the Kakatiya dynasty whose capital was at Warangal. Mohammed succeeded to the Delhi throne upon his father's death in 1325.

Mohammed Tughluq was a scholar versed in logic, philosophy, mathematics, astronomy and physical sciences. He had knowledge of medicine and was skillful in dialectics. He was also a calligrapher. Ibn Batuta (Moroccan traveller) visited him during his reign.

RULE OF TUGHLUQ

Tughlaq was committed to maintaining the Sultanate's expansion into the newly conquered provinces of peninsular India. To strengthen the sultanate's hold on its southern parts, Tughluq early in his reign moved the capital from Delhi to Devagiri, 700 miles (1500 km) south in the Deccan, renaming Devagiri as Daulatabad. Instead of moving just his government offices there, he forcibly moved the entire population of Delhi to the new capital. The plan proved disastrous due to Mongol Attack on North.Inadequate water supply arrangements in Daulatabad; after only two years, the capital had to be shifted back again to Delhi. Multitudes died during the two moves, and it was said that Delhi was a ghost town for years after the move back. "When I entered Delhi, it was almost like a desert", wrote the famed North African travel writer, ibn Battuta. Tughluq also introduced token currency for the first time in India, modelled after the Chinese example, using brass or copper coins, backed by silver and gold kept in the treasury. However, very few people exchanged their gold or silver coins for the new copper ones. Moreover, the tokens were easy to forge, which led to heavy losses. It is said that after the plan failed, there were heaps of copper coins lying around the royal offices for years.

CAMPAIGN AGAINST MOKHADAJI GOHIL IN GUJARAT

Mohammed bin Tughluq was very ambitious and he was planning to attack surrounding countries, probably China. To fund his campaign he decided to accumulate wealth. He started to move his wealth from Devagiri to Delhi through the Gujarati port of Khambhat. During that time Mokhadaji Gohil ruled nearby Ghogha and Piram Bet (presently near Bhavnagar). In 1347, he got information about moving of treasure by the Delhi Sultanate through Khambhat. His navy seized the port and looted the Delhi Sultanate's cargoes. Tughluq sent his army to defeat Mokhadaji Gohil, who skillfully waged a naval war from his base at Piram Bet. The sultanate's army's strategy was to cordon Piram Bet, but they were not well experienced in naval warfare and were easily defeated. Thereafter, Mohammed bin Tughluq himself came to Gujarat to take charge.

He established his base in Ghogha and resolved not to leave until Mokhadaji was killed. During the initial few months he didn't taste any success in his efforts to capture Piram Bet. He therefore schemed to entice Mokhadaji to come ashore in order to engage him in land battle. To this end he recruited a rich Vaishnav merchant of Khambhat, who was promised trade benefits if he could convince Mokhadaji to come on land to fight. The merchant went to Piram and emotionally told Mokhadaji that the local people felt very oppressed by the sultan's occupying army, and wished to wage battle for Mokhadaji if the latter would come to them. Mokhadaji heeded the plea, lost the battle, was taken prisoner near Khadarpar village, and was beheaded near Ghogha. But his force continued to fight. Mohammed bin Tughluq is said to have been so upset to witness the horrible scene of a beheaded Mokhadaji in battle, that he didn't sleep for many nights.

COLLAPSE OF THE EMPIRE

Tughluq died in 1351 on his way to Thatta. He had lived to see his empire fall apart. During the latter years of his reign new kingdoms broke away in the Deccan, such as the Bahmani kingdom founded by Hasan Gangu.

EXPERIMENTS WITH COINAGE

Muhammad bin Tughluq is known for his active interest in experimenting with coinage. He memorialized himself and his activities through his coinage and produced more gold coins than had his predecessors. The coins boasted fine calligraphy. He issued a number of fractional denominations.

The large influx of gold from his plundering of south Indian campaign led him to increase coinage weights. He enlarged the gold dinar from 172 grains to 202 grains. He introduced a silver coin, the *adlis*, which was discontinued after seven years due to lack of popularity and acceptance among his subjects.

All his coins reflect a staunch religiosity, with such inscriptions as "The warrior in the cause of God", "The trustier in support of the four Khalifs-Abubakkar, Umar, Usman and Ali". The *kalimah* appeared in most of his coinage. Both at Delhi and at Daulatabad coins were minted in memory of his late father. There were also mints at Lakhnauti, Salgaun, Darul-I-Islam, Sultanpur (Warrangal), Tughlaqpur (Tirhut), and Mulk-I-Tilang. More than thirty varieties of billion coins are known so far, and the types show his numismatic interests.

Unique among his coinage was the "forced currency". Tughluq had two scalable versions, issued in Delhi and Daulatabad. The currency obeyed two different standards, probably to satisfy the local standard which preexisted in the North and in the South respectively. Tughluq's skill in forcing the two standards of currency is remarkable. He engraved "He who obeys the Sultan obeys the compassionate" to fascinate people in accepting the new coinage. Inscriptions were even engraved in the Nagari legend, but owing to the alloy used, the coinage underwent deterioration. As well, the copper and brass coins could easily be forged, turning every house into a mint. Tughluq subsequently withdrew the forged currency by exchanging it with bulls and gold.

RELIGIOUS TOLERANCE

Muhammad bin Tughluq was relatively liberal and permitted Hindus and Jains to settle in Delhi. The policy was reversed by his nephew Firuz Shah Tughluq.

THE CONSOLIDATION OF MUSLIM RULE

According to generally accepted accounts, Ghiyasuddin Tughluq, who became sultan of Delhi in September, 1320, was the son of a Turkish slave of Balban and a Jat woman. With a distinguished record as a defender of the sultanate against the Mongols, he faced first the task of restoring the authority of the Delhi government, which had been weakened during the disorders that followed Alauddin's death. In the south, the tributary raja of Warangal had declared his independence; Ghiyasuddin met the challenge by annexing his kingdom. The governor of Bengal had also revolted, and while suppressing this rebellion Ghiyasuddin expanded his boundaries by the conquest of Tirhut (the ancient Mithila), which had remained outside Muslim rule. This was his last campaign, however, for he was killed in 1325 in the collapse of a victory pavilion erected to celebrate his triumphal return from Bengal.

The son who succeeded him was Muhammad Tughluq, whose character was a puzzle both to contemporary and later historians. Highly gifted and accomplished, and possessing great purity of character, he endeavored throughout his reign to create a just and orderly society. Instead, he soon gained a reputation for barbarous cruelty, and his rule brought misery to his people and greatly weakened the power of the Delhi Sultanate.

Admittedly this was due partly to natural calamities, for his reign coincided with a long period of drought which in intensity and extent was one of the worst the subcontinent has ever known. From 1335 to 1342 there was widespread famine, and although the king tried to deal with the situation by opening poor-houses and distributing free grain, the problem was beyond his resources.

But his misfortunes were not all due to natural and unavoidable causes. A man of ideas, he continually conceived new schemes; and if they were not well received, he lost patience and resorted to ferocious cruelty to enforce them. The most famous incident of this kind occurred in 1327.

He had decided, in view of repeated rebellions in the south, that it was necessary to shift the capital to a more central place. He selected Devagiri, which he named Daulatabad, as the new seat of government, and he forced the Muslim inhabitants of Delhi to migrate to the new capital.

Many perished on the long march to Daulatabad, and eventually the sultan allowed them to return to Delhi. On the face of it, the operation seems to have been an act of folly, yet there is no doubt that the migration of a large Muslim population drawn from all sections of society helped to stabilize Muslim rule in the south. Like many of his schemes, it failed, not because his idea was wrong, but because his organization was not adequate to carry it out.

Another controversial measure was the sultan's issue of token currency. The prolonged famine, the expensive wars, and royal liberality had severely strained the exchequer. Muhammad Tughluq's solution was to issue brass and copper tokens in place of silver coins. Again, the idea was probably sound enough, and one that has been adopted everywhere in the modern world. However the measure was too unfamiliar and too complex for fourteenth-century India. The result was severe dislocation of the economy. Counterfeiting became common and as Barani says, "every Hindu's house became a mint." The king had the good sense to acknowledge his failure, and the token currency was withdrawn from circulation after three or four years. Its introduction and failure neither enhanced public confidence in the sultan nor restored economic prosperity to the country.

There were widespread rebellions throughout Muhammad Tughluq's reign, and the vast empire which Alauddin Khalji and Ghiyasuddin Tughluq had governed with success began to fall apart. Early in his reign he had to deal with the revolt of Baha-ud-din Gurshashp, a cousin who was given shelter by the Hindu rajas of the south. Muhammad Tughluq sent a powerful force against the defiant rajas, annexed Kampili, sacked Dvarasamudra, and forced its ruler to surrender Gurshashp and to reiterate his submission to the government of Delhi.

The cousin's fate was indicative of the sultan's treatment of rebels. He was flayed alive, his flesh was cooked with rice and was sent to his wife and children, while his skin, stuffed with straw, was exhibited in the principal cities of the kingdom. But even such ferocious punishments did not prevent rebellion; perhaps they drove men to rebel out of desperation and fear.

In 1335 Mabar, in the extreme south, became independent, followed three years later by Bengal. The Hindu rajas in the south organized a confederacy, and in 1336 Vijayanagar became the nucleus of a powerful Hindu state. A year later, when the Muslim chiefs in the Deccan set up the independent Bahmani kingdom, the entire area south of the Vindhyas was lost to Delhi. In the same year Gujarat and Kathiawar revolted, but the sultan was able to quell the rebellions in these two areas. Next it was Sind, and in 1351 he was marching towards Thatta to put down the revolt when he fell ill and died. As Badauni says, "The king was freed from his people and they from their king."

While the breakup of the Delhi Sultanate began in the reign of Muhammad Tughluq, the disasters which overtook him during the last years of his reign need not be the only basis for assessing his character and abilities. Until extreme irritation at the failure of his plans had warped his judgment, driving him to revolting cruelties, he had tried, as a man of ideas, to steer his course according to certain intelligent plans and considerations.

His policy toward the Hindus, for example, was conciliatory, and he had tried to introduce social reforms, such as the abolition of sati. He appointed a Hindu as governor of Sind, and employed others in high positions. The Jain chroniclers remember with gratitude the respect with which he received their theologians. When northern India was afflicted by the seven-year famine, he built a new town on the Ganges near the worst affected area, giving it the Hindu name of Svargdvara, the "Gate of Heaven."

Muhammad Tughluq's greatest achievement was in the south. Previous rulers, particularly Alauddin Khalji, had established suzerainty over the Hindu princes of the south, but in general had left them in possession of their territories as long as they paid tribute. Muhammad Tughluq, however, set out to end Hindu rule in the south. Warangal and Madura had already been incorporated in the Tughluq dominions, and now Kampili and a large part of the Hoysala dominions shared the same fate. Not all of these conquests were maintained, for even during Muhammad's lifetime a powerful Hindu reaction led to the foundation of Vijayanagar, but much remained. Above all, the creation of Daulatabad out of the old fortress city of Devagiri gave the Muslims a great stronghold.

Mention must be made also of the attempt by Muhammad Tughluq to establish links with other Muslim countries. Among the many distinguished visitors who came to Delhi at this time perhaps the most famous was Ibn Battuta, the Moorish traveller who was appointed chief judge in the capital. He has left an interesting account of the capital as well as of places in Sind, Multan, and the Punjab which he visited on the way to Delhi. He was sent on a diplomatic mission to China, and although he did not return to India, his *Book of Travels* is a useful source for the history of Indo-Islamic society.

Muhammad Tughluq's successor was his cousin, Firuz Tughluq, who reigned from 1351 to 1388. While the commencement of the Tughluq rule had seen a new emphasis on orthodoxy, Firuz's reign saw an even greater attempt to govern India in conformity with Islamic law. Until Aurangzeb, in fact, no other ruler made such a serious endeavor to champion orthodoxy as a guide for the state. The study of Islamic law was encouraged, and Firuz attempted to enforce the law not only among orthodox Muslims, but also among sects such as the Ismaili Shias and the non-Muslims. For the first time jizya was levied upon the Brahmans, who had hitherto remained exempt from the tax. On appeal, the king reduced the amount to be levied from 10 tankas to 50 jitals, but maintained the tax as a legal formality.

In this support of orthodoxy Firuz was probably swayed by personal religious beliefs, even though he was not, in his private life, a strict follower of the Islamic code. Probably he was conscious also that one reason for Muhammad Tughluq's failures was lack of support from the powerful religious leaders, and therefore he was anxious to win them to his side.

The measures by which Firuz helped to gain a reputation for orthodoxy were of a formal nature; the developments which shed luster on his reign were the steps taken in the furtherance of public welfare. In many ways he was the ablest of the Muslim rulers of Delhi previous to Akbar, and contemporary historians describe at length the steps he took to assist agriculture, promote employment, and secure the happiness and prosperity of the people. He initiated extensive irrigation schemes, digging five canals to distribute the water of the Sutlej and Jhelum over a large area. One of these continues to be used up to the present day. Also he set up an employment bureau where young men who were without work in the city of Delhi gave their qualifications, and occupations were found for them.

The greatest monuments of Firuz's rule, however, are the buildings and the towns founded by him. He is credited with the erection of 200 towns, 40 mosques, 30 colleges, 30 reservoirs, 50 dams, 100 hospitals, 100 public baths, and 150 bridges. He built a magnificent new capital near Delhi, and the two important towns of Jaunpur and Hissar were founded by him. He set up a regular Department of Public Works, which erected new buildings and took steps to restore the structures of former kings. He removed two gigantic monolithic pillars of the emperor Ashoka, one from a village in the Ambala District and the other from Meerut, and had them set up near Delhi. He also showed his interest in India's past by having translations made of a number of Sanskrit books which he found during his conquest of Kangra in 1361.

But Firuz did little to prevent the disintegration of the sultanate which had already set in during the last years of the reign of his predecessor. The process was speeded by his death, for a civil war broke out between his son and grandson. The Hindu chiefs threw off their allegiance and governors of provinces became independent. The weakness of the kingdom invited foreign invasion and in 1398 Timur, the Barlas Turkish chief who ruled at Samarqand, invaded India. He had no intention of staying in India, but came, as had the invaders of four centuries before, to take back slaves and booty. After terrible destruction, including the sacking of Delhi, he returned home, but he had helped to destroy the Delhi Sultanate. Possibly it could not have survived long in any case, but certainly Timur's raid effectively prevented the Tughluqs from regaining their control.

The familiar story of dynastic decay thus repeated itself. In the decade following Firuz's death, six sultans briefly occupied the throne. The last of the Tughluq line, Mahmud, fled from Delhi during Timur's invasion. Although he returned after his departure, managing to stay on the throne until 1413, he was not able to ensure the succession to a member of the house.

FIRUZ SHAH TUGHLAQ

Firoz Shah Tughlaq, 1309-1388 in Delhi, was a Muslim ruler of the Tughlaq Dynasty from 1351 to 1388. He was the son of a Hindu Rajput princess of Dipalpur. His father's name was Razzab (the younger brother of Gazi Malik). Gazi Malik means Gayasuddin Tughluq. He succeeded his cousin Muhammad bin Tughluq following the later's death from a fatal illness, but due to widespread unrest Firuz's realm was much smaller than Muhammed's. Firuz was forced by rebellions to concede virtual independence to Bengal and other provinces. He was known as an iconoclast.

BIOGRAPHY

The "Tarikh-i-Firuz Shah" is a historical record written during his reign that attests to the systematic persecution of Hindus under his rule. In particular, it records atrocities on Hindu Brahmin priests who refused to convert to Islam: "An order was accordingly given to the Brahman and was brought before Sultan. The true faith was declared to the Brahman and the right course pointed out. but he refused to accept it. A pile was raised on which the Kaffir with his hands and legs tied was thrown into and the wooden tablet on the top. The pile was lit at two places his head and his feet. The fire first reached him in the feet and drew from him a cry and then fire completely enveloped him. Behold Sultan for his strict adherence to law and rectitude."

Under his rule, Hindus who were forced to pay the mandatory Jizya tax were recorded as infidels, their communities monitored and, if they violated Imperial ordinance and built temples, these were destroyed. In particular, an incident in the village of Gohana in Haryana was recorded in the "Insha-i-Mahry" (another historical record written by Amud Din Abdullah bin Mahru) where Hindus had erected a deity and were arrested, brought to the palace and executed en-masse.

In 1230, the powerful Ganga Vanshi Hindu King of Orissa, Anangabhima III consolidated his rule and proclaimed that an attack on Orissa constituted an attack on the king's god. A sign of Anangabhima's determination to protect Hindu culture is the fact that he named his new capital in Cuttack "Abhinava Varanasi." His anxieties about further Muslim advances in Orissa proved to be well founded. In 1361, the Indian region of Orissa was conquered by the Delhi Sultan Firoz Shah and he destroyed the Jagannath temple and the stone deity of Krishna, but the indigenous wooden image of the deity was saved.

Firoz probably learnt many lessons from his cousin Muhammad's rule. He decided not to reconquer areas that had broken away. He decided to keep nobles and the Ulema happy so that they would allow him to rule his kingdom peacefully. In fact, there were hardly any rebellions during his rule. We come to know about him from a 32-page brochure he wrote. Firoz allowed a noble's son to succeed to his father's position and jagir after his death. The same was done in the army, where an old soldier could send his son, son-in-law or even his slave in his place. He won over the Ulemas by giving them grants of revenue, which gave him political power. He increased the salary of the nobles.

He stopped all kinds of harsh punishments such as cutting off hands. Firoz also lowered the land taxes that Muhammad had raised. Firuz's reign has been described as the greatest age of corruption in medieval India. It can be imagined from the fact that Firuz once gave a golden tanka to a distraught soldier so that he could bribe the clerk to pass his sub standard horse. The case of Imadulmulk Bashir, the minister of war who began his career as an inherited slave of Firuz, in course of his service is said to have accumulated wealth to the tune of thirteen crores, when the state's yearly income was six crores and seventy-five lakh tankas.

He was the first Muslim ruler to think of the material welfare of his people. Many rest houses, gardens and tombs were built. A number of madrasas (Islamic schools which provided Koranic education) were opened to encourage literacy. He set up hospitals for the free treatment of the poor. He provided money for the marriage of girls belonging to poor families. He commissioned many public buildings in Delhi. He built over 300 villages and dug 5 major canals for irrigation bringing more land under cultivation for growing grain and fruit.

Hindu religious works were translated from Sanskrit to Persian. He had a large personal library of manuscripts in Persian, Arabic and other languages. He brought 2 Ashokan Pillars from Meerut and Topara, carefully wrapped in silk, to Delhi. He re-erected one of them in his palace at Firoz Shah Kotla.

He had about 180,000 slaves, who had been brought from all over the country, trained in various arts and crafts. They however turned out to be undependable. Transfer of capital was the highlight of his reign. When the Qutb Minar struck by lightning in 1368 AD, knocking off its top storey, it was replaced by the existing two floors by Firoz Shah Tughlaq, faced with white marble.

Firoz Shah's death led to many rebellions. His lenient attitude had weakened the sultan's position. His successor Ghiyas-ud-Din Tughluq II could not control the slaves or the nobles. The army had become weak. Slowly the empire shrank in size. Ten years after his death, Timur's invasion devastated Delhi.

GHIYAS-UD-DIN TUGHLUQ II

Ghiyas-ud-Din Tughluq II was a Muslim Turkic ruler of the Tughlaq Dynasty (1388-1389). He succeeded Firuz Shah Tughluq in 1388 AD, immediately after his death. However, Ghiyas-ud-Din Tughluq II was not a capable ruler, and failed to successfully manage and control his empire.

He was eventually murdered in 1389 and succeeded by Abu Baker. Even so, none of the successors were strong leaders, and the Tughlaq Dynasty eventually came to its end in 1398.

ABU BAKER

Abu Baker was a Muslim Turkic ruler of the Tughlaq Dynasty (1389) and the younger son of Firuz Shah Tughluq. After Ghiyas-ud-Din Tughluq II (who had succeeded Firuz Shah Tughluq) was murdered, Abu Baker became ruler of the Tughlaq empire. However, his brother, Nasir ud din Muhammad Shah III, also desired to be ruler, and struggled against Abu Baker over the control of the throne. Eventually Abu Baker was defeated, and Nasir ud din Muhammad Shah III succeeded him as king, reigning from 1390 to 1394.

TIMUR AND HIS INDIAN CAMPAIGN

Timur was a 14th-century conqueror of much of western and central Asia, and or Pirnazar founder of the Timurid Empire and Timurid dynasty (1370–1405) in Central Asia, which survived until 1857 as the Mughal Empire of India.

A descendant of Mongol conquerors, Timur-whose tribe had become Turkicized in identity and language and Persianized in culture and religion-aspired to recreate the empire of his ancestors. He was a military genius who loved to play chess in his spare time to improve his military tactics and skill. And although he wielded absolute power, he never called himself more than an emir.

Timur was in his lifetime a controversial figure, and remains so today. He sought to restore the Mongol Empire, yet his heaviest blow was against the Islamized Mongol Golden Horde. He was more at home in an urban environment than on the steppe.

He styled himself a ghazi yet some Muslim states, e.g. the Ottoman Empire were impacted severely by his wars. A great patron of the arts, his campaigns also caused vast destruction. Timur told the qadis of Aleppo, during the sack of that newly-conquered city," I am not a man of blood; and God is my witness that in all my wars I have never been the aggressor, and that my enemies have always been the authors of their own calamity."

NAME

His full name in the Arabic tradition of *ism, nasba, and nisbat* was *Timur bin Tara!ay Barlas*. *Timur* means "iron" in the Chagatai language and in Mongolian (compare *Temujin* "ironworker", the given name of Genghis Khan). The term *Temur* is ultimately derived from a Buddhist Hybrid Sanskrit word **eimara* ("iron").

At the point he reached adulthood he was better known and called as *Timur Gurkani, Gurkan* being the Persianized form of the original Mongolian word *kurugan*, "son-in-law", the title bestowed upon his ancestors due to the fact, that first person in Timur's ancestors who was by the name "kara-sharnoban", embraced Islam and married the daughter of Chagatai Khan, the son of Genghis Khan, thus became son-in-law of Chagatai Khan.

Various Persian sources use a byname, *Tîmûr-e Lang* which translates to "Timur the Lame", as he was lame after sustaining an injury to the leg in battle. During his lifetime his enemies used to tease him with it, much to Timur's discomfort. In the West, he is commonly known as *Tamerlane,* which derives from his Persian byname.

Timur was also the great grandfather of Babur, the founder of the Mughal Dynasty.

EARLY LIFE

Timur was born in Transoxiana, in City of Kesh (an area now better known as Shahrisabz, 'the green city,'), some 50 miles south of Samarkand in modern Uzbekistan. His father Taraqai was a little landowner and belonged to the Barlas, a nomadic Turkized Mongol tribe in the steppes of Central Asia. They were remnants of the original Mongol hordes of Genghis Khan, many of whom had embraced Turkic or Iranian languages and customs. Timur was a Muslim, his official religious counsellor was the Hanafite scholar 'Abdul-Jabbar Khwarazmi. He also constructed one of his finest buildings at the tomb of Ahmed Yesevi, an influential Turkic Sufi saint who was spreading Sunni Islam among the nomads.

MILITARY LEADER

In about 1360 Timur gained prominence as a military leader whose troops were mostly Turkic tribesmen of the region.. He took part in campaigns in Transoxania with the Khan of Chagatai, a fellow descendant of Genghis Khan. His career for the next ten or eleven years may be thus briefly summarized from the *Memoirs*. Allying himself both in cause and by family connection with Kurgan, the dethroner and destroyer of Volga Bulgaria, he was to invade Khorasan at the head of a thousand horsemen. This was the second military expedition which he led, and its success led to further operations, among them the subjection of Khwarizm and Urganj.

After the murder of Kurgan the disputes which arose among the many claimants to sovereign power were halted by the invasion of the energetic Jagataite Tughlugh Timur of Kashgar, another descendant of Genghis Khan. Timur was dispatched on a mission to the invader's camp, the result of which was his own appointment to the head of his own tribe, the Barlas, in place of its former leader, Hajji Beg.

The exigencies of Timur's quasi-sovereign position compelled him to have recourse to his formidable patron, whose reappearance on the banks of the Syr Darya created a consternation not easily allayed. The Barlas were taken from Timur and entrusted to a son of Tughluk, along with the rest of Mawarannahr; but he was defeated in battle by the bold warrior he had replaced at the head of a numerically far inferior force.

RISE TO POWER

Tughlugh's death facilitated the work of reconquest, and a few years of perseverance and energy sufficed for its accomplishment, as well as for the addition of a vast extent of territory.

It was in this period that Timur reduced the Jagatai khans to the position of figureheads, who were deferred to in theory but in reality ignored, while Timur ruled in their name. During this period Timur and his brother-in-law Husayn, at first fellow fugitives and wanderers in joint adventures full of interest and romance, became rivals and antagonists. At the close of 1369 Husayn was assassinated and Timur, having been formally proclaimed sovereign at Balkh, mounted the throne at Samarkand, the capital of his dominions. This event was recorded by Marlowe in his famous work *Tamburlaine the Great*:

Then shall my native city, Samarcanda...

Be famous through the furthest continents,

For there my palace-royal shall be placed,
Whose shining turrets shall dismay the heavens,
And cast the fame of lion's tower to hell.

A legendary account of Timur's rise to leadership, recorded among the Tatar descendants of the Qypchaq Khanate in Tobol, goes as follows:

One day Aksak Temür spoke thusly: "Khan Züdei (in China) rules over the city. We now number fifty to sixty men, so let us elect a leader." So they drove a stake into the ground and said: "We shall run thither and he who among us is the first to reach the stake, may he become our leader". So they ran and Aksak Timur (since he was lame) lagged behind, but before the others reached the stake he threw his cap onto it. Those who arrived first said: "We are the leaders". (But) Aksak Timur said: "My head came in first, I am the leader". In the meanwhile an old man arrived and said: "The leadership should belong to Aksak Timur; your feet have arrived but, before then, his head reached the goal". So they made Aksak Timur their prince.

It is notable that Timur never claimed for himself the title of khan, styling himself amir and acting in the name of the Chagatai ruler of Transoxania. Timur was a military genius but sometimes lacking in political sense. He tended not to leave a government apparatus behind in lands he conquered, and was often faced with the need to conquer such lands again after inevitable rebellions.

PERIOD OF EXPANSION

Timur spent the next 35 years in various wars and expeditions. He not only consolidated his rule at home by the subjugation of his foes, but sought extension of territory by encroachments upon the lands of foreign potentates. His conquests to the west and northwest led him among the Mongols of the Caspian Sea and to the banks of the Ural and the Volga. Conquests in the south and south-West encompassed almost every province in Persia, including Baghdad, Karbala and Northern Iraq.

One of the most formidable of Timur's opponents was another Mongol ruler, a descendant of Genghis Khan named Tokhtamysh. After having been a refugee in Timur's court, Tokhtamysh became ruler both of the eastern Kipchak and the Golden Horde. After his accidence, he then quarreled with Timur over the possession of Khwarizm and Azerbaijan. However, Timur still supported him against the Russians and in 1382 Tokhtamysh invaded the Muscovite dominion and burned Moscow.

After the death of Abu Said, ruler of the Ilkhanid Dynasty, in 1335, there was a power vacuum in the Persian Empire. In 1383 Timur started the military conquest of Persia. He captured Herat, Khorasan and all eastern Persia by 1385 and captured almost all of Persia by 1387. These conquests were characterised by exceptional brutality. For example, when Isfahan surrendered to Timur in 1387, he initially treated it with relative mercy as he commonly did with cities that surrendered without resistance. However, after the city revolted against Timur's punitive taxes by killing the tax collectors and some of Timur's soldiers, Timur ordered the complete massacre of the city, killing a reported 70,000 citizens. An eye-witness counted more than 28 towers, each constructed of about 1,500 heads.

In the meantime, Tokhtamysh, now khan of the Golden Horde, turned against his patron and invaded Azerbaijan in 1385. This action would cause a counter by Timur that would become the Tokhtamysh–Timur war. In the initial stage of the war, Timur won a victory at the Battle of the Kondurcha River, however Tokhtamysh and his army were allowed to escape.

After Tokhtamysh's initial defeat, Timur then invaded Muscovy to the north of Tokhtamysh's holdings. Timur's army burned Raizan and advanced upon Moscow, only to be pulled away before reaching the Oka River by Tokhtamysh's renewed campaign in the south. In 1395, at the Battle of the Terek River, Tokhtamysh's power was finally broken concluding the titanic struggle between the two monarchs.

In this Tokhtamysh–Timur war, Timur first led an army of over 100,000 men north for more than 700 miles into the uninhabited steppe, then west about 1000 miles, advancing in a front more than 10 miles wide. The Timurid army almost starved, and Timur organized a great hunt where the army encircled vast areas of steppe to get food.

Tokhtamysh's army finally was cornered against the Volga River in the Orenburg region and destroyed. During this march, Timur's army got far enough north to be in a region of very long summer days, causing complaints by his Muslim soldiers about keeping a long schedule of prayers in such northern regions. Timur during the course of his campaign destroyed Sarai, the capital of the Golden Horde, and Astrakhan, subsequently wrecking the Golden Horde's economy based on Silk Road trade.

INDIAN CAMPAIGN

Timur began a trek starting in 1398 to invade the reigning Sultan Nasir-u Din Mehmud of the Tughlaq Dynasty in the north Indian city of Delhi. His campaign was politically pretexted that the Muslim Delhi Sultanate was too tolerant toward its Hindu subjects, but that could not mask the real reason being to amass the wealth of the Delhi Sultanate.

Timur crossed the Indus River at Attock (now Pakistan) on September 24, 1398, but Timur's invasion did not go unopposed and he did meet some resistance during his march to Delhi, by the Governor of Meerut. Timur was able to continue his relentless approach to Delhi, arriving in 1398 to combat the armies of Sultan Mehmud, already weakened by an internal battle for ascension within the royal family.

The Sultan's army was easily defeated on December 17, 1398. On this day the army of Sultan Mahmud Khan had prepared 120 war elephants armoured with chain mail. He had put poison on the tusks, which put fright into the Tatar lines. Timur took action and the Tatars dug out a trench in front of their positions. Timur then took his camels and placed all the wood and hay he could on their backs. When the war elephants charged he lit the camels on fire and then prodded them with iron sticks. They charged at the elephants howling in pain. Timur had understood that elephants were easy creatures of panic. Faced with the strange specter of the burning camels flying straight at them with flames leaping from their backs, the elephants turned around and stampeded back toward their own lines. Timur entered Delhi and the city was sacked, destroyed, and left in ruins. Before the battle for Delhi, Timur executed a large number of captives, mostly Hindus.

Timur himself recorded the invasions in his memoirs, collectively known as Tuzk-e-Taimuriy. In them, he vividly described the massacre at Delhi:

In a short space of time all the people in the Delhi fort were put to the sword, and in the course of one hour the heads of 10,000 infidels were cut off. The sword of Islam was washed in the blood of the infidels, and all the goods and effects, the treasure and the grain which for many a long year had been stored in the fort became the spoil of my soldiers. They set fire to the houses and reduced them to ashes, and they razed the buildings and the fort to the ground....All these infidel Hindus were slain.

Their women and children and their property and goods became the spoil of the victors. I proclaimed throughout the camp that every man who had infidel prisoners should put them to death, and whoever neglected to do so should himself be executed and his property given to the informer. When this order became known to the ghazis of Islam, they drew their swords and put their prisoners to death. One hundred thousand infidels, impious idolaters, were on that day slain. Maulana Nasiruddin Umar, a counselor and man of learning, who, in all his life, had never killed a sparrow, now, in execution of my order, slew with his sword fifteen idolatrous Hindus, who were his captives....on the great day of battle these 100,000 prisoners could not be left with the baggage, and that it would be entirely opposed to the rules of war to set these idolaters and enemies of Islam at liberty... no other course remained but that of making them all food for the sword.

Timur further describes as below in Tuzk-e-Taimuriý how he and his army massacred the Hindus population of Delhi after conquering it.

The savage Turks fell to killing and plundering, while the Hindus set fire to their houses with their own hands, burned their wives and children in them and rushed in to fight and were killed... All day Thursday and throughout the night nearly 15,000 Turks were engaged in slaying, plundering and destroying. When Friday morning dawned, my entire army, no longer under control, went off to the city and thought of nothing but killing, plundering and making prisoners. The sack was general during the whole day, and continued throughout the whole day Saturday, the seventeenth (Dec 17), the spoil being so great that each man secured from fifty to a hundred prisoners, men, women and children, while no soldier took less than twenty. There was likewise an immense booty in rubies, diamonds, pearls and other gems; jewels of gold and silver... gold and silver ornaments of the Hindu women obtained in such quantities as to exceed all account. *Excepting the quarter of the Sayyids, the scholars, and the other Mussulmans, the whole city was sacked.*

As per Malfuzat-i-Timuri, Timur targeted Hindus. In his own words, "Excepting the quarter of the saiyids, the 'ulama and the other Musalmans [sic], the whole city was sacked". In his descriptions of the Loni massacre he wrote, "Next day I gave orders that the Musalman prisoners should be separated and saved."

Timur explains his objective behind the Indian campaign as below in *Tuzk-e-Taimuri*

My object in the invasion of Hindustan to lead an expedition against the infidels... (so that) the army of Islam might gain something by plundering the wealth and valuables of the Hindus... we may convert to the true faith the people of that country, and purify the land from the filth of infidelity and polytheism; and that we may overthrow their temples and idols and become ghazis and mujahids before God.

Timur left Delhi in approximately January 1399. In April he had returned to his own capital beyond the Oxus (Amu Darya). Immense quantities of spoils were taken from India. According to Ruy Gonzales de Clavijo, 90 captured elephants were employed merely to carry precious stones looted from his conquest, so as to erect a mosque at Samarkand - what historians today believe is the enormous Bibi-Khanym Mosque. Ironically, the mosque was constructed too quickly and suffered greatly from disrepair within a few decades of its construction.

LAST CAMPAIGNS AND DEATH

Before the end of 1399, Timur started a war with Bayezid I, sultan of the Ottoman Empire, and the Mamluk sultan of Egypt. Bayezid began annexing the territory of Turkmen and Muslim rulers in Anatolia. As Timur claimed sovereignty over the Turkmen rulers, they took refuge behind him. Timur invaded Syria, sacked Aleppo and captured Damascus after defeating the Mamluk army. The city's inhabitants were massacred, except for the artisans, who were deported to Samarkand. This led to Timur's being publicly declared an enemy of Islam.

In 1400 Timur invaded Armenia and Georgia. More than 60,000 people from the Caucasus were captured as slaves, and many districts were depopulated.

He invaded Baghdad in June 1401. After the capture of the city, 20,000 of its citizens including Muslims were massacred. Timur ordered that every soldier should return with at least two severed human heads to show him (many warriors were so scared they killed prisoners captured earlier in the campaign just to ensure they had heads to present to Timur). After years of insulting letters passed between Timur and Bayezid, Timur invaded Anatolia and defeated Bayezid in the Battle of Ankara on July 20, 1402.

Bayezid was captured in battle and subsequently died in captivity, initiating the 12-year Ottoman Interregnum period. Timur's stated motivation for attacking Bayezid and the Ottoman Empire was the restoration of Seljuq authority. Timur saw the Seljuks as the rightful rulers of Anatolia as they had been granted rule by Mongol conquerors, illustrating again Timur's interest with Genghizid legitimacy.

Timur's army ravaged Western Anatolia, with Muslim writers complaining that the Timurid army acted more like a horde of savages than that of a civilized conqueror. After the Battle of Ankara, Timur did take the city of Smyrna, a stronghold of the Knights Hospitalers, thus he referred to himself as ghazi. Timur was furious at the Genoese and

Venetians whose ships ferried the Ottoman army to safety in Thrace. As Lord Kinross reported in *The Ottoman Centuries*, the Italians preferred the enemy they knew to the one they did not.

By 1368, the Ming had driven the Mongols out of China. The first Ming Emperor Hongwu demanded, and received, homage from many Central Asian states paid to China as the political heirs to the former House of Kublai. Although Timur more than once sent to the Ming Government tributes after he had imprisoned the Chinese envoys for several months, he wished to restore the Mongol Empire, and eventually planned to conquer China. To this end, Timur made an alliance with the Mongols of the Northern Yuan Dynasty and prepared all the way to Bukhara. The Mongol leader Enkhe Khan sent his grandson Oljei Temur, also known as Buyanshir Khan. In December 1404, Timur started military campaigns against the Ming Dynasty and detained the Ming envoy, but he was attacked by fever and plague when encamped on the farther side of the Sihon (Syr-Daria) and died at Atrar (Otrar) in mid-February 1405. His scouts explored Mongolia before his death, and the writing they carved on trees in Mongolia's mountains could still be seen even in the 20th century.

Although he preferred to fight his battles in the spring, Timur died enroute during an uncharacteristic winter campaign against the ruling Chinese Ming Dynasty. It was one of the bitterest winters on record; his troops are recorded as having to dig through five feet of ice to reach drinking water. Records indicate though, that for part of his life at least, he was a surreptitious Ming vassal and that his son Shah Rukh visited China in 1420.

He ruled over an empire that, in modern times, extends from southeastern Turkey, Syria, Iraq, Kuwait and Iran, through Central Asia encompassing part of Kazakhstan, Afghanistan, Armenia, Azerbaijan, Georgia, Turkmenistan, Uzbekistan, Kyrgyzstan, Pakistan, North-Western India, and even approaches Kashgar in China. Northern Iraq remained predominantly Assyrian Christian until attacked, looted, plundered and destroyed by Timur leaving its population decimated by systematic mass slaughter.

All churches were destroyed and any survivors forcefully converted to Islam by the sword. Of Timur's four sons, two (Jahangir and Umar Shaykh) predeceased him. His third son, Miran Shah, died soon after Timur, leaving the youngest son, Shah Rukh. Although his designated successor was his grandson Pir Muhammad b. Jahangir, Timur was ultimately succeeded in power by his son Shah Rukh. His most illustrious descendant Babur founded the Mughal Empire and ruled over most of Pakistan and North India. Babur's descendants Humayun, Akbar, Jahangir, Shah Jahan and Aurangzeb, expanded the Mughal Empire to most of the Indian subcontinent along with parts of modern Pakistan and Afghanistan.

Markham, in his introduction to the narrative of Clavijo's embassy, states that his body "was embalmed with musk and rose water, wrapped in linen, laid in an ebony coffin and sent to Samarkand, where it was buried." His tomb, the Gur-e Amir, still stands in Samarkand, though it has been heavily restored in recent years. Timur had carried his victorious arms on one side from the Irtish and the Volga to the Persian Gulf, and on the other from the Hellespont to the Ganges River.

CONTRIBUTIONS TO THE ARTS

Timur became widely known as a patron to the arts. Much of the architecture he commissioned still stands in Samarkand, now in present-day Uzbekistan. He was known to bring the most talented artisans from the lands he conquered back to Samarkand, and is credited with often giving them a wide latitude of artistic freedom to express themselves.

According to legend, Omar Aqta, Timur's court calligrapher, transcribed the Qur'an using letters so small that the entire text of the book fit on a signet ring. Omar also is said to have created a Qur'an so large that a wheelbarrow was required to transport it. Folios of what is probably this larger Qur'an have been found, written in gold lettering on huge pages.

Timur was also said to have created Tamerlane Chess, a variant of shatranj (also known as medieval chess) played on a larger board with several additional pieces and an original method of pawn promotion. These pieces included the camel, siege-weapon, giraffe, and several others as well as boasting a complicated system involving the ability to exchange pawns for certain pieces should they reach the other side of the board. Timur's mandating of Kurash wrestling for his soldiers ensured for it a lasting and legendary legacy. Kurash is now a popular international sport and part of the Asian Games.

7

Architecture During Delhi Sultanate

The architecture of the Delhi sultanate represents a gradual evolution from an imported Afghan style using unfamiliar materials to a developed Indo-Islamic style which formed the basis of later Mughal architecture. The first building of the Delhi sultanate was the Quwwat al-Islam Mosque complex built by Qutb al-Din Aibak out of the remains of twenty-seven destroyed Hindu temples. The arcades were supported by two tiers of Hindu temple pillars placed one on top of the other to achieve the desired height. They were built in a trabeated construction and in 1199 an arched facade was added to the east side of the sanctuary to give it the familiar appearance of a mosque. However, the arches of the screen were built out of corbels rather than voussoirs whilst the decoration consisted of Quranic inscriptions contained within dense Hindu-style foliage. In the same year Qutb ud-Din began the famous Qutub Minar which has become one of the potent symbols of Islam in India. Other work carried out at this time was the construction of the Great Mosque of Ajmer which like the Delhi Mosque employed re-used Hindu columns and later had an arched screen added to the front.

Ala al-Din in particular devoted a great deal of attention to the mosque by extending the area of the sanctuary as well as beginning a new minaret on the same design as the Qutub Minar but more than twice the size. Unfortunately Ala al-Din was unable to finish his work and the only part completed is a monumental gateway. Other work carried out by Ala al-Din was the foundation of Siri, the second city of Delhi.

Several new cities were founded including Fatehabad, Hissar and

Jaunpaur as well as the third, fourth and fifth cities of Delhi. Also at this time the influence of Sultanate architecture was felt in the Deccan when Muhammad Tughlaq II moved his capital to Daulatabad. Characteristic features of this architecture are massive sloping fortification walls with pointed crenulations and the development of the tomb as the focus of architectural design. One of the more important tombs is that of Khan Jahan built in 1369 which incorporates Hindu features into an Islamic form. The tomb has an octagonal domed form with chhajjas, or projecting eaves, on each side and domed chhatris on the roof.

Nevertheless, many of the buildings are sophisticated structures like the tomb of Sikander Lodi which uses a double dome form so that the dome may have a significant form on the outside without disrupting the proportions of the interior (a technique later used in the Taj Mahal). The tomb is also the first Indian tomb to form part of a formal garden which became the established format under the Mughals. In addition to the centralised architectural styles developed during the Delhi sultanate several vigorous regional traditions also developed.

The four most significant styles are those of Gujarat, Kashmir, the Deccan and Bengal. The style of Gujarat developed independently for over 200 years from its conquest by the Khaliji sultan Ala al-Din Shah in the early fourteenth century to its incorporation in the Mughal Empire in the late sixteenth century. Characteristic features of Gujarati architecture are the use of Hindu methods of decoration and construction for mosques long after they had ceased to be fashionable in Delhi. After the conquest of Gujarat, the Mughal emperor Akbar adopted this style for his most ambitious architectural project, Fatehpur Sikri. Less well known but equally distinctive is the architecture of Kashmir where the first Islamic conquest was in the mid-fourteenth century.

The significant features of Kashmiri architecture are the use of wood as the main building material and tall pyramid-shaped roofs on mosques. The third major regional style is the architecture of the Deccan in southern India. Decaying architecture is characterised by massive monumental stonework, bulbous onion-shaped domes and elaborate stone carving, including vegetal forms, arched niches and medallions. Far to the east, in the region of Bengal and modern Bangladesh, a distinctive architecture developed using baked brick as the main building material Other characteristic features of Bengal include the use of the curved do-chala and char-chala roofs which were later incorporated into imperial Mughal architecture under Shah Jahan.

Alai Darwaza: The Alai Darwaza is a magnificent gateway built by Ala-ud-din Khalji of the Delhi Sultanate, having exquisite inlaid marble decorations and latticed stone screens. It highlights the remarkable artisanship of Turkish and local artisans who worked on it. The Alai Darwaza was an important part of the project undertaken by Ala-ud-din Khalji in his quest to decorate the Qutab complex.

The Alai Darwaza represents a new style of architecture, popularly referred to as the Indo-Islamic style of architecture. The Indo-Islamic style is neither a local variant of Islamic art, nor a modification of Hindu art, but it is an assimilation of both the styles, though not always in an equal degree. It is so because each region in India has its own form of Indo-Islamic architecture, which varies from place to place and there is no standardisation. On the other hand, Islamic art itself was a composite style, which had various Muslims influences-Turkish, Persian, and Arabic.

Though both the Indian and Islamic styles have their own distinctive features, some common characteristics made fusion and adaptation easy. Both the styles favour ornamentation and buildings of both styles are marked by the presence of an open court encompassed by chambers or colonnades. The Qutab Minar, the Quwwat-ul-Islam mosque, and the tomb of Iltutmish, which were constructed by different rulers of the Slave dynasty (1193-1290), heralded the birth of Indo-Islamic architecture. Of these monuments, the Qutab Minar is a tower symbolising the victory of the first Muslim rulers of India over the indigenous people. This fluted tower with floral patterns and Quranic inscriptions around in a flowing calligraphic style was the first monument of the Indo-Islamic style of architecture.

The Quwwat-ul-Islam mosque was the first mosque to be built in India and is made up of the remnants of 27 Hindu and Jain temples, broken down by the Muslim rulers of the Delhi Sultanate. It is also a representation of Muslim power. The tomb of Iltutmish was the first Islamic tomb to be built in India. As the concept of a domed tomb was new to the indigenous craftsmen, the resultant structural flaws in the building let to the collapse of the dome-the first one to have been built in India. Thus, one can say that the monuments belonging to the Slave dynasty mixed two cultures.

The Alai Darwaza is a perfect specimen of architecture belonging to the period of the Delhi Sultanate. It was built in 1311, by Ala-ud-din-Khalji, of the Khalji dynasty (which ruled the Delhi Sultanate from AD 1290 to AD 1316). The Alai Darwaza was a part of Ala-ud-din-Khalji's extension of the Quwwat-ul-Islam mosque. It was one of the four grand gateways; the other three could not be completed because of the death of Ala-ud-din in AD 1316.

The main structure of the Alai Darwaza consists of a single hall 34½ feet on the inside and 56½ feet on the outside. The domed ceiling rises to a height of 47 feet. The three doorways on the east, west, and south are lofty pointed arches, in the shape of a horseshoe, which rise above the flanking side bays. The entrance to the north is of an indigenous character, as its arch is semi-circular in shape. The overall outlook and proportions of the Alai Darwaza is pleasing to the eye. The recessed corner arches of the attractive horseshoe forms, supporting a simple spherical dome on top of the square chamber, are an especially happy solution to the perpetual problem of supporting a good dome. It would be well worth noting that the earlier attempts at raising the dome, particularly the tomb of Iltutmish, had been unsuccessful. The dome of the Alai Darwaza, in this respect, is a notable achievement.

The plinth on each side is beautifully carved with floral and geometric patterns in both white marble and red sandstone, creating a superb polychrome effect. Perforated latticework window screens (jali) are set in the recessed windows on both sides of the entrances. These marble screens set off the monotony of the vertical lines of calligraphic ornamentation. The most charming aspect of surface decoration is the lace-like interweaving of floral tendrils, repeated with a flawless symmetry on all the three entrances, elegantly designed and perfectly built. The northern entrance is semi-circular with a shallow trefoil in its outline. The facade is elaborately ornamented in sensuous carving and patterns, characteristic of the pre-Turkish days (the first Muslim rulers of India came from Turkey). The Alai Darwaza also shows the influence of Seljuk art. The Seljuks had started fleeing Western Asia after Mongol invasions in the 12th century AD and had reached Delhi for protection. The 'spear-headed' embellishment on the three entrances is of particular importance in this regard. In addition, the surface ornamentation has been done with an eye for lavishness and detail.

Siri Fort: Ala-ud-din Khalji was a great patron of architecture and to him goes the credit of getting the Siri Fort in Delhi constructed. The fort was mainly built by Ala-ud-din to protect the people of his capital from the frequent invasions of the Mongols, who easily penetrated the weak defences of India's borders time and again to reach all the way up to

Delhi. He succeeded in his mission of protecting his subjects after building the Siri Fort. Ala-ud-din Khalji built Siri Fort not only as the imperial capital of his kingdom, but also to protect the people of his capital city from the threat of the Mongols marauders. Siri Fort was a formidable fort, having strong Ramparts and unassailable walls. The fort also served as the administrative centre of the Delhi Sultanate, under the rule of Ala-ud-din Khalji (AD 1296-1316).

The kingdom of Delhi was constantly threatened by hoards of Mongol tribesmen who had been descending in waves to loot India since the 13th century. The Slave dynasty (AD 1193-1290), which was the first dynasty of the Delhi Sultanate, also faced this threat in the later half of its reign. Balban, the last important ruler of this dynasty successfully countered the Mongol threat.

In the course of time, the reins of the Delhi Sultanate passed into the hands of the Khalji Dynasty (AD 1290-1316). Ala-ud-din Khalji ascended the throne of the Delhi Sultanate in AD 1296. He was a strong monarch, who was constantly expanding his empire.

Ala-ud-din was also a great builder. He built the fort city at Siri, which served as the administrative centre of the Khalji kingdom and was the first city in Delhi to be built by the Muslim rulers of India.

The rulers of the Slave dynasty, who were the first Muslim rulers of India and the first dynasty of the Delhi Sultanate before the Khiljis, used Lal Kot, the fort city of the last Hindu rulers of Delhi. He also began to put into shape his grand plans of beautifying the Qutab Minar complex. He added the Alai Darwaza, a magnificent gateway with inlaid marble decorations and latticed stone screens, which showcases the remarkable craftsmanship of the Turkish artisans who worked on it. He also planned to build the Alai Minar, which was conceived as a greater tower than the already existing Qutab Minar but the construction of this tower was abandoned after the completion of the 24.5-meter high first story.

The Mongols under their leader Taraghai plundered Delhi in AD 1303, and almost captured it. However the marauders did not capture the city and without reason turned back and left. Meanwhile, Ala-ud-din Khalji was away from Delhi, busy in one of his military campaigns in the Deccan region in South India. Returning back to Delhi from his Deccan campaign, Ala-ud-din Khalji decided to build a defensive fortress at Siri with strong fortified Ramaparts and impregnable bastions. This was the third fort to be built within the city of Delhi. The construction of the Siri Fort and the city within it began in AD 1304. The place he chose was a plain ground around five km to the north-east of the Qutab Minar where forces attacking or defending Delhi used to camp.

Tamurlane, who invaded Delhi in AD 1398, found Siri a magnificent fortress and damaged it. Later on, Sher Shah Suri (an Afghan chieftain from eastern India who ruled Delhi from AD 1540-1555 and was a contemporary of the second Mughal Emperor, Humayun) took construction material from Siri to build his own city. Only some portions of the Siri walls can be seen today as all else has been destroyed and stones have been removed.

ART AND ARCHITECTURE OF DELHI SULTANATE

Art and architecture of Delhi Sultanate was the period when the Delhi Sultanate flourished in India. This period brought with it new styles of architecture and art to India which were quickly absorbed into the set up present previously. There are reasons for events to move in this direction. The new ideas and the existing Indian styles had several common features, thus enabling them to become accustomed to one another. Both mosque and temple possess large open courtyards and several other temples were converted into mosques by some of the foreign invaders, which formed a mixture of both Indian and foreign styles. The Delhi Sultanate brought two new architectural ideas, the pointed arch and the dome. The dome forms the major decorative component in Islamic buildings, and soon the same was introduced in several other structures. The true or pointed arch used during this period, was totally dissimilar to that of the arches which were being constructed within the country before.

The primitive Indian style of making arches was to first construct two pillars and then the same would be cut at interval to hold 'plug in' projections. There would also be a series of squares which would step by step decrease in size forming an arch. The new artisans brought in the true arch. This was accomplished by forming the middle stone a key stone and to other stones allocates the load to the two pillars. The idea of the dome was also newly introduced. This was slowly perfected and one of the striking examples is the dome of the famous Taj Mahal in Agra. The dome at first started out in the form of a conical dome in the Mehrauli region in Delhi and finally developed the final bulbous onion shape on the Taj Mahal. The dome effect was attained by an interesting process.

At first, a square base was constructed and then at changing angles more squares adds up to the base. It thus creates a rough dome effect which was plastered in order to form it fully round and after that the squares were removed. Concrete was also used abundantly by opening up new opportunity. Concrete helped the builders to construct larger and massive structures stretching over a vast area. The local craftsmen of India were soon given training on Persian styles of art which they utilized to decorate the structures. The artisans also at times put in some of their own ideas, and soon the Hindu traditional motifs like the lotus were introduced into the Islamic buildings. Several other instances like the Islamic buildings utilized more advanced pointed arch, they also adapted for the purpose of decoration a variant of the Hindu arch.

The early period of the Sultanate, namely the Slave dynasty in India and the Khiliji dynasty formed a number of exquisitely designed structures, with delicate works of art adorning them. In the Tughlaq period, the temper was less decorative and more austere and simple. This is assigned in part to the Tughlaq's religious ideas and the depleted state finances. The Lodis and the Sayyids who came after the Tughlaqs brought the more lavish styles with the Lodis bringing in the new concept of double dome. A new decorative style was also introduced by them, mainly borrowed from Persia, enameled tiles, with grey sandstone. Terra-cotta decorative work remained popular in the period. The period was marked with great experimentation, and a majority of the artists and engineers in India were eager to learn from the flood of new ideas entering the country at that time. The indigenous technique was retained by them and at the same time they also absorbed several new thoughts coming in their way. Thus, two different ideas mixed to form a coherent whole. Under the Delhi Sultanate major developments were made in music as Indian and Arab forms mixed with the traditions of Persia and Central Asia.

This syncretism led to the formation of a new type of music in north India quite dissimilar to that of the traditional Indian music, which retained its hold in the south. Much of the credit for this synthesis can be attributed to Amir Khusrau, the poet whose fame gave prestige to the new music, and also to the interest of the Chishti Sufis. At the independent court of Jaipur, music received special attention. At Jaunpur the last Sharqi king, Sultan Husain, was considered to be the founder of the Khiyal or romantic school of music, which went on to blossom under the Mughals.

At Gwalior under Raja Man Singh the chief musician was a Muslim who systematized Indian music in the light of the changes it had undergone since the advent of the Muslims. Little is known about in the field of education and the detailed curriculum of the madrasas, but it appears that medicine was accorded high importance.

The earliest surviving work, written in the year 1329, by Zia Muhammad, Mazmua-i-ziai, is based on Arabic and Indian sources, and gives local equivalents of Arab medicines. Others followed with combinations of Arab, Greek and Indian works, bringing together the medical knowledge of three cultures.

Very few literary works have survived from the period of the Sultanate. With the exception of a number of major pieces by poets like Amir Khusrau or Hasan, the only enduring works were those included in general histories, like the poems of Sangreza, the first poet of eminence born in India, or Ruhani's poem of the conquest of Ranthambhor by Iltutmish. Perhaps the most important literary contribution during the Delhi Sultanate was in the field of history.

Ancient Indian culture produced no historical literature, so surviving Muslim works are vital primary sources. These works are richly varied. While many glorify or exaggerate the role of their royal patrons, the basic historical facts are sound. The historian Baruni is particularly notable for his fascinating insights into the political philosophies of different monarchs and for his portrayal of individual personalities. With the collapse of the power of the Sultanate in the 15th century, the rise of the provincial kingdoms fostered the growth of regional languages. While Hindu rulers had patronized Sanskrit language as the language of religion and the Epics, Muslim rulers supported the common languages of the people. Ironically, it was the Muslims who were responsible for the first translations of the Sanskrit Epics into the provincial languages.

HINDU ARCHITECTURE UNDER DELHI SULTANATE

Specimens of Hindu architecture during the period of Delhi Sultanate are found in the north India in Rajasthan as the Hindus could maintain their political existence in the north India only. The Vijayanagara Empire which was established in the south later on revived the glory of the Hindus and magnificent architectural edifices were raised by their rulers. Most of the buildings and temples of the Vijayanagara Empire wee destroyed by the Muslims. Among the architectural wonders that survives are the Vitthala temple which was constructed by Krishnadeva Raya.

It is a beautiful temple and one of the finest buildings in the south India. The other notable buildings built by the Hindus are found only in Rajasthan. Rana Kumbha of Mewar erected many forts, palaces and other buildings, the best known among which is the fort of Kumbhalgarh and the Kriti Stambha. Part of this pillar is built in red stone and some portion is made of marble. It has been regarded as the most remarkable tower in the country.

Another beautiful specimen of Hindu architecture is the tower at Chittor known as the Jain Stambha which is richly ornamented with beautiful carvings and lattice works. Many other forts and palaces were built by the Rajput rulers at different places. The forts though exist at present but the palaces have perished.

The Hindus learnt a lot about the art of construction from the Muslims but kept their architectural style free from their influence. Therefore, their buildings maintained their separate identity and were different from the buildings of the Muslim rulers.

In the south the rulers of the Vijayanagara further elaborated the art of constructing gopurams (gateways of temples). Tall and massive gopurams were constructed at the temples of the south during the period of the Delhi Sultanate. Different rulers also constructed mandapas over the temples which have been regarded as fine specimens of architecture.

The Kalyana Mandapa at Vellore has often been described as the richest and the most beautiful structure of its kind. Similar beautiful mandapas were constructed in the temples of Sri Varadarajasvami and Ekambaranatha at Kanchipuram and in the Jambukesvara near Trichinopoly. Thus the Hindus helped in the growth of architecture in their own way. Unlike the Muslims who mostly constructed tombs, minarets, palaces, forts and mosques, the Hindu architectural specimens constituted mainly of temples, pillars, forts, palaces, gopurams and mandapas in the temples. However no positive efforts ware made for the fusion of Hindu and Muslim architecture, yet the synthesis took place and the new style of architecture which emerged came to be known as Indo-Islamic architecture.

IMPERIAL STYLE OF ARCHITECTURE UNDER DELHI SULTANATE

Imperial style of architecture developed and gained prominence during the period of Delhi Sultanate. Qutub-ud-din Aibak constructed few monuments which have the imprint of both Hindu and Muslim art. Even during the reign of Iltutmish and Ala-ud-din Khilji, there were several specimens of architecture which were built. The Tughlaqs also played an imperative role in the thriving of the imperial style of architecture.

Qutub-ud-din Aibak constructed the Quwat–ul–Islam mosque at Delhi and another mosque at Ajmer called the Dhai Din Ka Jhonpra. The first was raised at the site of a destroyed temple and the other at the location of a ruined college of Sanskrit. Therefore, both these mosques have the impression of both Hindu and Muslim art. Sultan Iltutmish and Ala-ud-din Khilji added to the Quwat-ul-Islam mosque. The construction of the Qutub Minar though started by Aibak but it was completed by Iltutmish.

The planning of this monument was purely Islamic and was originally intended to serve as a place for the muazzin but afterwards, it became famous as a tower of victory. Qutub Minar is an impressive building and according to many historians it is one of the most perfect examples of a tower known to exist anywhere in the world. Iltutmish constructed a tomb on the grave of his eldest son which is known as Sultan–Ghari. He also built Hauz-i-Shamsi, Shamsi-Idgah, Jami Masjid at Badaun and the Atarkin-ka-Darwaza at Nagaur (Jodhpur). He made additions to Quwat-ul-Islam and Dhai Din Ka Jhonpra. Balban built his own tomb and the red place at Delhi. His construction marked a notable landmark in the development of Indo-Islamic architecture.

A number of magnificent buildings were constructed under the reign of Ala–ud–din Khilji. He had good economic resources and his buildings were constructed with perfectly Islamic viewpoint and have been regarded as few best examples of Islamic art in India. Ala–ud–din founded the city of Siri, built a palace of thousands of pillars within it, Jamait Khan Mosque at the shrine of Nizam–ud–din Auliya and the famous Alai Darwaza at the Qutub Minar. The Alai Darwaza is considered as one of the most treasured possession of Islamic architecture. Ala–ud–din known constructed a magnificent tank covering an area of nearly seventy acres, known as Hauz-i-Alai or Hauz-i-Khas near his newly constructed city of Siri in the vicinity of the old city of Delhi.

The Tughlaqs were puritanical in taste and thus their buildings were devoid of any ornamentation. Ghiyas-ud-din constructed the new city of Tughlaqabad in the east of the Qutub area, his own tomb and a palace which was constructed in golden bricks. Muhammad Bin Tughlaq constructed the new city of Jahanpanah near the city of old Delhi, the fort of Adilabad and few other buildings at Daultabad. But all his buildings have been destroyed.

The only two buildings which remain are the Sathpalahbund and the Bijai-Mandal. Among the distinguished buildings constructed by Firoz Tughlaq are the new city of Firozabad near the old city of Delhi, the palace fort known as Kotla Firoz Shah within it.

During his reign, a noble at the court, Khan-i-Jahan Jauna Shah constructed the tomb of his father, Tilangani, the Kali Masjid and the Khirki Masjid in the city of Jahanpanah. A striking building known as Lal-Gumbad, was constructed by Nasir-ud-din Muhammad Tughlaq Shah at the grave of Kabir-ud-din Auliya. Among the buildings constructed by Lodi and Sayyid Sultans, are the tombs of Mubarak Shah Sayyid, Muhammad Shah Sayyid and Sikandar Lodi. Most of the buildings raised by Sultans of the Delhi Sultanate which includes palaces and forts have been destroyed. Only a few tombs, mosques and minars have existed so far. The buildings which are good specimens of early imperial style of architecture in India and the best among them are the Qutub Minar and the Alai-Darwaza.

BUILDING CONSTRUCTION IN DELHI SULTANATE

The first thing the Muslim Sultanate of Delhi started on was construction of impressive buildings. It aimed at overawing the people of the land with the greatness and might of the new Islamic regime. This could be achieved by constructing huge Muslim edifices with the wealth obtained from war and materials from Hindu buildings after destroying them.

Architecture was considered as the visual symbol of Muslim political power with which the Turks wished to impress and overawe the conquered people. It denoted victory with authority. Wherever the Muslim conquerors marched or ruled in Central Asia or India, they constructed edifices both gigantic and delicate. The important fact to note in this connection is that slaves were drafted to construct the buildings.

And so thousands of slaves were drafted to construct the edifies (many even now extant as monuments), so as to complete the work in the shortest possible time. Surely, the task could be accomplished only by pressing into service thousands and thousand of slaves captured in early victories who were made to do the job. The congregational mosque at Delhi named, purposefully, as the Masjid Quwwatul Islam (Might of Islam), was commenced by Aibak in 592/1195 within two years of its conquest. It was built with materials and gold obtained by destroying 27 Hindu and Jain temples in Delhi and its neighbourhood. A Persian inscription in the mosque testifies to this. The mosque at Ajmer erected by Qutbuddin Aibak soon after its occupation and known as the *Arhai din ka Jhonpra,* was also built from materials obtained from demolished temples. The Qutb Minar, planned and commenced by Aibak sometime in or before 1199 and completed by Iltutmish, was also constructed with similar materials, "the sculptured figures on the stones being either defaced or concealed by turning them upside down." *"In this improvisation,"* rightly observes Habibullah, *"was symbolised the whole Mamluk history"* (emphasis added).

How many slaves were needed to accomplish the task on these three and the other buildings of Qutbuddin Aibak and Iltutmish such as mosques, *madrasas,* mausoleums, *qasrs* and tanks (*e.g.* Hauz-i-shamsi) in and outside Delhi? It is difficult to determine but easy to conjecture their numbers, for these two sultans had embarked on constructional activity on a very large scale. It is known that Alauddin Khalji, another great builder, had 70,000 slaves working on his buildings, as attested to by the contemporary chronicler Ziyauddin Barani. Alauddin built "masjids, minars, citadels and tanks". But his Qutb Minar alone was an edifice more than equal to all his undertakings. Thus the men working on the buildings of the first two sultans were probably not less than those of Alauddin Khalji; they may have been probably more. These slaves were to dismantle standing temples, very carefully, stone by stone, carry the carved columns, shafts and pillars to the new sites of construction, and raise the new structures. Although Hasan Nizami says that temples were demolished with the help of elephants and one elephant could haul stones for which 500 men were needed, yet it has to be recognised that not many mechanical devices were available. Most of the work was done by human hands and muscles. The task was delicate and the slaves were freely flogged for any damage to stone slabs thus carried. The *korrah* (whip) of Bernier was not an invention of Shahjahan's time; it had been there all along during Muslim conquest and rule.

Hindu masons and architects were expert builders, they created wonderful specimens of architecture. About the temples of India, Alberuni says that his own people "are unable to describe them, much less to construct anything like them". Indian builders would never have liked to destroy their own splendid creations and dismantle their own sacred temples, to build in their instead mosques and minars for foreign invaders and rulers. But they had no choice. All Turkish slaves from abroad had become masters in India as kings, nobles, army officers and even soldiers, lording over the native workers who had been reduced to the position of slaves. Furthermore, Hindu masons and labourers turned slaves under the new dispensation had to do the work in record time. Barani in his enthusiasm hyperbolically says that during Alauddin's reign a palace could be built in 2-3 days and a citadel in two weeks. It was considered a matter of pride for a newly crowned king to build a city of his own to give name and fame to himself and his dynasty. The old city of Iltutmish was abandoned by Balban who built the Qasr-i-Lal or the Red Palace, and Kaiqubad built the city of Kilughari. "It is their custom," writes Ibn Battuta, "that the king's palace is deserted on his death... and his successor builds a new palace for himself." The slaves had often to do double the work, destroy Hindu buildings and construct new ones from the materials of earlier ones. In those times people lived in congested localities for reasons of security. A city used to get dirty and uninhabitable after a few years because of lack of means of disposing off garbage and filth. Ibn Battuta and Babur affirm that all was destroyed because of moisture. It is because of this reason also that it was thought better to found and shift to a new town where everything was clean and tidy. Hindu slaves toiled as scavengers and cleaners in old cities. They toiled with blood and sweat to create new ones.

Muhammad Tughlaq and Firoz Tughlaq were as keen as Aibak, Iltutmish and Alauddin about founding new cities, raising new buildings and repairing old edifices of earlier Muslim rulers. Shams Siraj Afif counts Firoz's builders among the 180,000 (or about 2 lakh) slaves of Firoz Tughlaq, but the break up for various duties would point to there being separate contingent of masons and builders with 12,000 slaves as stone-cutters alone. Even the shifting of the two Ashokan pillars to Delhi required the services of a few thousand men (*chandin hazar admi*). No wonder the invader Timur (1399 C.E.) found in India exquisite Muslim buildings, and enslaved thousands of craftsmen and builders many of whom he took with him to Samarqand to construct edifices similar to the Jama Masjid built by Firoz Shah and the Qutb Minar built by Aibak. But after his departure from India new slaves soon replaced those taken away by Timur, and every sultan and noble embarked on building enterprises as usual.

Besides the Sultanate, new independent Muslim states sprang up all over the country throughout the fifteenth century. In all of them feverish architectural activity was carried on with the help of local slaves. At the centre, Sultan Sikandar Lodi is credited with constructing mosques in almost all important cities including Lahore, Karnal, Hansi, Makanpur

(District Kanpur) besides many in Delhi and Agra. In addition to the tombs in Lodi Gardens in Delhi, there are also so many other nameless tombs belonging to the Lodi period. Sikandar Lodi, like Firoz Tughlaq before him, is credited with constructing a canal in 1492-93 and a Baoli in Rajasthan. In "Mathura and other place" like Allahabad and Banaras he turned temples into mosques, and established Muslim Sarais, colleges and bazars in Hindu places of worship. Like Firoz Tughlaq, Sikandar was also a great repairer and conserver of old Muslim monuments. An inscribed frieze at the entrance doorway of the Qutb Minar credits him with repairing this edifice in 1503 (909 H).

We have spoken about only some of the architectural works of just five sultans of Delhi-Aibak, Iltutmish, Alauddin Khalji, Firoz Tughlaq and Sikandar Lodi-and noted that thousands and thousands of slaves were required for their construction. It is unnecessary to repeat that all Muslim rulers were great builders and the number of slaves engaged on building cities, mosques, Sarais, tombs of every sultan and noble and Sufi Shaikh in Delhi and other cities of the Sultanate ran into thousands. Same was the case with the buildings of the provincial and independent kingdoms into which the Sultanate of Delhi broke up.

"There was a strain of artistic feeling which ran through the successive generations of the ruling Mughal house in India," observed E. Maclagan in 1932. This artistic feeling found its greatest manifestation in their architecture. And those who built had unbounded command of both money and slaves. Babur writes that "680 men worked daily on my buildings in Agra... only; while 1491 stone-cutters worked daily on my buildings in Agra, Sikri, Biana, Dulpur (Dholpur), Gwalior and Kuil (Aligarh). In the same way there are numberless artisans and workmen of every sort in Hindustan." Some workers were wage-earners, for says he at another place, "Gifts were made to the stone-cutters, and labourers and the whole body of workmen in the way customary for master-workmen and wage-earners of Agra." But as discussed elsewhere slaves were preferred to servants and wage-earners, and the *Korrah* was the surest leveller of artisan, handicraftsman, servant and slave. From the days of Babur to those of Shahjahan during whose "august reign, when... lovely things reached the zenith of perfection," money in millions and slaves in thousands were employed on erecting the hundreds of huge Mughal buildings still extant.

The opulent grandees in the provinces esteemed it an honour and obligation to adorn towns and cities of the regions under their control with magnificent buildings. The law of escheat encouraged them to spend lavishly. Pelsaert perhaps has the last word on it. "I have often ventured to ask great lords," says he, "what is their true object in being so eager to amass their treasures, when what they have gathered is of no use to them or to their family (because of escheat)... I have urged they would share it with the poor, who in this country are hundreds of thousands, or indeed innumerable [including of course the slaves]... Their answers have been based on the emptiest worldly vanity..." Buildings they constructed with great zest-gardens, tombs, and palaces - "they build them with so many hundreds of thousands ... Once the builder is dead, no one will care for his buildings, but every one tries to erect buildings of his own, and establish his own reputation alongside that of his ancestors. If all these edifices were attended to and kept in repair, the lands of every city, and even village, would be adorned (covered) with monuments; but as a matter of fact the roads leading to the cities are strewn with fallen columns of stone."

INDO-ISLAMIC CULTURE : STARTING

The Qutb was the first monumental stamp of Islamic architecture in India and was the start of a long relationship between indigenous craftsmen and their Mamluk masters. The grandiosity of its concept encouraged several rulers to continue adding to the structure and adding further stages.

The Arhai-din-ka Jhompra: Shams-ud-Din Iltutmish (A.D. 1211-1236), succeeding to the throne after Qutb-ud-Din's death in a freak polo accident, was an energetic builder. The first of his notable works was the addition of a facade to the Adhai-din ka Jhonpra (literally, hut of two-and-a-half days) mosque built by his predecessor at the military encampment of Ajmer in Rajasthan. Built on the same principles as the Quwwatul Islam at Delhi, this mosque at Ajmer is larger. The facade is similar to the one at the Qutub, but here the similarity ends. The central arch at Ajmer is straighter-Tudor Gothic-and the side arches are multifoil and cusped, a common feature in other Islamic work outside India. The main stylistic difference is evident in the It was not long, however, before several other additions and alterations were made on the same site.

The first of these was by Iltutmish, who doubled the size of the original enclosure of the Quwwatul Islam mosque, and added another screen of five arches to define the qibla (the axis towards Mecca). This screen, though superficially the same as in the original mosque, has better stood the ravages of time. The main differences are in the detail, with the carving using a purer Islamic vocabulary, though here too, in the sinuous curves, the hand of the indigenous craftsman is seen. The floriform low relief at the Qutb gives way to a far more geometric, rigid style. This is by no means an advance over the Qutb mosque. The arches seem almost a regression to a purer, stricter form of Islam with their monolithic and sombre appearance. Two broken minarets over the main arch resemble the Qutb in their flutings.

ILTUTMISH AND SULTAN GHARI'S TOMBS

Iltutmish constructed his own tomb as well as that of his son Nasiruddin Mohammed-the so-called Sultan Ghari or 'Sultan of the Cave'. This is probably due to the subterranean tomb chamber. The octagonal platform above was probably intended to support a pillared pavilion, the whole of which has disappeared or was never built. This platform was surrounded by a square masonry arcade on a high plinth, and according to Percy Brown, it has "such a grim and martial appearance that one of its more remote purposes may have been to serve as some kind of advanced outwork to the main fortress of the capital".

The second main contribution of Iltutmish was his own tomb, a little to the north-west of the enlarged mosque at the Qutb, built a little before A.D. 1235. A square 42 feet in side and with a height of almost 30 feet, its plain and unadorned exteriors belie its interior-the whole of which is covered from top to bottom on all four sides by rich carvings almost rivaling Hindu temple sculpture on the sandstone-clad walls. The cenotaph and the three arches of the mehrab towards the west (marking the direction of Mecca) are both in marble, again a dispute on the Quranic inscriptions.

Architecturally speaking, Iltutmish's tomb is interesting as it reveals quite clearly the first attempt in India to solve the 'dome on a square' problem-or in other words, how do you support a circular shape on a square base? In this case, a 'squinch' was employed-a half-arch/dome spanning across the corners of the square base and making the square an octagon.

This can be repeated to transform the octagon into a sixteen-sided figure on which the base of the dome may rest. That the dome, if ever fully built, subsequently collapsed was a testimony to the fact that the it was imperfectly constructed-however an important start had been made and future attempts in this direction were to grow ever more confident.

After the death of Iltutmish, there is little to be seen architecturally from the early years of the Delhi Sultanate. The main reason for this were the squabbling successors of the Sultan ruling for too short a time for any effective architectural patronage. There was thus an interregnum of 60 years-with one exception. This is the tomb of Sultan Balban of the extremely short-lived 'House of Balban' (A.D. 1266-1287).

Now a ruined and totally unremarkable structure in the extreme south of Delhi, this tomb is notable because it introduced for the first time in India the principle of the true arch with radiating voussoirs. This is not only a significant structural advance, but also a sociocultural one. For it indicated that slowly but surely the Muslim rulers were ceasing to regard North India as invaded territory. Delhi was becoming a city of repute attracting men of art and learning, craftsmen, poets and historians. The early steps of creating a distinct Indo-Islamic culture were under consideration.

The Great Alai Minar: Ala-ud-Din, true to form, felt compelled to increase even further the size of the Quwwatul Islam mosque. His scheme called for increasing the size of the enclosure four times, providing ceremonial entrance gateways on each side, and a great minar, twice the size of the Qutb-the Alai Minar. It would have been clear to anyone less megalomanic- with a vision less obscured by self-exaltation-that such a grandiose project would be impossible in the Sultan's lifetime. Indeed, the Alai Minar today is a stump (albeit a magnificent one-we can well imagine the proportions of the tower had it ever been finished), its rubble core clearly showing as it rises up to one story.

The Alai Darwaza: The only part of Ala-ud-Din's scheme which was completed was the southern ceremonial entrance-named the Alai Darwaza after its builder. It is clear from its appearance and construction that a fresh new influence was at work-this is a piece of Muslim architecture hitherto unknown in India. Historians have traced its genealogy to the architecture found in Asia Minor under the rule of the Seljuks in the early centuries of the second millennium.

The breakup of the Seljuk empire under the weight of Mongol invasions caused craftsmen and builders to be scattered far and wide, and among the places offering sanctuary was the Delhi Sultanate. Because of its revolutionary construction, the Alai Darwaza served as a model for many of its successors. The first innovation in the gateway was the system of walling, alternating between one course of stretchers-stone laid with its longer ends facing outward-and one course of headers-stone laid with its longer end going deep into the wall. The header course enabled the walling to penetrate into the rubble core and thus make the wall as a whole stronger. This method of walling was to continue and was a typical characteristic of Mughal building. The second innovation was the true arch. This imported arcuated tradition was to play an important role as it was to provide the prototype for successive Sultanate tombs.

Alai Darwaza is a rectangular building on high plinth into which steps have been cut to access the interior. The three outer faces are very similar with a tall arch over the steps. The plinth is carved in bands, and the wall surface above is divided into two stories, each further subdivided into rectangular panels. The lower of these panels have a recessed arch while the upper ones into smaller rectangles. At each point, the articulation is marked by a mixture of sandstone and marble arabesque and decorative carving.

However, by far the most imposing feature of these facades is the central arch, rising to nearly the whole height of the structure. In shape it is rare-a horseshoe or keel arch. Around its outer rim is a band of inscribed white marble. The intrados or the inner rim of the arch shows its most distinctive feature-a fringe of lotus-bud carving.

The inner facade, facing the mosque and Qutb Minar, is different. For one, the opening is not a keel arch but a true semi-circular one, and for another it is clear that in its sensual and plastic decoration the indigenous craftsman was given a much freer hand. The interior of the structure is no less remarkable for its technological innovation. First started in the tomb of Iltutmish, the weight of the dome is transferred to the square base by the same mechanism-the squinch.

In this case, the squinch consists of five recessed arches gracefully transforming the square into the octagon, and the octagon into a sixteen sided figure. Among the other architectural work of Ala-ud-Din, little remains except fragmentary and crumbling structures. And though the work of the Khiljis was not entirely confined to the capital city of Delhi, the influence of local workmen in the provinces and the eventual decline of the Khalji dynasty meant that these were never as remarkable nor of as high a standard as the Alai Darwaza at the Qutb.

ISLAMIC ARCHITECTURE: REGIONAL VARIATIONS

In and around Delhi Islamic architecture retained much of the characteristics in both form and detailing of Persian Islam, with only the court at Delhi able to attract and pay the best Muslim architects and artisans from abroad. As one moves away from the main power centre, the regional Islamic satraps-whether governors of the Delhi Sultanate or newly-independent Sultan-patronised an architecture which slowly began to assume a very different identity.

This identity was not constant throughout, but varied from place to place, and depended chiefly on : the distance from Delhi, which determined the level of dilution of 'pure' Islamic principles; the economic condition of the regime, responsible for the quality of finished and materials used; the local artisans available in the region and their specialisation and experience; and local Hindu architecture, which served as direct or indirect inspiration for Muslim examples. If the Qutb Minar merely had sinuous carving which hinted at the Hindu craftsman at work, examples further away from Delhi illustrated both a riot of carving as well as formal aspects directly influenced by Hindu architecture. The main areas that produced a substantial body of architecture and can be said to have evolved a 'style' of their own are Gujarat, Punjab, Bengal, Malwa, Kashmir and some parts of south India.

QUTB MINAR

The Qutab Minar a tower in Delhi, India, is at 72.5 meters the world's tallest brick minaret. It is situated in the Qutb complex, amidst the ruins of ancient Hindu temples which were destroyed and their stones used to build the Qutb complex and minar. Construction commenced in 1193 under the orders of India's first Muslim ruler Qutubuddin Aibak, and the topmost storey of the minaret was completed in 1386 by Firuz Shah Tughluq. The Qutb Minar is notable for being one of the earliest and most prominent examples of Indo-Islamic architecture.

It is surrounded by several other ancient and medieval structures and ruins, collectively known as Qutb complex. The complex is listed as a UNESCO World Heritage Site and is one of the most popular tourist destinations in Delhi, and was also India's most visited monument in 2006, as it attracted 3.9 million visitors, even more than the Taj Mahal, which drew about 2.5 million visitors

STRUCTURE

The Qutab Minar is tall with 378 steps leading to the top. The diameter of the base is 14.3 meters wide while the top floor measures

2.75 meters in diameter. Surrounding the building are many fine examples of Indian artwork from the time it was built in 1193. A second tower was in construction and planned to be taller than the Qutb Minar itself. Its construction ended abruptly when it was about 12 meters tall. The name of this tower is given as Alai Minar and construction of recent studies shows that this structure has been tilted in one direction. It is made of red sandstone all the way except for two stories at the top. This part is of white marble and was made by Firoz Shah Tughlaq. He had decided to put a prominent finish to the magnificent minar.

HISTORY

Inspired by the Minaret of Jam in Afghanistan and wishing to surpass it, Qutbuddin Aibak, the first Muslim ruler of Delhi, commenced construction of the Qutb Minar in 1193, but could only complete its base. His successor, Iltutmish, added three more stories and, in 1386, Firuz Shah Tughluq constructed the fifth and the last story. The development of architectural styles from Aibak to Tughluq are quite evident in the minaret. Like earlier towers erected by the Ghaznavids and Ghurids in Afghanistan, the Qutb Minar comprises several superposed flanged and cylindrical shafts, separated by balconies carried on Muqarnas corbels. The minaret is made of fluted red sandstone covered with intricate carvings and verses from the Qur'an. The Qutb Minar is itself built on the ruins of the Lal Kot, the Red Citadel in the city of Dhillika, the capital of the Tomars and the Chauhans, the last Hindu rulers of Delhi. The complex initially housed 27 ancient Hindu temples which were destroyed and their debris used to build the Qutb minar. One engraving on the Qutb Minar reads, "Shri Vishwakarma prasade rachita" (*Conceived with the grace of Vishwakarma*), this is thought to have been engraved by the enslaved Hindu craftsmen who built the minar.

The purpose for building this monument has been variously speculated upon. It could take the usual role of a minaret, calling people for prayer in the Quwwat-ul-Islam mosque, the earliest extant mosque built by the Delhi Sultans. Other possibilities are a tower of victory, a monument signifying the might of Islam, or a watch tower for defence. Controversy also surrounds the origins for the name of the tower. Many historians believe that the Qutb Minar was named after the first Turkish sultan, Qutubuddin Aibak, but others contend that it was named in honour of Qutbuddin Bakhtiar Kaki, a saint from Transoxiana who came to live in India and was greatly venerated by Iltutmish.

The nearby Iron Pillar is one of the world's foremost metallurgical curiosities, standing in the famous Qutb complex. According to the traditional belief, anyone who can encircle the entire column with their arms, with their back towards the pillar, can have their wish granted. Because of the corrosive qualities of sweat the government has built a fence around it for safety. The minar did receive some damage because of earthquakes on more than a couple of occasions but was reinstated and renovated by the respective rulers. During the rule of Firoz Shah, the minar's two top floors got damaged due to earthquake but were repaired by Firoz Shah. In the year 1505, earthquake again struck and it was repaired by Sikandar Lodi. Later on in the year 1794, the minar faced another earthquake and it was Major Smith, an engineer who repaired the affected parts of the minar. He replaced Firoz Shah's pavilion with his own pavilion at the top. The pavilion was removed in the year 1848 by Lord Hardinge and now it can be seen between the Dak Bungalow and the Minar in the garden. The floors built by Firoz Shah can be distinguished easily as the pavilions was built of white marbles and are quite smooth as compared to other ones.

HAUZ-I-SHAMSI

Hauz-i-Shamsi is a water storage reservoir or tank built by Iltumish of the Slave Dynasty in 1230 AD, at a location revealed to him in a dream by the Prophet Muhammad. A palace called the Jahaz Mahal was built on the eastern edge of the same reservoir during the Lodi dynasty period in the 16th century as a retreat or Inn for use by pilgrims. Also at the edge of *Hauz* is the tomb of 17th century Persian writer in the Mughal court, Abdul-Haqq Dehlavi. The monuments are situated in Mehrauli, Delhi.

LEGEND

A popular legend narrated is of Iltumish's dream in which Prophet Muhammad directed him to build a reservoir at a particular site. When Iltumish inspected the site the day after his dream, he reported to have found a hoof print of Muhammad's horse. He then erected a pavilion to mark the sacred location and excavated a large tank (reservoir) around the pavilion to harvest rain water.

Another version of the legend linked is that the Holy Prophet appeared in a dream not only to Iltumish but also to the Muslim sufi saint Khawaja indicating the same particular location, where the hoof print of

Muhammad's horse was imprinted, for the construction of a water tank. Since drinking water supply was acute in the newly founded capital of Iltumish (the first medieval city of Qila Rai Pithora of Delhi) a tank was dug at the location indicated in the dream, which resulted in water jetting out from a spring source. It was, thereafter, named as Hauz-i-Shamsi, and Khawaja, the saint who divined it, came to be known as Hazrat Qutbuddin Bakhtiar Kaki or simply 'Kaki'. The name Kaki was attributed to him by virtue of this keramat (miracle). The Khawaja died in 1235 AD. He is buried in Mehrauli (near the Qutab Minar) and it is inferred that Qutub Minar was also named after him. His dargah or tomb is considered one of India's oldest and revered shrines. His exalted divinity has also been extolled by Moinuddin Chishti who had said: Kaki was such an exalted divine person that even Moinuddin Chishti had decreed that those coming to seek his blessing should first pay homage to the former. The practice is still adhered to.

RESERVOIR

Hauz-i-Shamsi originally covered an area of 2 ha (4.9 acres). The domed pavilion constructed by Iltumish to mark the foot print of Prophet's horse located in the middle of the tank is a double storie structure made of red sandstone supported on twelve pillars. It could be approached only by boat (now a foot bridge exists). The original stone, on which the foot print of the horse of the Prophet was imprinted, was located at this pavilion. It has since been removed but replaced by a new one. In view of its religious significance, the water stored in the tank was considered sacred. Many famous emperors and saints have been buried on the periphery of the reservoir. Because of reduction in the size of the reservoir over the years, due to encroachments and siltation, pavilion's present location is seen in the eastern edge of the tank.

A Jharna or water fall emanating from the Hauz-i-Shamsi is located close to the Jahaz Mahal. It is identified as a significant water structure that had been developed by Nawab Ghaziuddin around 1700 AD as a pleasure garden during the Mughal rule. An underground pipe (still visible in ruins) supplied the runoff to the Jharna from Hauz-i–Shamshi. This was in addition to an open channel close by that carried the overflow of the tank to Tughlaqabad fort to enhance the drinking water supply. The Jharna structure was built in three parts (pictured - painting from Metcalfe's album). The first part consisted of the reservoir or the tank, the second part was the water fall and the last part consisted of the fountains. Akbar Shah II built the pavilion on the side and his son Bahadur Shah II added the central pavilion, more in the style of *hayat hakhsh* pool in the Red Fort. The Jharna, which was once the Mughal retreat and the highlight of the three day festival of the Phool Walon Ki Sair, is seen now partly in ruins and the surroundings have been encroached upon (25 families are reported to be living here now). The water fall is seen more in the form of a drain in need of urgent restoration measures.

TOMB OF ILTUTMISH

The tomb of Slave Dynasty ruler, Iltutmish, the second Sultan of Delhi, built 1235 AD is also part of the Qutb complex at Mehrauli. The central chamber is a 9 mt sq. and has squinches, suggesting the existence of a dome, which has since collapsed. The main cenotaph, in white marble is place on a raised platform in the centre of the chamber. The facade is known for its ornate carving, both at the entrance and the interior walls. The interior west wall has a prayer niche, *mihrab* decorated with marble, and a rich amalgamation of Hindu motives into Islamic architecture, such as bell-and-chain, tassel, lotus, diamond emblems.

BALBAN'S TOMB

The Tomb of Ghiyas ud din Balban is located in Mehrauli, New Delhi, India. Built in ca 1287 CE, in rubble masonry, the tomb is a building of historical importance in the development of Indo-Islamic architecture, as it was here that first true arch made its appearance in India, and according to many first true dome as well, which however hasn't survived, making *Alai Darwaza* built in 1311 CE, in near by Qutb complex, the earliest surviving true dome in India. Ghiyas ud din Balban (1200 – 1287) was a Turkic ruler of the Delhi Sultanate during the rule of Mamluk dynasty of Delhi (or Slave dynasty) from 1266 to 1287. The tomb of Balban was discovered in the mid-twentieth century.

ALAUDDIN KHILJI'S TOMB AND MADARSA

At the back of the complex, southwest of the mosque, stands an L-shaped construction, consisting of Alauddin Khilji's tomb dating ca 1316 CE, and a *madarsa*, an Islamic seminary built by him. Khilji was the second Sultan of Delhi from Khilji dynasty, who ruled from 1296 to 1316 AD.

The central room of the building, which has his tomb, has now lost its dome, though many rooms of the seminary or college are intact, and since been restored. It was the first example in India, of a tomb standing alongside a *madarsa*. Near by stands the Alai Minar, an ambitious tower, he started constructing to rival the Qutub Minar, though he died when only its first storey was built and its construction abandoned thereafter. It now stands, north of the mosque.

ALAI DARWAZA

The Alai Darwaza is a perfect specimen of architecture belonging to the period of the Delhi Sultanate. It was built in 1311, by Ala-ud-din-Khilji, of the Khilji dynasty (which ruled the Delhi Sultanate from AD 1290 to AD 1316). The Alai Darwaza was a part of Ala-ud-din-Khilji's extension of the Quwwat-ul-Islam mosque. It was one of the four grand gateways; the other three could not be completed because of the death of Alauddin in AD 1316.

The main structure of the Alai Darwaza consists of a single hall 34½ feet on the inside and 56½ feet on the outside. The domed ceiling rises to a height of 47 feet. The three doorways on the east, west, and south are lofty pointed arches, in the shape of a horseshoe, which rise above the flanking side bays. The entrance to the north is of an indigenous character, as its arch is semi-circular in shape. The overall outlook and proportions of the Alai Darwaza is pleasing to the eye. The recessed corner arches of the attractive horseshoe forms, supporting a simple spherical dome on top of the square chamber, are an especially happy solution to the perpetual problem of supporting a good dome. It would be well worth noting that the earlier attempts at raising the dome, particularly the tomb of Iltutmish, had been unsuccessful. The dome of the Alai Darwaza, in this respect, is a notable achievement.

The dome was constructed on highly scientific principles. A series of squinches of pointed shape, one recessed within the other, in the upper section of each angle of the hall, changes the square into an octagon, and then the octagon into the circle of the dome with an interweaving sixteen-sided shaft formed by a bracket at each end of the octagon. With use of complex geometric calculations, the load of the dome has been gracefully conveyed to the ground-from the circle to the sixteen-sided shaft, from the latter to the octagon and then onto the four walls of the square chamber.

The plinth on each side is beautifully carved with floral and geometric patterns in both white marble and red sandstone, creating a superb polychrome effect. Perforated latticework window screens (jali) are set in the recessed windows on both sides of the entrances. These marble screens set off the monotony of the vertical lines of calligraphic ornamentation. The most charming aspect of surface decoration is the lace-like interweaving of floral tendrils, repeated with a flawless symmetry on all the three entrances, elegantly designed and perfectly built.

The northern entrance is semi-circular with a shallow trefoil in its outline. The facade is elaborately ornamental in sensuous carving and patterns, characteristic of the pre-Turkish days (the first Muslim rulers of India came from Turkey). The Alai Darwaza also shows the influence of Seljuk art. The Seljuks had started fleeing Western Asia after Mongol invasions in the 12th century AD and had reached Delhi for protection. The 'spear-headed' embellishment on the three entrances is of particular importance in this regard. In addition, the surface ornamentation has been done with an eye for lavishness and detail.

Though the Alai Darwaza stands isolated at the southern end of the Qutab complex, with the Qutab Minar behind it, it appears a fitting part of the grand structures of the Delhi Sultanate.

HAUZ KHAS COMPLEX

Hauz Khas Complex in South Delhi houses a water tank, an Islamic seminary, a mosque, a tomb and pavilions built around an urbanized village with medieval history traced to the thirteenth century of Delhi Sultanate reign. It was part of Siri, the second medieval city of India of the Delhi Sultanate of Allauddin Khilji Dynasty (1296-1316). The etymology of the name Hauz Khas in Urdu language is derived from the words 'Hauz': "water tank" (or lake) and 'Khas': "royal" -the "Royal tank". The large water tank or reservoir was first built by Khilji {the plaque displayed (pictured in the gallery) at the site records this fact} to supply water to the inhabitants of Siri. The tank was de–silted during the reign of Firuz Shah Tughlaq (1351-88). Several buildings (Mosque and madrasa) and tombs were built overlooking the water tank or lake. Firuz Shah's tomb pivots the L–shaped building complex which overlooks the tank.

In the 1980s, the Hauz Khas village, studded with domed tombs of Muslim royalty from the fourteenth century to sixteenth century, was developed as an upper class residential cum commercial area in the metropolis of South Delhi, India. It is now a major expensive tourist cum commercial area with numerous art galleries, posh restaurants and upscale boutiques.

HISTORY

The water tank that was excavated during Alauddin Khilji's reign (1296-1316) in the second city of Delhi to meet the water supply needs of the newly built fort at Siri, was originally known as Hauz-i-Alai after Khilji. But Firuz Shah Tughlaq (1351-88) of the Tughlaq dynasty re-excavated the silted tank and cleared the clogged inlet channels. The tank was originally of about 50 ha (123.6 acres) area with dimensions of 600 m (1,968.5 ft.) width and 700 m (2,296.6 ft.) length with 4 m (13.1 ft.) depth of water. When built, its storage capacity at the end of each monsoon season was reported to be 0.8 Mcum. Now the tank size has substantially reduced due to encroachment and siltation but is well maintained in its present state (pictured).

Feruz Shah who ruled from his new city called the Firuzabad (now known as Feroz Shah Kotla) - the fifth city of Delhi - was an enlightened ruler. He was known for "his keen sense of historical precedent, statements of dynastic legitimacy and the power of monumental architecture". He is credited with construction of new monuments (several mosques and palaces) in innovative architectural styles, irrigation works and renovating/restoring old monuments such as the Qutub Minar, Sultan Ghari and Suraj Kund, and also erecting two inscribed Ashokan Pillars, which he had transported from Ambala and Meerut in Delhi. At Hauz Khas, he raised several monuments on the southern and eastern banks of the reservoir.

In efforts made in the past by the Delhi Development Authority to develop Hauz Khas village, the inlets to the reservoir were blocked and consequently the lake had gone dry for several years. To rectify the situation, a plan was implemented in 2004 to store storm water generated at the southern ridge of Delhi behind an embankment and then diverting it into the lake. An outside source has also been tapped by feeding the water from the treatment plant at Sanjay Van into the lake. With these efforts initiated by The Indian National Trust for Art and Cultural Heritage (INTACH), the lake has been revived.

STRUCTURES

The notable structures built by Firuz Shah on the eastern and northern side of the reservoir consisted of the Madrasa (Islamic School of Learning - a theological college), the small Mosque, the Main tomb for himself and six domed pavilions in its precincts, which were all built between 1352 and 1354 A.D.

MADRASA

Established in 1352, the Madrasa was one of the leading institutions of Islamic learning in the Delhi Sultanate. It was also considered the largest and best equipped Islamic seminary anywhere in the world. There were three main Madrasa's in Delhi during Firuz Shah's time. One of them was the Firuz Shahi madrasa at Hauz Khas. After the sack of Baghdad, Delhi became the most important place in the world for Islamic education. The village surrounding the Madarsa was also called Tarababad (city of joy) in view of its affluent and culturally rich status, which provided the needed supporting sustenance supply system to the Madrasa.

The madrasa structure has an innovative design. It was built in L-Shape as one contiguous structure on the south and east edges of the reservoir complex. One arm of the L-shape structure runs in the North–South direction measuring 76 m (249.3 ft.) and the other arm runs in the East–West direction measuring 138 m (452.8 ft.). The two arms are pivoted at the large Tomb of Firuz Shah (pictured). At the northern end there is a small mosque. Between the mosque and the tomb two storied pavilions exist now on the northern side and similar pavilions on the eastern side, overlooking the lake, which were used as madrasa. The two arms are interconnected through small domed gateways passing through the tomb at the center. The North–South arm with balconies overlooking the reservoir is a two storied building with three towers of varying sizes. Ornamental brackets cover the upper storied balconies while the lower stories have corbelled support. Roof overhangs or Eaves (chajjas) are seen now only in the upper stories though it is said that they existed on both stories when it was built.

From each floor of the Madrasa, staircases are provided to go down to the lake. Many cenotaphs, in the form of octagonal and square chhatris are also seen, which are reported to be possibly tombs of teachers of the Madrasa. It is inferred that, though no regular curriculum could be cited, subjects taught in the Madrasa could have been *tafsix* (astronomy), *hadith* (mathematics), *qirat* (medicine), *ishlaq* (calligraphy), *kalàm* (grammar) and *fiqr* (oratory). Later on, Sanskrit was also taught. It is recorded that the first Director of the Madarasa was one Jalal al-Din Rumi who knew fourteen sciences, could recite the Quran according to the seven known methods of recitation and had complete mastery over the five standard collections of the Traditions of the Prophet. The madrasa was well tended with liberal donations from the Royalty. Timur, the Mongol ruler, who invaded Delhi, defeated Mohammed Shah Tughlaq in 1398 and plundered Delhi, had camped at this venue. Expressed in his own words, his impressions of the tank and buildings around Hauz Khas were vividly described as:

When I reached [the city's] gates, I carefully reconnoitred its towers and walls, and then returned to the side of the Hauz Khas. This is a reservoir, which was constructed by Sultan Feruz Shah, and is faced all round with stone and stucco. Each side of the reservoir is more than a bows-shot long, and there are buildings placed around it. This tank is filled by rains in the rainy season, and it supports the people of the city with water throughout the year. While his description of the place is correct but his ascribing construction of the tank to Firuz Shah was a misconception.

The madrasa is flanked by the reservoir in the northern front and by a garden on its southern side at the second floor level. The entry to the garden is from the eastern gate which paases through the Hauz Khas village. The garden houses six impressive pavilions. The pavilions with domes are in different shapes and sizes (rectangular, octagonal and hexagonal) and on the basis of inscriptions are inferred to be graves. A cluster of three hemispherical domes, a large one of 5.5 m (18.0 ft.) diameter and two smaller ones of 4.5 m (14.8 ft.) diameter, portray exquisite architectural features of foliated motifs on the drums with kalasa motifs on top of the domes. Each pavilion is raised on a plinth of about 0.8 m (2.6 ft.) and is supported by square shaped wide columns with entablature which have decorative capitals that support beams with projecting canopies. Ruins of a courtyard with a rectangular plan, are seen to the west of the three pavilions which are built of double columns. The pavilions and the court yard are conjectured to have been used as part of the madrasa in the past. Another striking structure in the garden, opposite to the Feruz Shah's tomb on the southern side, is a small eight pillared Chatri seen in the garden which has large cantilevered beams that supported flat eaves all round the small dome.

The northern end of the madrasa is secured to a small mosque. The qibla of the Mosque projects towards the reservoir by about 9.5 m (31.2 ft.). A domed gateway from the south east provides entry into three rooms of size 5.3 m (17.4 ft.) x2.4 m (7.9 ft.) whose utility is not traced. A "C"-shaped layout of a double row of pillars on a raised podium forms the prayer hall, which is open to the sky. The qibla wall seen clearly from the reservoir side has five mihrabs. The avant-garde setting of the central mihrab with a domed chhatri (cupola) with open sides is seen in the form of a pavilion projecting into the reservoir. The other mihrabs are set, on either side of the main mihrab, in the walls with grilled windows.

SIRI FORT

Siri Fort, in the city of New Delhi, was built during the rule of Ala-ud-Din Khalji of the Delhi Sultanate to defend the city from the onslaught of the Mongols. It was the second of the seven cities of medieval Delhi built around 1303 (stated to be the first entirely constructed by Muslims), which at present is seen only in ruins with a few remnants (pictured)

Near the Siri Fort ruins modern auditoriums, the Asiad Games Village Complex and residential and commercial establishments fill the modern landscape between the Khel Gaon Marg and the Auro Bindo Marg in the heart of South Delhi.

HISTORY

Alauddin is the best known of the Khalji dynasty because he extended his dominion to Southern India and established the second city of Delhi, Siri. He created Siri between 1297 and 1307 to defend against Mongol invasions of India and Delhi. In response he built Siri Fort, mimicked massive Turkish ones. The Fort served as the seat of his power during his campaigns to enlarge his territory. Due to frequent Mongolinvasions of West Asia, the Saljuqs took asylum in Delhi. The craftsmen of Seljuq dynasty are credited with this era's architectural monuments in Delhi.

Targhi, a Mongol ruler, besieged the Siri fort when Alauddin Khalji retreated during the Mongol expedition into India. Targhi could not penetrate the fortifications of the Siri Fort and he finally retreated to his Kingdom in Central Asia. But this attack forced Allauddin to strengthen his defences at the borders which enabled him to keep the Mongols away - Ali Beg and Tartaq and their army - after they attacked and plundered Punjab and Amroha. Alauddin deputed his two generals Ghazi Malik and Malik Kafur to repel the Mongol attack. The Mongol army was soundly beaten before they could return to Central Asia with their plunder; All the generals and soldiers of the Mongol army were captured and brought to Siri where they were trampled to death by elephants and decapitated. The Mongols tried to attack one last time in 1306 AD but Ghazi Malik (who was the Governor of Punjab) annihilated the entire attacking Mongol army (believed to be 50,000 strong).

Subsequent ruthless attacks by Allauddin's army, deep into Mongol territory in Kandahar, Ghazni and Kabul in Afghanistan ensured that Mongols would never attack India again. His military strategies were thus aimed at building an Indian Empire, which he had mostly succeeded. He consolidated his territory, ruled with military might for 20 years and was considered the "first real Emperor of India".

Siri, which is now a part of New Delhi, was later linked to the fortifications of Jahanpanah. Siri was then also known as "Darul Khilafat" or ''Seat of Califate'' In 1398 AD, Timurlane, the Mongol ruler who invaded Delhi, wrote in his memoirs, " the Siri is a round city. Its buildings are lofty. They are surrounded by fortifications built of stone and brick, and they are very strong - from the fort of Siri to that of Old Delhi, which is a considerable distance - there runs a strong wall built of stone and cement.

The part called Jahanpanah is situated in the midst of the inhabited city. The fortifications of the three cities (old Delhi, Siri and Tughlaqabad) have thirty gates. Jahanpanah has thirteen gates, Siri has seven gates. The fortifications of the Old Delhi have ten gates, some opening to the exterior and some towards the interior of the city."

LEGEND

According to the legend of Alauddin's war exploits, the name Siri given to the Fort was because the foundation of the fort was built on the severed heads ('Siri' in Hindi means "head") of about 8,000 Mongol soldiers killed in the war.

Another version of the legend refers to the war crimes committed by Allauddin when the Mongol army was defeated and the captured soldiers were brought to Siri and trampled by elephants, then their severed heads were hung on the walls of the Siri Fort.

STRUCTURE

Siri Fort was built 5 km (3.1 mi) to the north-east of the Qutab Minar on an old camp near Delhi. The first city is considered to be built by Muslims, it was in an oval shape; its ruins are presently seen in an area of about 1.7 km (0.7 sq mi).

Allauddin, the second ruler of the Khilji dynasty, laid the foundation for the City of Siri in 1303 AD. The structures built in Siri were stated to have had a fine imprint of the enthusiasm of the rulers of Khalji dynasty (particularly, the first three out of six Rulers of the Dynasty) with Allauddin's deep interests in architecture and his achievements supported by the imported skills of the artists of Saljuqs richly contributing to the efforts to build the new city. Legend states that Allauddin's prolific building involved engagement of 70,000 workers. The city was built with an oval plan with palaces and other structures. There were seven gates for entry and exit, but at present only the Southeastern gate exists.

The fort was once considered the pride of the city for its palace of a thousand pillars called the Hazar Sutan. The palace was built outside the fort limits, and had marble floors and other stone decoration. Its Darwaza (door) is supposed to have been beautifully decorated. In eastern part of the ruins there are remnants of flame shaped battlements, loop holes for arrows, and bastions, which were considered unique new additions of that period.

In the nearby Shahpur Jat village (pictured), some dilapidated structures of the period are seen. Tohfewala Gumbad Masjid (pictured) is one such structure whose ruins show the form of domed central apartment and sloping wall characteristic of Khaljis architecture.

Apart from building the Siri Fort, the citadel around it and the water supply system with a reservoir at Hauz Khas for providing water supply to Siri, his new city, Alauddin also expanded the building activity around the religious city of the first city complex of Qutb complex by making additions to the Quwwatul-Islam Mosque, which doubled its original size, additions to the Qutub Minar itself (Nagari inscriptions on the tower attribute to this tower as *"Vijaya sthamba"* or victory tower of Alauddin) and a grandiose plan of constructing a new Minar (tower) bigger (double) that of the Qutub Minar. This plan was left half completed, as may be seen from the ruins at the site, due to the death of Allauddin in 1316.

The destruction of the Fort is attributed to the local rulers who removed the fort's stones, bricks and other artifacts for their own buildings. In particular, Sher Shah Suri (1540-1545), of Pashtun Afghan descent from Eastern India (Bihar), took away material from Siri to build his own city.

The battered walls of the fort had a wider base on the outside. A protected passage was provided within the battered walls (now seen in ruins as pictured).

FIRUZ SHAH TOMB

Firuz Shah, who established the tomb, ascended the throne in 1351 (inherited from his cousin Muhammad) when he was middle aged, as the third ruler of the Khilji dynasty and ruled till 1388. He was considered a well-liked ruler. His wife was a Hindu lady and his trusted Prime Minister, Khan-i-Jahan Junana Shah was a Hindu convert. Firuz Shah assisted by his Prime Minister was responsible for building several unique monuments (mosques, tombs, pavilions), hunting lodges and irrigation projects (reservoirs) in his domains, apart from establishing and constructing a new Citadel (palace) in his new city of Firuzabad. Feruz died at the age of ninety due to infirmities caused by three years of illness between 1385 and 1388.

On his death, his grandson Ghiyasuddin was proclaimed as his successor to the throne. During his enlightened rule he abolished many vexatious taxes, brought in changes in the laws on capital punishment, introduced regulations in administration and discouraged lavish living styles. But the most important credit that is bestowed on him is for the large number of public works executed during his reign namely, 50 dams for irrigation across rivers, 40 mosques, 30 colleges, 100 carvansarais, 100 hospitals, 100 public baths, 150 bridges, apart from many other monuments of aesthetic beauty and entertainment.

Among the notable buildings of historical importance that he built within Hauz Khas precincts is the domed tomb for himself. The tomb which is very austere in appearance, is located at the intersection of the two arms of the L-shaped building which constitutes the madrasa. Entry to the tomb is through a passage in the south leading to the doorway. The passage wall is raised on a plinth which depicts the shape of a fourteen phased polyhedron built in stones.

Three horizontal units laid over eight vertical posts that are chamfered constitute the plinth. Squinches and muqarnas are seen in the solid interior walls of the tomb and these provide the basic support to the octagonal sherical dome of the tomb. The dome with a square plan - 14.8 m (48.6 ft.) in length and height - has a diameter of 8.8 m (28.9 ft.). The maximum height of the tomb is on its face overlooking the reservoir. The domed gateway on the north has an opening which has height equal to two-thirds the height of the tomb. The width of the gate is equal to one-third of tombs' width. The entrance hall has fifteen bays and terminates in another doorway which is identical to the gateway at the entrance.

This second doorway leads to the tomb chamber and cenotaph, which are accessed from the gateway through the L-shaped corridor. Similar arrangement is replicated on the western doorway of the tomb leading to the open pavilion on the west.

The ceiling in the dome depicts a circular gold medallion with Quranic inscriptions in Naksh characters. Foliated crenellations are seen on the outer faces of the base of the tomb. Interesting features seen on the northern and southern sides of the tomb, considered typical of the Tuglaq period layout, are the ceremonial steps provided at the ground level that connect to the larger steps leading into the reservoir.

The tomb, a square chamber, is made of local quartzite rubble with a surface plaster finish that sparkled in white colour when completed. The door, pillars and lintels were made of grey quartzites while red sandstone was used for carvings of the battlements. The door way depicts a blend of Indian and Islamic architecture. Another new feature not seen at any other monument in Delhi, built at the entrance to the tomb from the south, is the stone railings. There are four graves inside the tomb, one is of Feruz Shah and two others are of his son and grand son.

The tomb was repaired during the reign of Sikandar Lodhi in 1507 AD, as is evidenced from an inscription on the entrance. The main impression is one of solidity and lack of decoration (typical of Tuglaq style).

JAHANPANAH

Jahanpanah was the fourth medieval city of Delhi established in 1326–1327 A.D. by Muhammad bin Tughlaq (1321-51), of the Delhi Sultanate. To address the constant threat of the Mongols, Tughlaq built the fortified city of Jahanpanah (meaning: "Refuge of the World") subsuming the Adilabad fort that had been built in the fourteenth century and also all the establishments lying between Qila Rai Pithora and Siri Fort.

Neither the city nor the fort has survived. Many reasons have been offered for such a situation. One of which is stated as the idiosyncratic rule of Mohammed bin Tughlaq when inexplicably he shifted the capital to Daulatabad in the Deccan and came back to Delhi soon after.

The ruins of the city's walls are even now discerned in the road between Siri to Qutub Minar and also in isolated patches behind the Indian Institute of Technology (IIT), in Begumpur, Khirki Masjid near

Khirki village, Satpula and many other near by locations; at some sections, as seen at Satpula, the fort walls were large enough to have few in built store rooms to stack provisions and armory. The mystery of the city's precincts (complex) has unfolded over the years with later day excavations revealing a large number of monuments in the villages and colonies of South Delhi. Due to compulsions of urban expansion of the Capital City of Delhi, Jahanpanah is now part of the upscale urban development of South Delhi. The village and the wealth of ruins scattered all around are now enclosed by South Delhi suburbs of Panchshil Park South, Malviya Nagar, Adchini, the Aurobindo Ashram, Delhi branch and other smaller housing colony developments. It is hemmed in the North-South direction between the Outer Ring Road and the Qutb Complex and on the east-west direction by the Mehrauli road and the Chirag Delhi road, with Indian Institute of Technology located on the other side of the Mehrauli road as an important landmark.

ETYMOLOGY

Jahanpanah's etymology consists of two Urdu words, 'Jahan', "the world", and 'panah', "shelter", colloquially this means "Your lordship".

HISTORY

Mohammed bin Tughlaq, son of Ghiyasuddin Tughlaq who built Tughlaqabad, constructed his new city of Jahanpanah between 1326 and 1327 by encircling the earlier cities of Siri and Lal Kot with 13 gates. But what remains of the city and Adilabad fort are large ruins, which leave much ambiguity and conjectures regarding its physical status as to why and when it was built by Tughlaq. Some of the structures which have survived partially are the Bijay Mandal (that is inferred to have housed the Hazar Sutan Palace, now destroyed), Begumpur Mosque, Serai Shaji Mahal, Lal Gumbad, Baradari with other near by structures and scattered swathes of rubble masonry walls. From Ibn Batuta's chronicle of the period (he lived in Delhi from 1333-41) it is inferred that Lal Kot (Qutb complex) was then the urban area, Siri was the military cantonment and the remaining area consisted of his palace (Bijaymandal) and other structures like mosques, etc.. Ibn Batuta has reasoned that Muhammad Shah wished to see a unified city comprising Old Delhi, Siri, Jahanpanah and Tughlaqabad with one contiguous fortification encompassing them but cost considerations forced him to abandon the plan halfway. In his chronicle, Batuta also stated that the Hazar Sutan Palace (1000 pillared palace), built outside the Siri fort limits but within the Jahanpanah city area, was the residence of the Tughlaq.

Hazar Sutan Palace was located within the fortified area of the Jahnapanah in Bijaya Mandal (literal meaning: "Wonderful Mansion"). The grand palace with its audience hall of beautifully painted wooden canopy and columns is vividly described but it does no longer exists. The Fort acted as a safe haven for the people living between Qila Rai Pithora and Siri. Tughalqabad continued to act as Tughlaq's centre of government until, for strange and inexplicable reasons, he shifted his capital to Daulatabad, however he returned after a short period.

ADILABAD

Adilabad, a fort of modest size, built on the hills to the south of Tughlaqabad was provided with protective massive ramparts on its boundary around the city of Jahanpanah. The fort was much smaller than its predecessor fort, Tughlaqabad fort, but of similar design. Archeological Survey of India (ASI) in its evaluation of the status of the fort for conservation has recorded that two gates, one with barbicans between two bastions on the south-east and another on the south-west. Inside, it, separated by a bailey, is a citadel consisting of walls, bastions and gates within which lay the palaces.

The fort was also known as 'Muhammadabad', but inferred as a later day development. The two gates on the southeast and southwest of Adilabad fort had chambers at the lower level while the east and west gates had grain bins and courtyards at the upper floors. The fortifications built, linking with the other two city walls, was 12 m (39.4 ft.) in thickness and extended to a length of 8 km (5.0 mi). Another smaller fortress, called the Nai-ka-kot was also built at a distance of about 700 m (2,296.6 ft.) from Adilabad, with citadel and army camps, which are now seen only in ruins.

Tughlaq's primary attention to infrastructure, particularly of water supply to the city, was also well thought out. A structure (weir or tank) with seven sluices (Urdu: Satpula) was built on a stream that flowed through the city. This structure called the Satpula is still existing (though non–functional) near Khirki village on the boundary walls of Jahanpanah. Similar structures had also been built at Tughlaqabad and Delhi in Hauz Khas Complex, thus covering the water supply needs of entire population of Jahanpanah.

BEGAMPUR MOSQUE

Now, remnants of the city lie scattered in the Begumpur village, as a moot reminder of the ancient glory. The Begumpur Mosque, a vestige of the old city, of overall layout plan of 90 m (295.3 ft.) x94 m (308.4 ft.) size with the inner courtyard measuring 75 m (246.1 ft.) x80 m (262.5 ft.), is said to be patterned on an Iranian design planned by the Iranian architect Zahir al-Din al-Jayush. A majestic building in the heart of the city with a pride of place played a pivotal role of serving as a madrasa, an administrative centre with the treasury and a mosque of large proportions serving as a social community hub surrounded by a market area.

It has an unusual layout with three arch covered passages with a "three by eight" deep nine bay prayer hall on the west. Construction of this mosque is credited to two sources. One view is that it was built by Khan-i-Jahan Maqbul Tilangani, Prime Minister during Feroz Shah Tughlaq's rule, who was also builder of six more masjids (two of them in the close vicinity). The other view is that it was built by Tughlaq because of its proximity to Bijay Mandal and could probably be dated to 1351 A.D., the year Tughlaq died here. In support of the second view, it is said that Ibn Batuta, the chronicler of the period (till his departure from Delhi in 1341 A.D.) had not recorded this monument. The Mosque considered an architectural masterpiece has three gates, one in each of the three covered passages, in North, East (main gate) and South directions. The west wall which has the Mihrab, has Toghluqi style tapering minarets flanking the central high opening covered by a big dome. The entire passageway of the west wall has twenty five arched openings. The Mihrab wall depicts five projections.

The prayer hall has modest decorative carvings but the columns and walls are bland. The eastern gate approach is from the road level up a flight of steps to negotiate the raised plinth on which this unique mosque has been built with a four Iwan layout. Stone chajjas or eaves can also be seen on all the four arcades. The Northern entry with 1 m (3.3 ft.) raised entrance, probably linked the Mosque to the Bijayamandal Palace. The stucco plastering work on the mosque walls have lasted for centuries and even now show some tiles fixed on them at a few locations. The mosque was under occupation during Jahanpanah's existence till the seventeenth century. In the later period, encroachers had occupied the mosque but were cleared by the ASI in 1921. A shuttered by lane entry from the north has been interpreted as an approach that was used by the womenfolk of the Sultan's family for attending prayers in the mosque.

BIJAY MANDAL

Bijay Mandal is a building with a layout plan of 74 m (242.8 ft)x82 m (269.0 ft.) dimensions, with a well proportioned square dome. It cannot be categorized as a tower or a palace. It is a typical Toghlaqi structure with an octagonal plan built in rubble masonry (with massive battered sloping walls on east, west and southern directions) on a raised platform with door ways in each cardinal direction. The purpose of this unusual structure and the ruins of the Sar Dara Palace was described by Ibn Battuta as the palace with multiple chambers and the large public audience hall as the famed Hazar Sutan Palace. It was also interpreted as serving as an observation tower to monitor the activities of his troops. The ambience of the place presented it as place to relax and enjoy the scenic view of the environs. The inclined path around the monument was a walkway leading to the apartments of the Sultan. Two large openings in the living rooms of the floor were inferred as leading to the vaults or the treasury. On the level platform, outside the building in front of the apartment rooms, small holes equally spaced are seen, which have been inferred to be holes used to fix wooden pillars to hold a temporary *shamiana* (pavilion) or cover. The process of ushering people into the presence of the Sultan was devious and formal involving entry through semi-public places to private chambers to the audience hall. The debate on whether the Hazara Sutan Palace cited as existing during Allauddin Khilji reign and also during Togluq's time are one and the same palace, has not been conclusive. A plausible hypothesis is that the stone hall of the palace was built by Allauddin Khilji while the tower adjoining the stone buildings was surely built by Mohammed bin Toghluq.

Archeological excavations carried out by the Archeological Survey of India unearthed treasures from the vaults in the buildings, which date the occupation of this monument during Feruz Shah's reign and also by Sheikh Hasan Tahir (a saint) during Sikander Lodi's rule at the beginning of the 16th century. Also, excavations done in 1934 have revealed wooden pillar bases attributed to the Hazar Sutan Palace. Within the close precincts of the Bijaymandal, a domed building is seen which has a unique architectural facade of two openings on each of its three sides, interpreted as an annex to another building (based on underground passages seen in the adjoining structure). However, the purpose for which this dome was built is not known.

Kalusarai Masjid is located 500 m (1,640.4 ft.) to the north of the

Bijaymandal but it is in a highly dilapidated state (pictured) needing urgent attention for restoration in view of its heritage monument status. At present, it is occupied as a residential complex by a few families. The Masjid was built by the famous builder of Mosques Khan-i-Jahan Maqbul Tilangani, Prime Minister during Feroz Shah Tughlaq's reign, as one of his seven mosques; built in the same architectural style as the other six built by him. But even now the visible decorations of the mihrab appear to be more intricate than in his other mosques. When built with rubble masonry and plastered, the mosque had seven arched openings as the frontage, three bays depth wise and crowned by a sequence of low domes in typical Toghluqi architectural style.

SARAI SHAHJI MAHAL

Further to the east of Begumpur Masjid, in the Sarai Shahji village, Mughul period buildings are seen of which the Sarai Shahji Mahal is a distinguishing monument. The area surrounding this is scattered with decrepit gates, graves and a large slum area. A little distance from this place is the tomb of Shiekh Farid Murtaza Khan, who during Emperor Akbar's period, was credited with building a number of Serai's, a mosque and Faridabad village, which is now the present-day large city in Haryana.

OTHER NOTABLE STRUCTURES

Other notable structures in the Jahanpanah's ambit of 20 ha (49.4 acres) area in close vicinity of the present day Panchshila Public School are the following :

The Lal Gumbad, was built as a tomb for Shaikh Kabbiruddin Auliya (1397), a sufi saint who lived in the fourteenth century as a disciple of sufi saint Shaikh Raushan Chiragh-i-Delhi. The dome tomb was built with red sandstone. It is considered to be a small size replica of the Ghiyasuddin Tughlaq's Tomb in Tughlaqabad. The gateway to the tomb has a pointed arch with marble bands. It is also called the Rakabwala Gumbad because dacoits had stolen the finial on the roof of the tomb by climbing up over the iron rungs (called 'Rakab') on its western wall. Apart from these structures, the four walls of a mosque also are within the compound wall of the tomb.

The Sadhana Enclave are features Baradari an arched hall. Thought to have been built in the 14th century or 15th century, it is in a fairly well preserved condition. A Lodi period tomb is also seen nearby.

Further away from the Sadhana enclave on its opposite side, in Shiekh

Serai, three tombs are noted of which only one is well preserved, the squared domed tomb of Sheikh Alauddin (1541-42). The tomb building is raised on twelve columns with perforated screens on the facade has a large dome, creating a drum with sixteen faces. The ceiling of the tomb is well decorated with medallions in plaster on the spandrel of arches and within the parapets a merlon design.

THE CURSE OF NIZAMUDDIN AULIYA

Ghias-ud-din is usually perceived as a liberal ruler. However, he was so passionate about his dream fort that he issued a dictate that all labourers in Delhi must work on his fort. Saint Nizamuddin Auliya, a Sufi mystic, got incensed as the work on his *baoli* (well) was stopped. The confrontation between the sufi saint and the royal emperor has become a legend in India. The saint uttered a curse which was to resonate throughout history right until today: Ya rahey usar, ya basey gujjar (may it [the fort] remain unoccupied/infertile, or else the herdsmen may live here).

THE DEATH OF THE EMPEROR

Another of the saint's curses was Hunuz Dilli dur est (Delhi is still far away). The Emperor was engrossed in a campaign in Bengal at this time. He was successful and was on his way to Delhi. However, his son, Muhammad bin Tughlaq, met him at Kara in Uttar Pradesh. Allegedly at the prince's orders, a *shamiana* (roof) fell on the Emperor, who was crushed to death (1324 AD).

MAUSOLEUM OF GHIYATH AL-DIN TUGHLUQ

The 'Mausoleum of Ghiyath al-Din Tughluq' is connected by a causeway to the southern outpost of the fortification. This elevated causeway leads across a former artificial lake and is nowadays pierced by the Mehrauli-Badarpur road.

After passing an old Pipal tree, the complex of Ghiyath al-Din Tughluq's tomb is entered by a high gateway made up of red sandstone with a flight of steps. The actual mausoleum is made up of a single-domed square tomb (about 8 m x8 m) with sloping walls crowned by parapets. In contrast to the walls of the fortification made up of granite, the sides of the mausoleum are faced by smooth red sandstone and inlaid with inscribed panels and arch boders from marble. The edifice is topped by an elegant dome resting on an octagonal drum that is covered with white slabs of marble.

Inside the mausoleum are three graves: The central one belongs to Ghiyath al-Din Tughluq and the other two are believed to be those of his wife and his son and successor Muhammad bin Tughluq. In the north-western bastion of the enclosure wall with its pillared corridors is another octagonal tomb in similar style with a smaller marble dome and inscribed marble and sandstone slabs over its arched doors. According to an inscription over its southern entrance this tomb houses the remains of Zafar Khan. His grave has been at the site prior to the construction of the outpost and was consciously integrated into the design of the mausoleum by Ghiyath al-Din himself.

ARCHITECTURE

Tughluqabad still consists of remarkable, massive stone fortifications that surround the irregular ground plan of the city. The sloping rubble-filled city walls, a typical feature of monuments of the Tughluq dynasty, are between 10 and 15 meters high, topped by battlemented parapets and strengthened by circular bastions of up to two stories height.

The city is supposed to once have had as many as 52 gates of which only 13 remain today. The fortified city contained seven rainwater tanks. Tughluqabad is divided into three parts;

- the wider city area with houses built along a rectangular grid between its gates
- the citadel with a tower at its highest point known as Bijai-Mandal and the remains of several halls and a long underground passage
- the adjacent palace area containing the royal residences. A long underground passage below the tower still remains.

Today most of the city is inaccessible due to dense thorny vegetation.

An ever increasing part of the former city area is occupied by modern settlement, especially in the vicinity of its lakes. South of Tughluqabad was a vast artificial water reservoir within the fortified outpost of Ghiyath al-Din Tughluq's Tomb.

This well preserved mausoleum remains connected to the fort by an elevated causeway that still stands today. Well visible in the southeast are the remains of the Fortress of 'Adilabad, built years later in a similar style.

KHIRKI MASJID

Khirki Masjid, approached from the Khirki village in South Delhi and close to the Satpula or the seven arched bridge on the edge of southern wall of Jahapanah (the fourth city of Medieval Delhi), was a mosque built by Khan-i-Jahan Maqbul Tilangani, the Prime Minister of Feroz Shah Tughlaq (1351-1388) of the Tughlaq Dynasty. The word 'Khirki' prefixed to masjid is a Urdu word that means "window" and hence is also called "The Masjid of Windows".

The Masjid, which is in a quadrangular shape, was built as a fortress with an unusual fusion of Islamic and traditional Hindu architecture. It is said to be the only mosque in North India, which is mostly covered; the totally covered mosque of the Sultanate period is, however, in South India at Gulbarga in North Karnataka.

HISTORY

Khan-i-Jahan Junaan Telangani and Feroz Shah Tughlaq were intensely committed towards building architectural monuments. Together, they planned and built several tombs and mosques. Telangani in particular, was credited with building seven mosques of unique designs. The inference drawn for his interest to build mosques was that he was impelled by the fact that he was a Hindu convert who willed to prove himself true to his converted Islamic religion. The regal mosque built by him was the Khirki Masjid. Constructed in the Jahapanah city, it is a novel cross–axial mosque in Tughluqian architectural style built more like a fortress. There are no specific inscriptions on the Mosque on its construction date, though the name of the builder is inscribed on the eastern gate of the Mosque as 'Khan-e-Jahan Junaan Shah'. Therefore, in the absence of "epigraphic and literary" evidence (though one recent web reference mentions 1375 and another 1380) for its provenance, a research study has been provided by Welch and Howard in their paper titled "The Tughluqs: Master Builders of the Delhi Sultanate". The study has conjectured the year of building by comparing with many other large mosques of this period. It is dated between 1351 and 1354 when Feroz Shah Tughlaq, during his stay in Jahapanah, ordered this mosque to be built as "his pious inaugural contribution to the Capital".

ARCHITECTURE

The Mosque has a 52 m^2 (170.6 ft.) x52 m^2(170.6 ft) square plan in an area of 87 m^2 (936.5 sq ft.). It is raised on a plinth of 3 m (9.8 ft.). There are four open courtyards (square in size of 9.14 m (30.0 ft.) on each side) encircled by arcades built with 180 square structural columns and 60 pilasters, which run in north–south direction and divides into aisles. The open court yards are the source of light and ventilation to the internal prayer spaces. The roof is partitioned into 25 squares of equal size with 9 small domes in each square (totalling to 81 domes) and alternated by 12 flat roofs to cover the roof. There are four open courts.

This internal layout gives a spectacular view, which is a photographers delight. The four corners of the mosque are adorned with towers with three protruding gateways, one in the middle of each face, with tapering turrets flanking each gate. The southern gate, with imposing steps at the main entrance, exhibits a combination of arch and trabeated construction. It has an ornamental rectilinear frame. The turrets flanking the southern and northern gates are circular in shape; the articulation on these gives them a three storied appearance. The main gate, which leads to the qibla on the western wall, has a projecting mihrab.

Above the vaulted first floor cells, ubiquitous arch windows (carved out of stone guard) with perforated screens or jalis or tracery, known as "Khirkis"", are seen on the second floor. However, the foyer in front of the mihrab is not well lighted since light from the latticed windows on the second floor do not penetrate this space. The approach to the roof of the mosque is from the east gate, and the view from the roof leaves a lasting impression of the geometrical design of the Mosque. The mosque's walls are of rubble masonry construction with plastered surface on the outside. The interior walls are bland but provided with traditional carved stone screens. The symmetrically designed admirable mosque is considered as one of "the finest architectural compositions of the Sultanate history." It was considered Firuz Shah's architectural benefaction. The importance of the Khirki Masjid's architectural elegance has been considered a precursor to the intensely metaphorical Mughal architecture (1526-1857), with the Lodhi period's (1451-1526) architecture – the Delhi Sultanate's last dynasty – marking the transition.

MOTH KI MASJID

Moth Ki Masjid is a mosque located in Delhi, and was built in 1505 by Wazir Miya Bhoiya, Prime Minister during the reign of Sultan Sikander Lodi (1517–26). It was a new type of mosque developed by the Lodi dynasty in the fourth city of the medieval Delhi of the Delhi Sultanate. The name of the mosque literally translated into English language means 'Lentil Mosque' and this name tag 'Lentil' has an interesting legend. This mosque was considered a beautiful Gumbad structure of the period.

The mosque is now completely enclosed within the modern locality of South Extension Part II, Uday Park and Masjid Moth comprising residential and commercial establishments in the urban setting of South Delhi.

LEGEND

It is famously narrated that when Sultan Sikandar Lodi was on a visit to a mosque in the vicinity of the present location of the Moth Ki Masjid for prayer, he knelt over a grain of moth (a kind of lentil), which had been dropped by a bird. A seed so honoured by His majesty must not be thrown away. It must be used in the service of God. So he took the moth seed and planted it in his garden for further growth. Over the years, the process of repeated planting and replanting of the moth seeds was carried out. In this process, the seeds multiplied several times. The Wazir finally sold the rich harvest and earned good money. With the proceeds of the sale he built the mosque after seeking permission from the Sultan to construct the Mosque. Impressed by the ingenuity of his minister, Sikandar Lodi laid the foundation for building the mosque.

Another version of the legend is that Sikandar Lodhi on one of his visits to the area played a prank on his Prime Minister by giving him a gift of a grain of moth (lentil). The Wazir accepted the gift in good grace and instead of throwing it away planted it in his garden. Over the years repeated plantation resulted in a rich harvest that provided a surplus income to the Wazir. Thereafter, the wazir, with the revenue earned from the lentil grains, decided to build a mosque. On completion, he invited the Sultan to visit the mosque and narrated the sequence of events which lead to the building of the mosque. Impressed by this unique achievement, the Lodi named the mosque as "Moth Ki Masjid" or the Mosque from the Moth Lentil.

STRUCTURE

Raised on a high plinth, the mosque has a square layout. It is approached from the eastern side street of village Moti Masjid, through an exquisitely designed gate made of red, blue, black and white coloured sandstones arranged in a neat design. In particular, the arch of the gateway has a Hindu arch within a Muslim arch.

Up the gateway steps, the entry is into a large courtyard of 38.6 m (126.6 ft.) width surrounded by walls. Within the courtyard, on the western side is the main shrine or the mosque with the rectangular prayer hall porch, which has a facade of five arched openings. The corners of the rectangular prayer hall are adorned with double storied towers. The towers have arched openings at the rear end of the roof with domed octagonal chhatris (the Cenotophs) on the related walls. The west side wall is provided with tapering turrets that depict a sophisticated outline (pictured).

The Cenotophs were the first of its kind to be built in India and since then these have been replicated in several other monuments, even in the Deccan. There are three impressive domes inside the prayer hall with the Mihrab located on the west qibla wall of the central dome, which is the largest of the three domes. The Mihrab depicts Quranic inscriptions in flora Nakashi in Iranian design. Turrets project out of the qibla. The central dome is supported on squinches. The domes on both flanks are borne on muqarnas pendentives. Carved panels of red sandstone and white marble and plaster, as well as glazed tiles embellish the walls of the mosque. The overall effect of the Mosque has been best described as: epitomizes in itself all that is best in Architecture of the Lodis and displays a freedom of imagination, a bold diversity of design, an appreciation of contrasting light and shade and a sense of harmony in line and colour, which combine to make it one of the most spirited and picturesque buildings of its kind in the whole range of Islamic art.

It is also said that it was the private mosque of the builder.

An unusual feature of this mosque built in Indo–Islamic style of architecture is that it has an austere design with no minarets, calligraphic decorations and embellishments, which are otherwise traditional features of mosques. The dome is semicircular and windows have latticework screens. An architectural appreciation of the structure vis-a-vis the five arched facade of domes of the period aptly infers:

the rapid crystallization of the earlier concept. Firstly, it is considerably larger than its predecessor. Secondly, the articulation of the recessed arches is far more adept. Thirdly, embellishment has been done using elegant niches on the columns abutting the arches. Another important feature is the use of better material and colour, as if the masons were trying for something more permanent and forceful.

SULTAN GHARI

Sultan Ghari was the first Islamic Mausoleum (tomb) built in 1231 AD for Prince Nasiruddin Mahmud, eldest son of Iltumish, in the "funerary landscape of Delhi" in the Malakapur village (near Vasant Kunj). Iltumish was the first Sultan of the Slave Dynasty who ruled in Delhi from 1210 to 1236 A.D. The area where the Ghari (meaning: cave) tomb is situated, was part of the first city of medieval Delhi known as the Slave Dynasty that ruled during the period 1206 to 1290. This area is now part of the Qutb complex. The Slave Dynasty was the forerunner under the early Delhi Sultanate that ruled from 1216 to 1516. This dynastic city was followed by creation of other five cities of Delhi ruled by different dynastic rulers of the Delhi Sultanate, namely, the Khilji dynasty (1290-1320), the Tughlaq dynasty (1320-1413), the Sayyid dynasty (1414-51), and the Lodi dynasty (1451-1526). The rule of the Mughal Empire then followed and lasted from 1526 to 1857.

The crypt or the tomb is implanted in a Ghari (cave), approached by winding steep stairs made of stone, and supported by pillars and flooring. The cave is covered by an unusual octagonal roof slab. The exterior of the tomb structure built in Delhi sandstone with marble adornment exhibits a walled area with bastions (towers) on corners, which impart it the look of a fortress in aesthetic Persian and Oriental architecture.. The other tombs inside the Ghari have not been identified.

HISTORY

Iltumish, ruling from Delhi since 1210 A.D., invaded eastern India in 1225 A.D. to capture Laknauti (now a ruined city in West Bengal called Gaur). The resultant battle ended in signing of a Treaty between Izaz, the then ruler of Eastern India (Bihar and Bengal) and Iltumish; the former ruler agreeing to pay a surety of 80 lakh tankas (silver currency), 38 elephants, mint and issue of coins in the name of Iltumish and accepting Sultan's suzerainty over the region. Before returning to Delhi, Iltumish divided the region into Bihar and Lakhnauti, and installed Alauddin masud jani as his feudatory in Lakhnauti. But Jani's control was short lived as he was overthrown by Iwaz soon after Iltumish's departure.

There after, Iltutmish deputed his eldest son prince Nasiruddin Mahmud to fight Iwaz. In the battle which took place near Lakhnauti, Iwaz was trounced and executed in 1227 A.D., along with his nobles. Prince Nasiruddin Mahmud who was then appointed as governor of Lakhnauti province, merged his original province of Oudh with Bengal and Bihar, and established his capital at Lakhnauti. This act of his coupled with the fact that he was son of Iltumish enhanced his prestige in the province. As a reward, he was given the honorific title of 'Malik-us-Sharq' (king of the

East) by Iltutmish. His rule was short lived, eventful and he could consolidate his territory. But after a short rule of 18 months, Nasiruddin Mahmud was killed. Immensely grieved by the death of his favourite eldest son, Iltumish built a tomb called the Sultan Ghari in memory of his son, in 1231 A.D., close to the Qutb complex. Five years later, Iltumish died in the year 1236 and his tomb can be seen in the Qutb complex. His two other sons, namely Ruknuddin Feroze Shah (died 1237 A.D., after he was deposed) and Muizzudin Bahram Shah (was killed in 1241 A.D.) who ruled for short periods, before and after their famous sister Razia Sultan ruled Delhi, were also buried in separate Chhatris (cenotaphs), just next to the Sultan Ghari. One of the two Chhatris (pictured) is restored while the other has been destroyed. Some archelogical findings reported by the Archeological Survey of India are a) the inscription of 1361 recording the excavation of a tank on the occasion of a marriage, b) a stone linga (phallic symbol of Lord Shiva the Hindu God in a lintel and c) a dilapitated mosque of Sultan Feroz Shah Tughlaq's time and a few scattered remnanats of the Moghul period.

WORSHIP AT THE TOMB

The tomb is a revered place for devotees of both Hindu and Muslim religious communities of the nearby villages of Mahipalpur and Rangpur since they consider the tomb as the dargah of a saintly 'peer'; a visit to the tomb is more or less mandatory for newlyweds from these two villages. Because of the religious veneration, the monument is maintained better by the local people than the Archeological Survey of India who are the formal custodians to maintain the heritage structure.

Thursday is a special day for worship at this tomb when devotees, both Hindus and Muslims, visit the shrine, which represents a festive display of Hindu - Muslim syncretism of religious tolerance.

Every year, on the 17th day of the Islamic month of Ziqad (month occurring between Ramadan and Eid festivals), the "Urs (death anniversary) of Nasiruddin Shah" is held when pilgrims from all parts of Delhi visit the tomb.

PROVINCIAL ARCHITECTURE UNDER DELHI SULTANATE

Provincial architecture under the Delhi Sultanate prospered in the hands of the Muslim rulers in the provinces. They built tombs, palaces, mosques, forts etc. in their kingdoms which were highly inspired by the Delhi or the imperial style of architecture. Due to limited financial resources, the provincial rulers could not afford the opulence to their building as was provided by the Sultans of Delhi. The local circumstances also influenced the provincial style of architecture. In Multan there are four notable buildings which were built during this period namely the shrine of Shah Yusuf-ul-Gardizi, the mausoleum of Bahlul Haqq, the tomb of Shams-ud-din and the tomb of Rukn-i-Alam built up by Ghiyas-ud-din Tughlaq. Among all these architectural specimens the tomb of Rukn-i-Alam has been regarded as the most magnificent one.

In Bengal, mostly bricks were used in the construction of the buildings. The prominent buildings of Bengal are the Adina Masjid built by Sikandar Lodi at Pandua, the Eklakhi Mausoleum at Hazarat Pandua, the Gunamant and the Darasbari mosques at Gaur, the Lotan Masjid and the Bari Sona Masjid at Gaur, the Sath Gumbad mosque at Bagerhat (Khulna district), the tomb of Rukn Khan at Debikota, the Qadam Rasul at Gaur built by Nusrat Shah, the Dakhil-Darwaza at Gaur and the tomb of Jalal-ud-din Muhammad at Pandua. The most important features of the Bengal Style of architecture were the use of pointed arches on pillars, Hindu decorative designs and adaptation of Hindu architecture to Islamic art.

The rulers of Sharqi dynasty at Jaunpur deeply patronised architecture and a number of good buildings were raised during their rule which were endowed with certain superior features of both the Hindu and Islamic architecture. The salient features of the buildings constructed in Jaunpur were square pillars, small galleries and absence of minarets. The fort and the palace of Ibrahim Naib Barbak are the most prominent specimen of architecture under the Delhi Sultanate. Among buildings constructed by the Sharqi rulers, are the Atala Masjid completed by Ibrahim Shah Sharqi, the Jami Masjid built by Husain Shah and the Lal Darwaza mosque which depicts the best features of provincial architecture. The buildings in Malwa bear similarity with those which were constructed by the Sultans of Delhi.

The fort of Mandu has been regarded as a beautiful protected city. The most notable buildings of Mandu are the Jami Masjid, the Hindola Mahal, the Ashrafi Mahal, the tower of victory and the tomb of Sultan Hushang constructed by Sultan Mahmud Khilji, the Jahaz Mahal and palace of Baz Bahadur and his queen Rupmati. The buildings in Malwa have their own distinct style and occupy a respectable place among the architectural style of provinces during this period. In Gujarat the best combination of Hindu and Islamic architecture are found.

The capital city of Ahmedabad was founded by Sultan Ahmad Shah and certain beautiful buildings were erected there. Most noteworthy buildings of Gujarat are the Jami Masjid at Cambay, the mosque of Hilal Khan Kazi at Dholka, the Jami mosque and tomb of Ahmad Shah at Ahmedabad, the tomb of Habit Khan and Sayyid Alam, the Tin Darwaza, the Rani-Ka-Hujra, the mosque of Dariya Khan and Alif Khan, the Dholka Masjid and the tomb of Shaikh Ahmad Khatri which is six miles away from Ahmedabad.

The city of Champaner contains beautiful buildings and the mosque built up by Mahmud Begarha has been regarded as the best among them. Certain innovative features were added to the style of architecture of Gujarat during the rule of Mahmud Begarha.

In Kashmir, a pleasant blend of Hindu and the Muslim architecture was found. The most notable buildings constructed here during this period are the tomb of Mandani, the Jami Masjid at Srinagar and the mosque of Shah Hamadan. The rulers of Bahamani dynasty constructed splendid buildings within their territories. Their buildings represent a fair amalgamation of Hindu and Islamic architecture. The noteworthy buildings among them are the mosques at Bidar and Gulbarga, the tomb of Muhammad Adil Shah, known as the Gol Gumbaz, the Chand Minar at Daultabad and the college constructed by Mahmud Gawan at Bidar.

8

Administrative and Political System of Delhi Sultanate

ADMINISTRATION OF DELHI SULTANATE

The King was the head of the Central Administration in Delhi Sultanate. The monarch had the last say in the legislative, executive and judicial matters. For smooth administration, the administration was further divided into provinces. The administration of the Delhi Sultanate primarily depended on the Shariat or the laws of Islam. The finance of the dynasty was largely depended on the revenue system of the Delhi Sultanate.

CENTRAL ADMINISTRATION OF DELHI SULTANATE

The central administration of the Delhi Sultanate consisted of the office of the Sultan. Other ministers like the naib, the vazir, Diwani-i-risalat, Dabir-i-khas, Ariz-i-mumalik, Sadr-us-Sudur, Qazi-ul-quzat and Barid-i-mumalika.

Besides, there were also several other departments and the Sultan appointed their officers to carry on specific duties. The sultan was the head of the state and enjoyed unlimited powers in every sphere of state activity. The naib also enjoyed equivalent position as that of the Sultan.

The vazir was the Prime Minister of the state and headed the financial department. Ariz-i-mumalik was the head of the department of diwani-i-arz and in that capacity was the controller-general of the military department.

Diwani-i-risalat was the minister of foreign affairs and Sadr-us-Sudur was the head of the religious department. The Vakil-i-dar-mahal looked after the officials of the palace; the Barbak maintained the tradition of the court and its glamour; Amir-i-hajib looked after the visitors to the Sultan; Amir-i-shikar-i-shahi arranged for the hunting parties of the Sultan; Amir-i-majlis-shahi looked after the festivals of the state; and Sar-i-jahandar was the Sultan's bodyguards.

ADMINISTRATION OF PROVINCES OF DELHI SULTANATE

The empire of the Delhi Sultanate was divided into province foe the convenience of the administration. They were called Iqtas. The number of Iqtas was not fixed and there was no uniformity in their administration. The head of the Iqta was addressed by various names such as naib Sultan, nazim, muqti or wali. The walis or the muqtis enjoyed the same powers in relation to their Iqtas as the Sultan enjoyed in the Empire.

Besides the muqti, there were other officers of the central government in every Iqta. There was a vazir, an ariz and a qazi in every Iqta. By the end of the 13th century there was no smaller administrative unit than Iqta. After that Iqtas were divided into smaller units called shiqqs, which were put under shiqqdars. The shiqqs were further divided into parganas.

FINANCIAL SYSTEM OF DELHI SULTANATE

The financial system was an important part of the administration of the Delhi Sultanate. Five categories of taxes were collected by the Sultan. Ushr was a land tax which was collected from the Muslim peasants. Kharaj was a land tax which was charged from the non Muslim peasants. Khams was one fifth of the booty captured in the war or one fifth of the produce of mines or buried treasure that was found. Jizya was a religious on the non Muslims. According to the Islam, a no Muslim had any right to dwell in the kingdom of a Muslim Sultan, but this concession was permitted after payment of the tax called Jizya. Zakat was a religious tax which was imposed only on rich Muslims and consisted of two and half per cent of their income. The main items of expenditure were expenses on the army, salaries of civil officers and the personal expenditure of the Sultan and his palace.

LAND REVENUE SYSTEM OF DELHI SULTANATE

Land revenue system of the Delhi Sultanate was based on the type and the measurement of the land. There were basically four kinds of lands.

The central government appointed revenue collector in each sub division called the shiq. He collected the revenue with the help of the hereditary officers of the village like chaudharis, muqaddams, patwaris etc. normally the peasants were asked to pay one third of the produce as land revenue. Ala-ud-din however collected half of the total produce from certain territories. Mostly the revenue was collected in cash. Except Ala-ud-din Khilji and Muhammad Bin Tughlaq no sultan of Delhi collected revenue based on the measurement of land.

MILITARY ADMINISTRATION OF DELHI SULTANATE

The power of the sultan depended on the army. Therefore every Sultan was forced to keep a large army at the center. There were four types of soldiers in the army of the Delhi Sultanate. The soldiers who were recruited by the center as soldiers of the army of the Sultan, the soldiers who were employed on a permanent basis by nobles and provincial governors, the soldiers who were appointed only in the times of war on a temporary basis and the Muslim soldiers who joined the army as volunteers at the time of war against the Hindus. The army primarily consisted of cavalry, infantry and elephants. The army of the Sultan had soldiers of different nationalities and diverse faith. The Persians, the Afghans, the Mongols, the Indian Muslims and the Hindus but the higher offices were mostly given to foreign Muslims.

ADMINISTRATIVE SYSTEM OF THE SULTANATE

A rapid survey of the three-hundred-year history of the Delhi Sultanate is likely to leave the reader with two impressions. One is of a political structure in which violence, based on a powerful fighting force, was the only support of a ruler's government; the other is that anything like a coherent political philosophy was completely lacking. What is becoming increasingly plain, however, as the period is studied in more depth, is that the sultanate under its abler rulers had a quite sophisticated administrative structure. In addition, the Turkish sultans were heirs to a tradition in which political theory had been considerably evolved, and there were many scholars in Islamic India who had given thought to both the general principles underlying government and the techniques of public administration. We know of the works of some of these writers only from casual references in other books, but a number which have survived suggest the background of thought against which the sultanate's actual administrative structure developed.

ADMINISTRATION OF JUSTICE

The administration of justice received attention quite early in the sultanate, and here as elsewhere traditional Islamic practice was modified to suit the peculiar problems of India. Four types of courts were normally recognized in Islamic society: the *diwan- i-mazalim*, the court of complaints, presided over by the ruler or his representative; the qazi's court, which administered the Holy Law of Islam; the courts of the muhtasib, or censor, which dealt with public morals and offenses against religious ordinances; and the *shurta*, or police courts. In India the third type of court gained in power and prestige under the Tughluqs, and later under Aurangzeb.

The first important judicial dignitary of the sultanate at Delhi to whom a reference is found in contemporary records was the *amir-i-dad*, or chief magistrate. He was a layman, and the office was usually reserved for a leading noble with special aptitude for judicial work.

Fakhr-i-Mudabbir suggested that only a member of the royal family, or a nobleman known for piety and learning, should be appointed to this post. A large salary was to be paid to him, as he might have to try complaints against governors and high commanders.

In the absence of the sultan, who functioned as supreme judge throughout Muslim rule, the *amir-i-dad* presided over the court of complaints, but his office had many other functions. He controlled the police, was responsible for public works, including the maintenance of the city walls, kept copies of documents registered with the qazi, and forbade covenants which transgressed the law.

If he felt that there had been a miscarriage of justice he could either draw the attention of the qazi to the fact or delay the execution of the decision until the matter was reconsidered by a fuller or a higher court; he also ordered the arrest of criminals, dealt with breaches of law, and tried cases, where necessary with the assistance of a qazi who functioned as a legal adviser.

While the system of dispensation of justice by the sultan or his representative continued, administration of justice by the qazis grew in importance and became a prominent feature of the Tughluq rule. The main concern of the qazi was civil disputes among Muslims, although later his jurisdiction was widened to include the supervision and management of the property of orphans and lunatics. Appointed by the central government, he was completely independent of the provincial governors.

The office of the *qazi-i- mumalik,* or chief judge, was normally held by the head of the ecclesiastical department, who was generally known as the *sadr- i-jahan.* It is not certain whether he heard appeals against the judgments of the qazis. He was also the sultan's legal adviser in matters relating to shariat, the holy law of Islam. With the monarch retaining the powers of appointment of the chief qazi, though the enlightened opinion and books on Muslim statecraft emphasize the importance of appointing only honest, pious, and well-qualified qazis in the realm, the sultan had the final say in the framing of the judicial structure.

Public opinion was critical of the appointment of chief qazis for considerations other than those of merit, and most of the kings took steps to uphold the prestige of the judiciary. The manner in which on one occasion Muhammad Tughluq appeared like an ordinary plaintiff in the court of a qazi and saluted him may be nothing more than a theatrical gesture, but such episodes built up the prestige of the courts and enabled the general public and the legal profession to realize what was expected of the judges.

Although under a despotic monarchy there were obvious limitations to the role which an individual could play, the jurists generally acted with courage and independence. When Jalaluddin Khalji wanted Sayyid Maula, who was accused of high treason, to vindicate himself by walking through fire, the jurists vetoed the idea by contending that fire did not distinguish between the innocent and the guilty.

The sultan bowed to their decision, though he later connived at Sayyid's murder. Similarly, in spite of Alauddin Khalji's reputation for ruthlessness, Qazi Mughis-ud-din did not fail to criticize his actions, and in spite of this condemnation, he rewarded the qazi. The sanctity attached to the office of qazi, as an expert in Islamic law, and the pressure of public opinion, encouraged an honest and independent judiciary, the need for which was universally recognized.

An important development during the sultanate was the crystallization of the Indo-Muslim legal tradition. The first important figure in the legal history of the Delhi Sultanate was Sayyid Nur-ud-din Mubarik, originally of Ghazni (d.1234). He was held in high regard by Sultan Muhammad Ghuri, and he maintained his position even though he was extremely critical of court etiquette and the mode of living adopted by Muslim rulers. He wanted Iltutmish to deal firmly with non-Muslims, and he condemned not only all heresy but also the study of philosophy. Barani often puts some of his own ideas in the discourses which he attributes to important personalities, but the puritanical, ascetic approach which he attributes to Nur-ud-Din Mubarik appears typical of the early days of Muslim India, when simplicity and piety found favour with the jurists and the ruling monarch.

A different type of personality, and one whose policy left a great mark on the history of Islamic law in India, was Qazi Minhaj- us-Siraj, the most important historian of the Slave dynasty. A native of Ghazni, he came to the subcontinent during the reign of Iltutmish and received many important assignments.

In the days of Iltutmish's successors, including Nasiruddin Mahmud, he held the important office of the chief qazi of the realm. It is said that the *sama* (ecstatic dances performed by groups similar to the "whirling dervishes") to which most orthodox lawyers objected, became prevalent in Delhi when Minhaj was qazi. A contemporary of Minhaj thought that he was not fit to be a qazi, but should have been the principal Sufi shaikh. These statements give a clue to his policies, for as he himself has recorded, he was so unpopular with other ecclesiastics that once they even attempted to have him assassinated.

In the light of these observations it is reasonable to infer that Minhaj was not rigid in the application of Islamic law, and that his long tenure as chief qazi contributed toward the evolution of a suitable modus operandi for the new Muslim government. His views on Islamic law in fact appear to have been in agreement with those of Balban.

Although personally punctilious in his religious observations, and careful about showing formal courtesy to religious leaders, Balban attached no importance to the views of ulama in political and administrative matters. He used to say that these things had to be decided in accordance with political considerations and not the views of jurists. According to Barani, "he would order whatever he considered to be in the interest of the realm, whether it was or was not sanctioned by Islamic law." Balban's practice and Minhaj's theory united to provide the flexibility needed by Islamic law if it were to operate in the peculiar conditions created by the existence of a tiny Muslim ruling class and a vast Hindu populace.

The tradition of strong common sense and a realistic approach to problems built up by Minhaj was maintained by his daughter 's son, Sadr-ud-din Arif, who was a deputy to the chief qazi for a long time, and whom Alauddin Khalji promoted early in his reign. According to Barani he was not distinguished for scholarship, but he was a strong executive officer who understood the temperament of the people, so that "in spite of the freed slaves who overran Delhi, it was not possible for anyone to resort to swindling, deception, or trickery before his court."

The man who most directly influenced the course of Indo- Muslim legal history was not a high official, as was Minhaj, but a scholar who introduced the systematic study of Islamic law into India. This was Maulana Burhanuddin, who brought with him to India from Balkh the *Hidaya*, the great legal textbook. This remained the basis of Muslim law for centuries, and was finally translated into English by officials of the East India Company. So great was Burhanuddin's reputation as a teacher that Balban, accompanied by his entire royal retinue, visited him after Friday prayers. Despite his orthodoxy, he was not particularly rigid in his application of Islamic law. On the crucial question of *sama*, the ecstatic dances, which remained the major legal controversy of the day and generally provided the dividing line between the mystics and the ecclesiasts, his practice was not different from that of the more tolerant Minhaj. "I have not committed any major sin in life," he said, "except hearing of *sama*, which I have heard and want to hear again, if I have an opportunity."

The popularity of *Hidaya* and other textbooks from Central Asia ensured that in legal affairs, as in much else, Muslim India followed the traditions of Central Asia. These books, which were brought to India mainly by refugees during Balban's reign, were in Arabic. With the efforts made by Firuz Tughluq to run the government according to Islamic law, it became necessary to have summaries and abstracts of Islamic law in Persian, the court language of Muslim India. We accordingly see a large number of manuals prepared in his reign, usually based on the compilations of the lawyers of Central Asia. In addition more substantial efforts for compilation of books on Islamic law in Persian and Arabic were made.

The earliest of such compilations prepared in India was in the time of Balban and was dedicated to him. Others were prepared during the Tughluq period but the most comprehensive digest compiled in Muslim India prior to the compilation of *Fatawa- i-Alamgiri* in Aurangzeb's reign was the *Fatawa-i-Tatar Khania*, named after the pious nobleman, Tatar Khan, who sponsored the compilation. Prepared by a committee of ulama, it consisted of thirty volumes. It attracted attention ouside the subcontinent, and a summary was prepared by Shaikh Ibrahim, the imam of the mosque of the Ottoman sultan, Muhammad the Conqueror, in Istanbul.

REVENUE AND FINANCIAL ARRANGEMENTS

The financial arrangements of the sultanate were in accordance with the normal Islamic theory and practice as inherited from the Ghaznavid predecessors, but they were modified in the light of local needs and usages. Land revenue was, as in Hindu India, the mainstay of the government.

Sultan Qutubuddin Aibak, the first Muslim ruler, fixed the state demand (*kharaj*) at one-fifth of the gross produce. In land revenue, as in other spheres, Balban laid down the administrative pattern for the sultanate. According to W. H. Moreland, one of the most careful students of Indian economic history, Balban "had grasped the main principles of rural economy in an Indian peasant- state, at a period when the environment afforded little scope for individual advance; he aimed at a peaceful and contented peasantry, raising ample produce and paying a reasonable revenue; and he saw that it was the king's duty to direct the administration with this object in view."

Under Alauddin Khalji, because of the need to build up a large army, the state demand was raised to one-half of the produce, the uppermost limit allowed by Muslim law. In the following reign the heavy demands were lowered.

The scale of demand in the reign of the first Tughluq king has been a matter of dispute. According to R. R. Tripathi, Ghiyasuddin Tughluq fixed the demand at 10 percent of the produce; according to Moreland, the relevant reference in the contemporary history refers to the limit of increase being 10 percent. I. H. Qureshi, on the other hand, holds that except for a few areas the general charge on land was a fifth of the produce, which was maintained from the earliest days of the sultanate until the end of Firuz Shah's reign. Under the Mughal rulers who followed Timur's precedent in charging a third of the produce as land revenue, the scale was raised and Sher Shah, who had seen the increase in the state demand under Babur and Humayun, followed their example.

Apart from the land revenue there were a number of local imposts imposed on various occasions. Orthodox Muslims considered them illegal, and the two monarchs who made an attempt to run the state in accordance with Islamic law, Firuz Tughluq and Aurangzeb, abolished these taxes. These imposts were of ancient origin, however, and most sultans permitted them. And when the rulers abolished them, they were realized by corrupt officials or even by panchayats. A tax which gained importance during Firuz's reign was the charge levied for use of canal water. Firuz was not the first to dig canals, but he was the first monarch to ask Muslim jurists whether an irrigation tax was lawful. The jurists' reply was in the affirmative, and so a 10 percent addition was made to the land revenue in cases where canal water was used for irrigation.

During the early period, when the subcontinent was being conquered and new areas were being occupied, the *ghanimah* (the spoils of war) provided an important source of state income. According to Islamic law, all booty should be collected and a fifth set apart for the state, the rest being distributed among the soldiers. Later the practice was reversed and four-fifths of the booty was appropriated by the state treasury. Firuz's ulama considered it illegal, and Firuz ordered the restoration of the old rate as fixed by the law.

The taxes which had a special religious significance in an Islamic state—zakat and jizya—have been the subject of much controversy, both as regards their nature and their actual imposition during Muslim rule in India. Zakat was imposed only on Muslims; it is not, strictly speaking, a tax in the normal sense, since its payment was an act of piety. Contemporary historians do not record that zakat was levied by the sultans of Delhi, and their silence has been taken to mean that the procedure, common to all Islamic states, was followed.

There were, at any rate, arrangements for the receipt of zakat, paid voluntarily by Muslims as a religious duty, and *Fiqh-i-Firuz Shahi* mentions a separate treasury for zakat. Toward the end of the sultanate, Sikandar Lodi abolished the zakat on grain and it was not renewed by any subsequent sultan. The question of jizya is even more complex, not only because of the lack of clarity in the contemporary records but also because of the strong emotional reaction that has been aroused in discussion concerning it. Under Islamic law, jizya was a tax levied on non- Muslims. This action can be interpreted as an equitable arrangement, since only Muslims had to pay zakat; and, in addition, they alone were liable to military service.

From this point of view it was, in the words of a modern historian, a poll tax levied on non-Muslims "in return for which they received protection of life and property, and exemption for military service." In the Quran jizya is used in the same sense as kharaj, meaning simply a tax, and the fact that early Muslim writers in India preserve this usage without attaching any technical significance to the term suggests that it was not levied during the first conquests. However it was later levied as a poll tax.

As such it was borrowed from Persia, where it was called *gezit*. The failure of the historians to indicate when jizya was paid cannot be taken as an indication, as has been sometimes suggested, that some rulers, notably Alauddin, did not levy jizya because they refused to accord the Hindus the status of zimmis, or protected peoples.

The reason jizya is not more definitely mentioned in the records is probably that for the sake of convenience in rural areas, where the population was overwhelmingly Hindu, jizya and kharaj, the land tax, were realized as a consolidated tax. In the early days of the sultanate the rulers had not built up an elaborate organization, and tax farming—through Hindu middlemen—was the normal means of recovery. It appears unlikely that apart from a comprehensive demand made on a village or a territory, separate or specific realization of jizya was feasible. Where jizya was recovered it was charged in three categories. The wealthy paid four dinars per head per annum, the middle groups two dinars, and the poor, one dinar. Women, children, and those on a bare subsistence level were excused.

Nothing better illustrates the practical approach of the early Muslim rulers to administrative problems than the cautious evolution of their coinage system. Muhammad Ghuri has usually been pictured as an ardent Muslim, zealous in the destruction of Hindu idols and the establishment of Islamic religion. Yet of the three of his coins which are extant, two are mere imitations of earlier Hindu coins, with even the figure of the goddess Lakshmi reproduced, the only distinguishing element being the sovereign's name inscribed in Indian characters. The third coin, though based on the dinar of the Muslim countries, bears a Devanagri legend and the figure of a horseman, much in the tradition of the Hindu coins. This evidence suggests that Muslim rulers, faced with the problem of establishing a new currency among a people unacquainted with the Muslim coinage system, much less with Arabic, disturbed existing usages and practices as little as possible. Not until sixty years after the conquest of Delhi did Balban finally complete the process, begun by Iltutmish, of replacing the Hindu device of the bull and horseman with the sovereign's name in Devanagari characters.

In the early days of the sultanate, the jital, an adaptation of the old dehliwala current before Muslim rule, was the token coin in use. Iltutmish introduced the silver tankah (which was replaced by the rupiah of Sher

Shah and Akbar), but even this innovation, in addition to its indigenous name, was linked to an Indian weight standard. Once the monetary system was established, the rulers introduced changes and improvements in the designs and legends of their coins and made them approximate to the normal Muslim coinage in legend and appearance. Apart from Muhammad Tughluq's unsuccessful effort to introduce token currency of mixed metals, the coins were made of pure metal and the state took precautions to maintain their purity and weight.

THE ARMY

An effective army was a vital feature of the administrative structure of the Islamic state in India; it is significant that Fakhr- i-Mudabbir 's book on government was largely a war manual. Good generalship, disciplined troops, and sound knowledge of warfare techniques had been responsible for the conquest of India, and the ablest of the sultans were aware that continuance of power depended upon these same factors. The steps taken by Balban to keep his troops in good trim, and by Alauddin Khalji to raise and maintain a large standing army, have been described by Barani. The cavalry was the backbone of the army, but the sultans did not confine their organization to the traditional pattern. They soon began to employ elephants on an extensive scale, and Balban considered a single war elephant to be as effective in battle as five hundred horsemen. The foot-soldiers (payaks) were mainly Hindus of the lower classes. The military grades were organized on a decimal basis: a *sar-i-khail* had ten horsemen under him; a *sipah salar* commanded ten sar-i-khails; an *amir* ten sipah salars; a *malik* ten amirs; and a *khan* ten maliks.

The use of naphtha and Greek fire was known from early times. Incendiary arrows and javelins as well as pots of combustibles were hurled against the enemy. The Delhi army used grenades, fireworks, and rockets against Timur, but although there are references to a crude form of cannon, and in the provincial kingdoms of Gujarat and the Deccan this weapon was properly developed, the sultanate of Delhi had not made much progress in the use of artillery. It was the neglect of this weapon which turned the scales against the Delhi forces in the battle of Panipat in 1526.

For maintaining the army, the important functionary within the central government was the *ariz*. Although Fakhr-i-Mudabbir, writing at the beginning of the sultanate, does not emphasize the office of ariz, possibly because it was directly under the wazir, by the time of Balban the position was independent of the wizarat. With the expansion of the empire and the growth of the military side of the government, the importance of the *ariz* increased. Not only did he function sometimes as the general of the forces, but he also acted as the chief recruiting officer and fixed the salary of each recruit. The commissariat was under him, and his office, *diwan-i-arz*, disbursed salaries to the troops. Even the poet Amir Khusrau and the other court officials who held a military rank received salaries from this office. Thus already under the sultanate we can see the beginnings of the Mughal system of placing all public servants on the army pay-list and giving them mansabs.

The *ariz-i-mumalik* was not the commander-in-chief, or even the senior general—the sultan named the generals for different campaigns—but it is not difficult to see in contemporary accounts the power and the importance of the head of the *diwan-i-arz*. Jalaluddin Khalji held this post before he ascended the throne, and the part played by Shaikh Farid, who held the corresponding position of mir bakhshi under Akbar, in securing the accession of Jahangir is well known.

POLITICAL THEORY

The earliest work of importance for the history of political thought of Muslim India was probably intended to be a blueprint for the first Muslim government at Delhi. It was written by a contemporary of Iltutmish, Fakhr-i-Mudabbir, who had spent a considerable part of his life at Lahore, where he met Sultan Muhammad Ghuri and Sultan Qutb-ud-din Aibak, to whom one of his works, a book on genealogies, was presented in 1206. The historical introduction to this work has been translated into English, but his more important work, variously styled *Adab-ul-Muluk wa Kifayat al Mamluk* (Rules for the Kings and the Welfare of the Subjects) or *Adab-ul-Harab wal-Shujaat* (Rules of Warfare and Bravery), has not yet been published in its entirety. It was undoubtedly intended to be a guide for rulers and administrators. The first part of this book deals with the privileges and responsibilities of kings, with separate chapters giving the qualifications and functions of different officers of state. The rest of the book is a manual dealing systematically and in some detail with the art of war. The work was presented to Iltutmish and, as the contemporary histories show, the government organization set up by him corresponded very closely to the structure visualized by Fakhr-i-Mudabbir.

Another early work, of which only an incomplete copy has survived, belongs to a different category. This is *Fatawa-i-Jahandari* (Rulings on Government) by Ziya-ud-din Barani (1285–1357), the greatest of fourteenth-century historians of Muslim India. A political phantasy consisting mainly of a number of discourses purporting to have been addressed by Sultan Mahmud of Ghazni to his successor, it was written after Barani had retired from the royal court in disgrace. It reflects Barani's bitterness against recent trends, his extremism, and his acute class-consciousness. He is bitter not only against the Hindus but also against the Muslim lower classes who, he believed, should not be "taught reading and writing, for plenty of disorders arise owing to the skill of the low-born in knowledge … For on account of their skill, they became governors, revenue collectors, auditors, officers and rulers." If the teachers disregard this edict, and it is discovered that "they have imparted knowledge or taught letters or writing to the low-born, inevitably the punishment for disobedience will be meted out to them."

Fatawa-i-Jahandari represents an individual's views, and made no impression on the course of Indo-Muslim history or political thought. Indeed, it is not referred to by any later writer or historian, and is not included in the fairly full list of Barani's works given by his contemporary, Amir Khurd. The importance of the book is partly personal, as an insight into the mind of Barani, and partly topical, as it gives his views in the context of the political and social situation then prevailing. In spirit and sentiments, *Fatawa-i-Jahandari* is in complete contrast with Fakhr-i-Mudabbir's book, which is throughout inspired by practical idealism, moderation and good sense.

Barani dealt at length with political philosophies of early Muslim rulers, statesmen, and religious leaders in his great historical work, *Tarikh-i-Firuz Shahi*. The long discourses on political affairs and statecraft contained in his book are dramatizations and expansions by an eloquent historian who is also a creative artist. Among the most interesting of these discourses are Nur-ud-din Mubarik Ghaznavi's advice to Iltutmish on the responsibilities of a Muslim "Defender of the Faith" (Din Panah); Balban's views on kingship, and his long lecture to his son, Bughra Khan, the governor of Bengal, on the relationship between the central and the provincial governments; Ahmad Chap's advice to Jalal-ud-din Khalji; Kotwal Ala-ul-Mulk's discourses at Alauddin's consultative assemblies; and Qazi Mughis's views on major political and legal problems of the day. They are presumably coloured by his own predilictions, and should not be treated as verbally authentic, but the views attributed to different rulers and dignitaries are so distinct and so much in character that they may be taken to represent generally the individual views of the persons to whom they are attributed.

To turn from theory to practice, the first comment that should be made on the Islamic state in India is that it was not a theocracy, as sometimes has been suggested. Aside from the question of the relevance of the concept of a theocracy to a society that does not recognize a priesthood, by the time the Delhi Sultanate was established the religious function of the caliph had ceased to be of much significance for the outlying Islamic world.

It is true that a few of the Delhi rulers obtained formal recognition of their titles from the caliph, but this pious legal fiction did not alter the reality. The temporal authority of the caliph at Baghdad dwindled to a mere shadow even within his own territories, and the actual reality of the Indian links with the caliphate may be judged by the fact that occasionally a caliph would have been dead for years before Delhi became aware of the event. The patents obtained by the rulers meant so little that at one time a caliph sent patents simultaneously to both rulers of Delhi and Bengal.

In any case the policy adopted by the early sultans under the stress of circumstances with which they were confronted could scarcely permit the growth of theocracy. Iltutmish, recognizing the essentially secular nature of the sultanate saw that under the conditions prevailing in India, it was not possible for him to be a "Defender of the Faith" except in limited spheres. Balban went even further. In spite of his courtesy to the leading ulama and his personal observance of religious practices, in matters of administration he was guided by the needs of the state, not Islamic law. Alauddin Khalji followed the same policy. "When he became sultan," Barani records, "he came to the conclusion that polity and government are one thing, and the rules and decrees of Islamic law are another. Royal commands belong to the sultan, Islamic legal decrees rest upon the judgment of the qazis and muftis." It was under the Tughluqs, particularly under Firuz, that Muslim jurists gained some recognition, but by then the pattern of Muslim rule in India had become firmly established.

The early ulama, realizing the complexity of the Indian situation and the need for strengthening the Muslim government, accepted Iltutmish's policy. Their lack of power may be judged by the fact that Raziyya ascended the throne of Delhi although Muslim legal opinion is firmly opposed to female rulers; it was left to a much later scholar, Shaikh Abdul Haq Muhaddis (1551–1642), in the more legalistic days of the Mughals, to criticize the selection of Raziyya and express surprise at the action of the contemporary jurists and Shaikhs in confirming it.

There was an equally glaring departure from the correct legal position in Qutb-ud-din Aibak's acceptance as sultan before his manumission. In general, then, the position was that so long as a sultan undertook to safeguard the honour and the observances of Islam, did nothing in open defiance of the principles of shariat, appointed qazis and made arrangements for religious education and observance of religious practices, the ulama did not interfere in the affairs of the state.

The use of the title "sultan" in itself indicates the transition from the quasi-theocratic caliphate to a secular institution. Although the process was implicit in the establishment and administration of the Umayyad caliphate, it was strengthened by the Persian belief in the divine right of kings. This idea, which had become dominant in Baghdad under the later Abbasids, was even more marked at Ghazni. At Delhi, in the early days of the Turkish rule, there was some opposition to it in orthodox Muslim circles, and Iltutmish was almost apologetic about his kingly role. The position completely changed with Balban, who was an advocate of Persian ideas, modelled his court after the Persian style, assumed the title of *zillullah*, and introduced Persian etiquette, court ceremonial, and festivities. With him Persian ideas of monarchy became dominant. The process was facilitated by the fact that the Hindus regarded a king as a representative of divine powers. These theories gave medieval rulers powers which occasionally were used arbitrarily, but a number of checks remained on the absolute exercise of authority by the sultan. For one thing, the Islamic theory curtails the law-making power of a ruler, and although there was nothing to stop an autocratic ruler from becoming a law unto himself, he could do so only in defiance of the system which gave him power. Even the autocratic Alauddin Khalji admitted that administration of justice was the concern of the Muslim jurists.

Equally important was the opinion of the nobility. The sultans consulted their chief nobles and the routine affairs of the state were left to them. Minhaj refers to a dignitary, Amir-i-Majlis, whose duty was to arrange meetings of the sultan's closest associates. Important questions were discussed freely, and some favourite royal schemes (such as Alauddin's proposal to establish a new religion) were ruled out. Together with the influence of public opinion and the natural desire of the sultan to maintain his position, the nobles in this way exercised a check on the theoretical absolutism enjoyed by him.

According to Muslim theory, held particularly by the Sunnis who formed the bulk of the Muslim population in India, election was the accepted method for selecting the ruler. This was rarely observed anywhere, and both Turko-Iranian and Hindu conceptions of sovereignty were opposed to it, but a form of limited election or acceptance was generally followed at Delhi. The oath of allegiance taken by the governors of the provinces, the principal nobles of the capital, and the chief theologians was taken as a symbol of the indirect consent of the mass of the people.

PROVINCIAL ADMINISTRATION

Although contemporary historians give meager details about the provincial governments, it seems a fair inference that the provincial administrative structure did not crystallize until the days of Sher Shah and Akbar. It is possible that this development was facilitated by the establishment of regional kingdoms in the original iqtas (regions) of the Delhi Sultanate. From the earliest period governors were appointed for large *iqtas* which later became provinces, but their responsibilities were mainly the maintenance of peace, establishment and extension of the authority of the government, and recovery of tribute from the Hindu chiefs and others.

The observance of state laws and the maintenance of order depended on the ability and the interest of the individual governor, and in some areas their authority must have been confined to main centers of administration and places easily accessible. The provincial boundaries were shifting and vague, and it was a long time before the territorial units took a stable form. Even the powers of all the governors were not identical. Governors in charge of bigger or more important areas or with special personal claims exercised wider powers than ordinary *muqtis* [=holders of *iqtas*] and were referred to as *walis*.

Before Balban's time, the governors were often semi-independent military chiefs of the territories conquered by them or by their ancestors, but even then many functions remained outside their domain. They were not given authority in religious and judicial affairs, nor were the local intelligence officers under their control. The governor's main concern was military control and revenue collection. With Balban the wizarat became more organized at the center and the provincial diwans were posted from Delhi, and a close check was exercised by the central government over the recovery and transmission of revenue. The provincial *sahib-i-diwan* was appointed by the sultan on the recommendation of the wazir, and submitted detailed statements of provincial accounts to the capital. On the basis of these statements the wazir's department settled the accounts with the *muqtis*. Even in the military sphere the powers of the provincial governors came to be regulated by the presence of the provincial *ariz* who was under the chief ariz at Delhi.

Balban had asserted the authority of the central government over the provincial chiefs, and Alauddin Khalji tried to introduce system and uniformity in the administration of the Doab (the fertile area between the Ganges and the Jamna), the most dependable source of state revenue. Ghiyas-ud-din Tughluq, who had a long experience of provincial administration in the Punjab, tried to improve the administration, but details of his provincial administration have not been recorded. Under his son, Muhammad Tughluq, we get details of the hierarchy of provincial officials, and this possibly follows a pattern introduced earlier. The empire consisted of twenty-four provinces divided into a number of *shiqs*, or rural districts. The next smallest unit after the shiq was the *pargana*, or group of villages. In a pargana and in the villages the old Hindu organization continued. The head of each pargana was a *chaudhari*, while a *Muqaddam* or a *mukhiya* was the head man of the village. The most important feature of Muslim administration in India was the acceptance of the local autonomy enjoyed by rural areas. This policy had been followed by Muhammad ibn Qasim in the earliest days of Muslim rule in the Sind and was maintained by the sultans of Delhi. Qutb-ud-din Aibak, who originally handed back Ajmer to a son of Prithvi Raj, first adopted the policy of appointing Hindu officers for the administration of the country. "The Hindu chief played such an important role in the rural life of the period that to many he was the government, whereas the sultan was almost a mythical figure."

The position of the nobility and the officers was so dominant in the early period that Minhaj, the historian of the period, devotes more space to an account of the principal officers of the realm than to the sultans. The existence of this bureaucracy made possible a large degree of stability in administration, and even in the periods of decline the succession of dynasties at Delhi was not usually reflected in changes of government at the local level.

Emphasis on administrative stability during the sultanate should not be taken as an indication that the period was peaceful or that normal judicial processes were always respected by either the sultans or their officials. Maintenance of control in a conquered area requires force, and, in addition, the ceaseless struggle for power that went on made violence commonplace. The smallest incident could be turned into a pretext for the drawing of the sword and the shedding of blood. Nor was violence confined to the cruel and heartless. Rulers such as Balban were not deficient in a sense of justice or in political ability, but these qualities did not deter him from severe punishments and free spilling of blood. At times a sense of justice and concern for the public welfare seemed to militate against human kindness. Once the deterrent theory of punishment was adopted and carried to extremes, all other human considerations gave way before it. In vain did the religious lawyers and intellectuals try to curb the extreme punishments inflicted by the sultans. Qazi Mughis argued before Alauddin Khalji that his punishments were unauthorized and opposed to Islam, and the historian Barani told Muhammad bin Tughluq that human life could be taken only for eight specific crimes, but the autocratic sultans listened unmoved.

Not only was human life held in little esteem, but there were abhorrent cases of torture and mutilation. In this Muhammad bin Tughluq, who was a highly educated monarch and enjoyed the company of intellectuals and philosophers, was the worst offender. Some of the punishments meted out by him—for example to his cousin Gurshashp—are truly revolting. The Moorish traveller Ibn Battuta wrote of him: "Notwithstanding all his modesty, his sense of equality and justice, and his extraordinary liberality and kindness to the poor, he had immense daring to shed blood. His gate was hardly ever free from the corpse of a man who had been executed. And I used to see frequently a number of people killed at the gate of the royal palace and the corpses abandoned there. ... The sultan used to punish all wrongs whether big or small and he would spare neither the men of learning and probity, nor those of high descent. Every day hundreds of people in chains with their hands fastened to the neck and their feet tightened were brought into the council hall. Those who were to be killed were killed and those who were to be tortured were tortured and those who were to be beaten were beaten. ... May God save us from calamity."

It is true that these punishments were reserved for treason, and it is also true that conditions in the medieval ages in other parts of the world were not very much better, but the position in Muslim India in this respect seems to have worsened distinctly during the hundred years or so following the death of Iltutmish. Possibly the instances of brutality and cruelty during the sultanate in the thirteenth and fourteenth centuries reflect the impact of the Mongols; certainly the extremes of ruthless severity associated with Muhammad Tughluq or even with Balban and Alauddin Khalji, did not exist in the days of Muhammad ibn Qasim, Aibak, and Iltutmish.

STRUCTURE OF GOVERNMENT

Fakhr-i-Mudabbir lists the principal dignitaries of the state as follows: wazir, *wakil-i-dar, amir-i-dad, amir-i-hajib, mushrif, mustaufi*, and *sahib-i-barid*. The *wakil-i-dar* (not to be confused with the wakil- i-sultanat of the Sayyid dynasty and the wakil-i-mutliq of the Mughals) was the controller of the household. The *amir-i-dad* (literally lord of justice) was the most important judicial dignitary. The *amir-i-hajib* is often designated as the chief chamberlain, but this does not fairly describe the functions and duties of this officer. He was the master of ceremonies at the court; no one could enter the royal presence without being introduced by one of his assistants, and all petitions were presented to the sultan through him. The post, therefore, was one of great prestige and was reserved for trusted nobles. One holder of this post, Balban, was the most powerful noble of his day. The *mushrif* was the accounts officer responsible for income, and the *mustaufi* for expenditure. The *sahib-i-barid* was in charge of communications and intelligence.

The chief minister of the sultan was called the wazir. Fakhr- i-Mudabbir considered the wazir a "partaker in sovereignty" and recommended that in his own technical domain he must be left free by the monarch. He describes the normal functions of the wazir in the following passage: "The kings know well how to lead expeditions, conquer countries, give rewards, and shine in the assembly or battlefield; but it is the domain of the wazir to make a country prosperous, to accumulate treasures, to appoint officials, to ask for accounts, to arrange for the stock-taking of the commodities in the karkhanas, and the census of horses, camels, mules, and other animals, to assemble and pay the troops and artisans, to keep the people satisfied, to look after the men of piety and fame and to give them stipends, to take care of the widows and the orphans, to provide for the learned, to administer the affairs of the people, and to organize the business of the state." This was the position in early days, when the wazir was in charge of the entire government, both the civil and the military departments and the functions which were later entrusted to Sadr-e-Jahan, but this arrangement underwent drastic changes in the light of practical experience. In view of the importance of the office, and to illustrate the administrative experiments that were carried on under the sultanate, it will be useful to sketch the history of the *wizarat* [=vazir-ship].

Although few details are known about administrative arrangements during the brief rule of Qutubuddin Aibak, presumably the practice of combining civil and military offices (which was introduced by the Ghaznavids at Lahore, and was continued under the Ghuris) remained in operation. This was also the position under Iltutmish. His first wazir, Nizam-ul-Mulk Junaidi, was in charge of all sections of the government, and in addition to his civil duties, was occasionally entrusted with military commands. During the troubled reign of Raziyya and her successors, Khwaja Muhazzab-ud-din used his influence with the weak rulers and his own capacity for intrigue to consolidate his position by taking all power out of the hands of the nobles. An attempt was made to curb the wazir 's powers by the creation of the post of naib (deputy of the realm), but this was unsuccessful and the wazir continued to be all-powerful. Muhazzab's opponents, therefore, joined forces and had him assassinated.

His death marks the close of a period in the history of the wizarat. The provincial governors and other administrative officers would not permit an individual selected for his ability in office to obtain so much power. His successors were selected for their docility. Balban, even before he became deputy, was more powerful than the wazir, and when he became sultan, he took away the military functions of the wizarat. The *rawat-i-arz* (the muster- master, who was originally in charge of the finances and records of military personnel) was made independent of the wazir.

Some fifty years later, Ghiyasuddin Tughluq made an even more interesting experiment. He created a board of three ex- wazirs, with the senior having the high title of malik-ul-wuzara (chief minister). Ghiyas consulted them in all important matters, but the routine work of the wizarat was carried on by Malik Shadi, his son-in-law.

With the general policy of the Tughluqs to approximate standard Muslim practice in all matters and with Muhammad Tughluq's preference for Arab and Persian ways, we notice a reversion to the earlier character of the wizarat. Khwaja Jahan, though essentially a civil servant, was occasionally entrusted with military duties. This change is more marked under Firuz, whose wazir fulfilled the Arab notion of an all-powerful wazir. Khan Jahan, a Hindu from Telingana who had accepted Islam at the hands of Hazrat Nizamuddin Auliya, exercised both civil and military powers. His position may be judged by Firuz's frequent remark that Khan Jahan was virtually the sultan of Delhi. After his death in 1372, his son became wazir and followed his father 's ideas for a long period, but this led to jealousy, and in 1387 he was killed in a quarrel with a noble. This also marked the end of Firuz Tughluq's power and the decline of the dynasty. Khwaja Jahan Sarvar-ul-Mulk, the wazir (1390–1394) of Muhammad Shah, exercised authority both in civil and military spheres, but realizing that the sultanate was tottering, he had one of the military leaders made wakil-i-sultanat, and he himself left for the eastern provinces, where he carved out a kingdom for himself in Jaunpur.

With the accession to power of the Lodi dynasty, the wizarat lost some of its importance, for Buhlul Lodi, with his tribal conception of kingship did not establish an organized wizarat. Sikandar Lodi, however, saw the impossibility of applying this tribal conception to a huge territory and had a regular diwan and a wizarat. His wazir, however, seems to have confined himself to civil work.

The developments that took place under the Mughals will be described later, but essentially their wizarat was based on Balban's model, with the holder of the office confined to civil duties. This meant that the wazir in the Indian Islamic state had less power than that assigned to him by Muslim political theorists, but the system worked fairly well. Indian tradition and the needs of the Islamic rulers favoured strong monarchs. It is probably true that the people, insofar as they had a preference, preferred an absolute monarch to an absolute wazir.

9

Socio-economic Conditions in Delhi Sultanate

SOCIAL CONDITION IN DELHI SULTANS PERIOD

As the rigid Islamic law could not be applied in India, the Sultans of Delhi allowed the Hindus to live in India as Zimmis which means people living under a contract as second rate citizens, Jizya was imposed on them. It was fairly high and amounted to 48, 24 and 12 silver coins for the rich, the average and poor Hindus respectively. Monks, beggars, blind men and children were exempted. Originally, Brahmans were also exempted but Firuz Tughlaq imposed Jizya even on them. The imposition of Jizya was considered as a badge of inferiority. The peculiar thing about the payment of Jizya was that the payers of that tax had to pay it personally to the Collector and behave humbly and obsequiously at the time of payment. The idea behind the payment of Jizya was that on account of sheer economic pressure and discriminatory treatment at the time of payment, the bulk of the Hindu's would one day be obliged to become Muslims, but that did not happen.

In addition to the payment of Jizya, the Hindus were not allowed to worship in open and carry on religious propaganda. Many legal disabilities were imposed on the Hindus. Their evidence in a court of law against Muslims was not considered worth anything. In social matters, Hindus were not given the respect due to their rank or position in life. During the reigns of Ala-ud-Din Khalji, Firuz Tughlaq and Sikandar Lodi, the Hindus were not allowed to put on fine clothes, ride on horseback or even to possess good arms. Sometimes, they were not allowed to chew betel or to put on the same kind of dress as the Muslims did. Hindus were forbidden from building new temples or repairing the old ones. Not only during war but even during peace-time, Hindu temples were razed to the ground and their images were broken to pieces.

Firuz Tughlaq writes that at a time of peace. He rode to the village of Maluh where Hindus had, gathered to worship by the side of a tank and a fair was being held. The Sultan not only stopped the worship and destroyed the idols but also ordered the worshippers to be put to death. Firuz Tughlaq also razed the Keshav Deva temple at Mathura to the ground at a time when there was no rebellion or disturbance of peace. When the Hindus rebuilt it, it was destroyed by Sikandar Lodi. Many sacred shrines of the Hindus in Northern India were destroyed by the Muslim rulers and their broken images and statues can be seen in various Indian museums. Mosques, mausoleums and tombs were built on the sites of the ancient Hindu shrines out of the material of those very shrines. Some of the Sultans like Firuz Tughlaq and Sikandar Lodi made it the chief object of their policy to convert the Hindus to Islam by offering them many inducements and exerting all kinds of pressure on them. Firuz Tughlaq announced that whoever embraced Islam and repeated the Kalima would be exempt from Jizya. He himself writes that his policy was successful and many Hindus became Muslims. The Muslims considered it as their duty to propagate Islam and to convert Hindus to their religion. Some of them offered temptations to the Hindus to become Muslims and some of them used force in their Jihad (Holy war) against Hinduism. There were many Mullahs who called for such a Jihad against the Hindus. The result was that the Hindus during the Sultanate period did not enjoy religious freedom, liberty of conscience worship.

No individual in the Sultanate was allowed to speak a word against the Prophet of Islam or point out any defect in Islam. Those who were guilty of such offences were put to death. In the reign of Sikandar Lodi, a Brahman maintained that both Hinduism and Islam were true religions and he was put to death. Islam did not allow the conversion of Muslim to Hinduism or the re-conversion of Hindu converts to Islam. Those who were guilty of seducing Muslims from their religion were put to death. A similar punishment was given to those who reconverted Hindu converts to Islam. The only Muslim ruler who showed exceptional toleration in this respect was Zain-ul-Abidin of Kashmir. Sometimes, Muslim rulers converted Hindus to Islam in large numbers. Sikandar, the ruler of

Kashmir, converted thousands of Hindus to Islam and expelled those who refused to become Muslims. Jalaluddin of Bengal (1414-1430) forcibly converted hundreds of Hindus and persecuted the rest. The same was done by Firuz Tughlaq and Sikandar Lodi.

Most of the Muslims in India were very orthodox in their religion and most of them were Sunnis. They considered the Shias also as their enemies like the Hindus. They suppressed the Shias, Karmanis, Mahadavis and other religious sects who were not Sunnis. Their leaders were persecuted in every way. Many of them were put to death. The Shia rulers of Bijapur and Golconda were persecuted. Firuz Tughlaq particularly persecuted the Shias. Their religious books were burnt by him in public. No Shia was taken in the service of the state. When the Karmanians revolted during the reigns of Iltutmish and Razia, they were put down ruthlessly. Many Sufi saints were also persecuted.

According to the law of Islam, the Hindus were not entitled to any kind of religious toleration. However, practical considerations compelled Mohammed-bin-Qasim, the conqueror of Sind and Multan, to accord to the Hindus of those provinces the same treatment as was given to the Christians and Jews in Arabia and other parts of the Caliphate. This practice was also followed by the Sultans to Delhi. However, as the Quran and the Hadis did not permit the Muslim rulers to allow Hindus to live under a Muslim Government but to give them the choice between Islam or death, the Ulama pressed the Sultans from time to time that the Quranic law should be enforced in India and the Hindus should be compelled either to embrace Islam or be butchered in cold blood.

There are many instances of such orthodox Ulama making this demand on the Sultans from time to time. During the reign of Iltutmish the Ulama made a united demand that the Hindus should be confronted with the choice of either embracing Islam or facing death. The Sultan referred the matter to his Wazir, Nizam-ul-Mulk Junnaidi. The Wazir agreed with the interpretation of law made by the Ulama but made the following recommendation : "At the moment India has newly been conquered and the Muslims are so few that they are like salt in a large dish. If the above orders are applied to the Hindus, it is possible that they might combine and a general confusion might ensue and the Muslims would be too few in number to suppress this general confusion, However, after a few years when in the capital and in the regions and the small towns, the Muslims are well established and the troops are larger, it will be possible to give the Hindus the choice of death or Islam."

In the reign of Ala-ud-Din Khalji, Qazi Mughis-ud-Din of Bayana made a similar demand in these words, "God has himself commanded their (Hindus) complete degradation in as much as the Hindus are the deadliest foes of the Prophet, The Prophet has said that they should either embrace Islam or they should be slain or enslaved and their property should be confiscated to the state. No one except the great Dr. Abu Hanifa allows the imposition of the Jizya upon the Hindus, while other scholars are of the opinion that there is no other alternative but death or Islam." It is clear from above that the Quranic law could not be enforced completely on above that the Quranic law could not be enforced completely on account of the vast numerical superiority of the Hindus and their military and economic strength. However, writers like Barani continued to lament that the fundamental Islamic law were ignored by the Sultans of Delhi.

Many causes were responsible for the conversion of Hindus to Islam. Some Hindus who came into contact with all powerful and prosperous Muslims, joined their faith. Some Hindus became Muslims to secure good jobs in the state. Some were tempted to become Muslims on account of the favours offered to them. Many Hindus were made Muslims through sheer force. Many Hindus of low castes became Muslims in order to raise their status, but their number was not large. There were very few Hindus who became Muslims as a result of the influence of the principles of Islam. One important reason was that there was at that time bitter hatred among Hindus against the Muslims who bad persecuted them and also humiliated them. There were many orthodox Hindus and they were so much devoted to their religion that the question of their embracing Islam could not arise. Although for about five centuries the Hindus and Muslims lived near one another they remained separate. The Hindus had to suffer terribly due to religious and political causes but they continued to oppose the Muslims. There is hardly any example of this period when a Hindu family established a matrimonial alliance with a royal family. In the 14th century, Tughril Shah forcibly married the daughter of Ranamal Bhatti and the consequences were disastrous. Feelings of enmity were aroused in the minds of the Hindus against the Muslims.

Not only the Sultans but other Muslims also considered it as their religious duty to convert Darul Harb (Land of the Kafirs) into Darul Islam (Land of the Muslims). Those Muslim rulers who tried to convert Hindus to Islam were praised by Muslim historians who belonged to the Ulama class. Instructions were issued to convert the Hindus to Islam. One of the reasons why that could not be done was that most of the time of the Sultans was spent in fighting against the Mongols and also in suppressing rebellions in various parts of the country.

There was a decline in the character of the Muslims. The Muslim invaders were brave people but as a result of their stay in India with a lot of money, power and luxury, they deteriorated. The early Muslim soldiers were prepared to sacrifice their lives for the sake of Islam and were ready to fight battles for the conquest of India. However, the luxurious life in India took away their courage and bravery. Too much of drinking and beautiful women finished their bravery. They lost their spirit of self-reliance. They lost self-respect and courage. Instead of being an asset, they became a burden to the state. They began to shun hard work and fighting. They became big landlords. They bad to pay only one-tenth of the produce to the state. As they got too much of wealth without exertion, their decline started. During the Sultanate period, the Mahayan form of Buddhism was prominent. Many scholars were born during this period. They put emphasis on Bhakti and not Nirvana. They acknowledged Buddha as the highest power. They worshipped Bodhisattavas. Buddhism had great influence in North-West and Central India. They had to struggle every day against the Brahman Pandits and philosophers. As a result of that, their influence declined.

There were four important Sampradaya, of Vaishnavism. Their names were Shri Sampradaya, Brahm Sampradaya, Rudra Sampradaya and Sanakadi Sampradaya, Ramanuja propagated Shri Sampradaya. His followers believed in Advaitvad. The original Guru of Brahm Sampradaya was Brahma but it was propagated by Madhavacharya. Its followers were Dvaitvadis. The followers of Rudra Sampradaya were Advaitvadi. It was propagated by Vishnuswami and Vallabhacharya. The followers of Sanakadi Sampradaya were Dvaita Advaitvadi. It was propagated by Nimbarkacharya.

There were many Sampradayas of Saivism. The important among them were Pasupat, Kapalik, Virsaiv, Shiv Sidhanta, Lingayat etc. Saivism was a very old religion and it spread in all parts of India. Many Sampradayas came into existence. The Saivas collected a lot of knowledge. They started the cult of Vam-Marg. When the Muslims attacked India, at that time Vijrayani Buddhists and Kapalik Saivas were spread from Bihar to Assam and Kalinga. As a result of the preachings of Sankaracharya, Buddhism lost its hold. Sankar gave Gyan Marg for the Pandits and worship for the ordinary people. In this way, he won over people belonging to all walks of life. There were some pandits who regarded the views of Sankar as not attractive and they put emphasis on Bhakti.

The religious order to which the Yogis belonged was known by different names : Gorakh-Panthi (followers of the path prescribed by Gorakhnath), Nath and Kanphata (split-eared). The literal meaning of the word Nath is master. The Yogis regarded Siva as Adi Nath (Original Master). There was nine human Naths who were really superior Yogis. To that category belonged Matsyendranath and Gorakhnath who were supposed to have attained immortality and as a consequence became objects of worship. The term Kanphata had reference to the practice of splitting the cars which tradition ascribed to Gorakhnath. A Siddha was a Yogi who had attained the stage of perfection, a semi-divine stage, through the practice of Yoga. The Siddhas were supposed to have acquired "extended life and miraculous powers." Usually, the Yogis used the sacred thread. A secular Yogi was known as Rawal. He earned his living by begging, fortune-telling, singing and similar practices. There was another sect of Yogis known as Aipanthis, i.e worshippers of the Mother Goddess. A female disciple of Gorakhnath named Bimla Devi was called Mai.

The Yogis were primarily devotees of Siva in the Bhairava form which represented his most terrible aspect, although some attention was paid to Vishnu. Sometimes Siva and Gorakhnath were identified. Gorakhnath was worshipped as a manifestation of Shiva in some Shaivite temples. In general, the Yogis worshipped many gods and goddesses of the Hindu pantheon. They also worshipped nine Naths and 94 Siddhas living in the Himalayas.

The Kanphata order admitted not only Sudras and low caste recruits but also Muslims. Caste restrictions were not observed in respect of inter-dining among the Hindu Yogis) but the Muslim Yogis took their food separately. Two principal vows had to be taken and those were to live by begging and to maintain celibacy.

The Gorakh-panthis succeeded in evolving an integrated system of thought and practice. They drew a clear line of distinction between a Yogi and a philosopher. Intellectual speculation had no relevance for a Yogi. He aimed at direct spiritual experience of the Truth on a supra-intellectual plane of consciousness. He devoted himself to the practice of various courses of self-discipline until he reached the stage of Samadhi which conferred upon a Yogi all that was worth knowing and attaining. It destroyed all fetters of Karma and all imperfections such as ignorance, ego, attachment, aversion and lust of life. That stage was called Nirvana.

The Yogi view of the world was not pessimistic. The world is not the creation of any Satanic force. It is not to be discarded as an evil. The constitution of the individual body is very important in the Yoga system.

The rigorous disciple of the Yoga system was very hard for the ordinary seeker. Hence, it degenerated to the level of self-delusion or even conscious fraud. Hatha Yoga became popular because it was supposed to bring miraculous powers which could be used for worldly purposes.

The view of the Muslim rulers in India was that the Hindus were their bitter enemies and were always scheming and organising instructions against them. Hence, they left no stone unturned to suppress them. The Hindus were made to pay high taxes and those were collected with great severity. Ala-ud-Din Khalji exacted 50% of their produce from the Hindus of the Doad. Most of the Hindus became poor and they had to struggle very hard to make their both ends meet. Their standard of living fell. They got no job in the state. Very few opportunities were given 'to them for rise in life. Sir Jadunath Sarkar has criticised in very strong words the treatment meted to the Hindus during the Sultanate period. The circumstances were such that there was no scope for the development and progress of the Hindus. Dr. Ishwari Prasad does not agree with his view. He admits that the Hindus were very badly treated during the Sultanate period and they had to face many difficulties even to save their religion. It is also true that they had to pay high taxes and were also humiliated. However, Dr. Ishwari Prasad maintains that the Hindus did their best to oppose the Muslims in every way. Moreover, all the Muslim rulers were not bad. It was during this period that many Hindu philosophers, writers, poets, saints and warriors appeared. It was during this period that we bad saints like Ramananda, Chatanya Mahaprabhu and Guru Nanak. Many Hindu poets added to the literature of India during this period. In spite of the various invasions, the Hindu did not Use their spirit. In spite of Muslim victories, Hindu culture continued to flourish. Their religion and philosophy continued to develop and grow. The writings of the Hindu scholars and saints of that period are a part of the great literature of the Hindus.

The Sufis challenged the orthodoxy of the Sunni. They believed in attaining God through love and devotion. The Muslims did not like the Sufis on account of their views. Most of the Sufis set up their own orders under their Shaikhs or Pirs. They spent all their time in devotion and prayers. The view of the Sufis was that the Ulama had not interpreted the Quran correctly and had given tip the principle of brotherhood of Islam. The Sufis and Ulama opposed each other. The Ulama criticised the Sufis on account of their broadmindedness. The Sufis called the, Ulama as opportunists who ran after the Sultans to win over favours. The Sufis did not revolt. They believed that good days were coming. The Sufis Firs were respected by the Hindus.

There were many similarities between the Sufis and saints of the Bhakti movement. Both of them put emphasis on the oneness of God and the desirability of devotion to God. They put all the emphasis on love to meet God. They realised the necessity of a Guru or Pir to achieve God. However, the Bhakti saints did not believe in the mysticism of the Sufis. They did not believe in remaining away from society and the common man. They wanted to solve the problems of the people and improving their condition.

Before the coming of the Muslims, there were Hindus, Buddhists and Jains in India. They bad different ways of living, worship and action. During the period, the influence of Jainism had declined. It was confined to Rajasthan and North-West parts of India. During this period, many Jain scholars wrote many books on their religion. It is true that further decline of Jainism was stopped but they could not complete with Mahayanism, Saivism and Vaishnavism.

RELIGIOUS POLICY OF DELHI SULTANATE

During the entire period of the Delhi Sultanate, Islam remained the religion of the state. The Sultans performed a religious duty along with his political obligation while administering the state. His duty was to convert the non Muslim territory to a Muslim land. Sultans like Firoz Tughlaq and Sikandar Lodi left no stone unturned to propagate Islam among their subjects. But to rulers like Ala-ud-din Khilji and Muhammad Bin Tughlaq, this was a secondary duty. All the rulers of the Delhi Sultanate pursued a discriminatory policy between their Muslim and non Muslim subjects the majority of who were Hindus.

In matters of land revenue the Muslims had to pay less than the Hindus. Even the Hindu traders paid double trade tax as compared to the Muslim traders. Foreign Muslims alone were entitled high offices of the state while the Hindus and even non-Muslims were not considered for them. The Hindus were unfavourably discriminated in the dispensation of justice. They had to pay the religious tax, Jizya. Restrictions were imposed on the religious pilgrimages of the Hindus. Hindu educational institutions, temples and images were destroyed, mosques were raised in their places and the religion of the Hindus was disrespected during the rule of most of the Sultans. Thus, the Hindus were not only referred to as Zimmis and Kafirs but also were treated as such in practice.

The period of the Delhi Sultanate was the period of struggle between the Hindus and the Muslims and they contested fiercely against each other both in politics and religion. The policy of the Sultans was that of religious intolerance. The religious propaganda adopted by the Sultans was mainly to defend their established empire in India. The Sultans acted according to the spirit of their age and that was natural and practical for them. But no Sultan of the Sultanate could realise that it was impossible to convert all Hindus to Islam or to destroy the strength of Hinduism by sheer physical force. This kept them devoid of loyalty and cooperation of the majority of their subjects. Though the religious administration of the Sultans suffered from certain defects yet it fulfilled the need of the time.

CULTURE UNDER DELHI SULTANATE

The culture of the Muslims was for long either an exotic one or a class culture confined to a certain group that basked in the sun-shine of the King's favour. The monotheism of Islam led to the birth of a similar movement among the Hindus. Certain aspects of 'Bhakti' movement were coloured by the iconoclastic character of Islam. Kabir was the most representative figure. Muslim architecture, painting and crafts had a certain originality which enriched the fabric of Indian culture. In the literary field the development of Urdu Language and the birth of historical writings are some of the colossal Muslim contributions to Indian culture. The dress, manners and food especially among the aristocracy in Northern India, underwent a certain reorientation in following the Muslims.

RELIGION UNDER DELHI SULTANATE

Religious scenario during the time of the Delhi Sultanate was an integral part of their culture. During the period of the Sultanate all ancient religious sect in India like the Vedic religion, Buddhism, Jainism, Vaishnavism, Shaivism and different Tantric sects existed in different forms.

LITERATURE UNDER DELHI SULTANATE

Literature during the period of Delhi Sultanate was produced not only in Sanskrit and Persian but also in other religious languages. The Sultans of Delhi and the rulers of provincial dynasties provided shelter to various scholars who produced historical, religious literature in other fields of knowledge. Al-beruni was a reputed Persian scholar at the time of Mahmud of Ghazni. The Hindu rulers of Warangal and the Vijayanagara Empire provided encouragement to Sanskrit literature. The one novelty of this period in literary field was the beginning of literature in different Indian regional languages.

ART AND ARCHITECTURE UNDER DELHI SULTANATE

Art and architecture made progress during the period the Delhi Sultanate. The architecture of the period of Delhi Sultanate can be categorised into the imperial style of architecture, the provincial style of architecture and the Hindu architecture. As a whole this period witnessed the growth of that style of architecture which was called the Indo-Islamic style of architecture. Thus, the culture under the dominion of the Delhi Sultanate was wide and varied and several factors which were responsible to shape the culture of that period.

SOCIETY OF DELHI SULTANATE

During the reign of the Delhi Sultanate, the society was divided into different sections. After the advent of the Muslims, the society constituted of the foreign Muslims, the Indian Muslims and the Hindus. Among them, foreign Muslims constituted the ruling class. The next part was that of the Indian Muslims who were either converted to Islam or were the descendants of the converted Muslims. The Hindus also formed the part of the society at that period and were divided among themselves on the basis of castes. The foreign Muslims enjoyed the most respected and the privileged section of the society. All high offices of the state were kept reserved for them. They yielded great influence in society and administration. But the foreign Muslims were not united. They belonged to different nationalities such as the Persians, the Afghans, the Arabs, the Turks, and the Abyssianians etc. The Turks claimed and maintained their superiority over all others up to the thirteenth century. Their position broke after the Khiljis captured the power of the state.

The foreign Muslims looked down upon the Indian Muslims because most of them were converted to Islam from among low-caste Hindus. The foreign Muslims regarded them neither of blue blood nor conquerors of this country. Therefore Indian Muslims were not given equal status with foreign Muslims either in society or in administration. During the total period of the Sultanate only few Indian Muslims enjoyed high offices of the state. The caste-system of the Hindus affected the Muslims, especially the Indian Muslims. They continued to maintain divisions among themselves on the basis of their previous castes. Thus, both the foreign and Indian Muslims were divided among themselves on the basis of their different nationalities and birth. The Muslims were also divided on the basis religious sect, education and professions. Sunnis and the Shiahs differed from each other on the basis of sects while soldiers and scholars were divided among each other on the basis of their professions. There was another class, the Ulema who constituted the religious community among the Muslims and claimed pre-eminence over all others.

The slave system was prevalent among the Muslims and the Hindus and slaves were sold am purchased in open market. The slaves were treated well though their property and lives were the property of their masters. The slaves of the Muslims were better off as compared to the slaves of the Hindus. The Sultans and nobles kept slaves in huge numbers, provided education and gave them training and opportunity to rise in their lives so that many of them rose to the position of prominence in the state. The women in the Hindu society enjoyed respect in the family and participated in the religious ceremonies. They received education and many of them had acquired scholarly fame. Yet, in general their status had deteriorated in the society and they suffered from many social evils.

There was no widow remarriage and the widows either became sati at the pyre of their husbands or passed their lives as women-hermits. The Purdah system and child marriages adversely affected the education and position of women in the society. Devadasi system was another social evil which was prevalent among the Hindus. Muslim women did not enjoy a respectable status in the society. Polygamy was extensively prevalent among the Muslims. Every Muslim had a right to keep at least four wives while the rich among them kept hundreds or thousands as wives or slaves. Purdah system was strictly observed among Muslim women. They were devoid of education because of this social custom. Generally the Hindus were vegetarians and the Muslims were non vegetarians. Among the Muslims, the Sufis, or the people who were under their influence avoided eating meat. Both the Hindus and the Muslims built good houses for themselves where all comforts of life were procured. There was a marked progress in the use of clothing and ornaments. All sorts of clothes made of silk, cotton and wool were used by the people and there was improvement in them. Both the Hindus and the Muslims liked to use ornaments. All types of ornaments from head to toe were used by both males and females and were made not only of gold and silver but of pearls, diamonds and precious stones. The people engaged themselves in all sorts of entertainments. Different sports such as hunting, duels among men, fighting among animals, horse-polo etc. were their usual entertainments. Fairs and religious festivals were also common among both Hindus and the Muslims.

The Hindus and the Muslims influenced each other in many fields. Historians have differed regarding the relations between the Hindus and Muslims during the period of the Sultanate. The Muslim rulers over their Hindu subjects according to Islamic-laws, and in no way tried to shape their administration and judicial system on a secular basis. Therefore, the Hindus could not expect to get justice or equality from their Muslim masters. Besides, except Ala-ud-din Khilji, all Sultans accepted the influence of the Ulema in matters of the state. It is acceptable that the common people wished to live a peaceful life and they had no religious or political ambition.

The religious preachers and saints of the Bhakti movement during this period and the saints who believed and preached religious tolerance belonged mostly to the class of the common people. The policy of religious intolerance of Sultans and the privileged position of the ruling class and the Ulema did not allow a happy synthesis between the culture and values of the Hindus and the Muslims and did not permit cordial relation between the two. Thus the culture, religion and the people had great impact in shaping the society of the Delhi Sultanate.

SOCIETY AND CULTURE UNDER THE SULTANATE

While the historians of the Delhi Sultanate have left full accounts that make possible a reconstruction of military and political affairs, unfortunately no such records exist for social and economic history. Scattered comments in the histories, however, as well as such works as the Travels of Ibn Battuta, the narrative poems of Amir Khusrau, and the table talk of Hazrat Nizamuddin, illuminate the social life of the time.

Muslim society during the period was dominated by the Turkish rulers and nobles who sought to maintain their position not only against non-Muslims or the Muslims of indigenous origin, but also against other non-Turkish immigrants, or over other Turks whose long separation from the Turkish homeland marked them off themselves. It can be argued that most of the sultans and nobles were ultimately Turkish in origin, even though they bear different designations, but the first hundred years of the Delhi Sultanate was clearly a period of Turkish supremacy: rule by groups that regarded themselves as Turks, and heirs of a definite cultural and historical tradition. During this time they produced not only three great rulers, Iltutmish, Alauddin Khalji, and Balban, but also a great poet—Amir Khusrau.

One of the most interesting features of Islamic society during the sultanate is the long struggle of Indian Muslims—Hindu and Buddhist converts or their descendants—to assert themselves. They tried to gain power in the middle of the thirteenth century, but Balban and other Turkish nobles were too powerful for them. Their position gradually improved under the Khaljis, and under the Tughluqs a distinct change can be seen. Ghiyasuddin Tughluq had an Indian mother, Muhammed Tughluq appointed a Hindu as the governor of Upper Sind, and the dominant personality of the reign of Firuz Tughluq was Khan-i-Jahan, a Hindu convert from Telangana.

Although it took a long time for the Indo-Muslims to reach positions of power, local usages and customs influenced social life and behaviour at an early period. The Indian *pan* (betel leaf) soon became popular among the Muslims; the use of spices for seasoning food became common; and standard Muslim dishes such as pilau were transformed. The newcomers also adopted Indian headgear; but, more significantly, religious ceremonies, especially those related to marriage and death, showed a definite Indian influence. The popularity of music, as well as its forms, reflected the local atmosphere.

The lives of the Muslim upper classes, especially in Delhi, were modelled on those of their Turkish and Persian counterparts, with the sports of a society that valued the horse—polo, riding, racing—being the chief outdoor amusements; these were the prerogatives of the rich. All classes enjoyed chess and backgammon, although the more orthodox regarded them with disapproval. Most of the Muslims, at least during the earliest period of the sultanate, were city dwellers, many of them attached to the garrisons. For this reason there was a good deal of communal life among the ordinary people. There were, for example, bakeries instead of individual kitchens, and hammams (Turkish baths) in the larger towns.

As for the Hindus, their social life was relatively unchanged, although during military operations they suffered losses in property and life. Even when the harsh laws of war gave place to peace, the Hindus were burdened by certain handicaps. The loss of sovereignty itself was a major loss, especially in the case of the Brahmans and the Kshatriyas. The sultanate period was more difficult for them than any other period of Muslim rule. The liberal and conciliatory policy adopted by Muhammad ibn Qasim had given place to a new relationship, and the integration of the Hindu population into the political and administrative structure was not to come about until later. Muslim conquest of Sind and Multan and even of Lahore and Peshawar had not led to the same tensions and conflicts which followed their domination over the heart of Aryavarta. Even the indirect effect of the Mongol invasion of Muslim lands led to a stiffening of attitude, as the Muslim refugees, who had suffered so much at the hands of the pagan Mongols, were not disposed to be friendly towards the non-Muslims of India.

All these factors make the sultanate a period of tensions and conflicts. The theory of Turkish racial superiority which held sway during the rule of early Slave kings was not favourable to the employment of Hindus—or even indigenous Muslims—in high civil and military appointments, as was the case under the Arabs in Sind or even under the Ghaznavids. It would, however, be wrong to think that the Hindus were completely excluded from service. In rural areas the Hindu landed aristocracy still occupied a position of prestige and power, and the muqaddams, the chaudharis, and the khuts had important roles in the administration.

The land system was not altered, and the Hindu peasant must have led much the same kind of life as he did before the coming of the Muslims. Trade and commerce also remained in Hindu control, for to the Muslim invader from Central Asia, the complex Hindu banking system would be unfamiliar and unworkable. The Hindu merchant might be heavily assessed, or, during a war have his movable goods confiscated, but he was too much a part of the intricate commercial structure to be easily replaced. The money-lender thrived under the new, as under the old, dispensation. We hear, for example, about the large incomes of the Muslim grandees and the splendor of their households, but Barani leaves us in no doubt that most, if not all, borrowed from the Hindu money lenders. "The maliks and the khans and the nobles of those days were constantly in debt, owing to their excessive generosity, expenditures, and beneficence.

Except in their public halls no gold or silver could be found, and they had no savings on account of their excessive liberality. The wealth and riches of the Multani merchants and the shahs [money lenders] were from the interest realized from the old maliks and nobles of Delhi, who borrowed money from them to the maximum limit, and repaid their debts along with additional gifts from their [lands]. Whenever a malik or a khan held a banquet and invited notables, his agents would rush to the Multanis and shahs, sign documents, and borrow money with interest." That the money lenders recovered their money along with interest (forbidden under Islamic law), is an indication of how vital they were to the system. Even the powerful Alauddin Khalji who, seeing the danger to his government from the power of the Hindu rural chiefs, made a determined attempt to curb their power and reduce their wealth, found it necessary to make Hindu traders the main instrument of his price control measures.

ECONOMY UNDER DELHI SULTANATE

Economic condition of India was affluent under the reign of the Delhi Sultanate. In fact the enormous wealth tempted Mahmud of Ghazni to invade India several times and each time he got immense treasure from here. Malik Kafur, during the reign of Ala-ud-din Khilji, brought so much wealth in plunder from south India that the value of currency fell down in the north. The Sultans, the rulers of the independent provincial kingdoms and the nobles possessed vast wealth and lived a life of luxury and pleasure. There are many beautiful mosques, palaces, forts and monuments which were built during this period and this could not have been possible without the economic prosperity of the country.

AGRICULTURE

Agriculture was a major occupation at that time. Land was the source of production. Produce was generally sufficient. The village was a self-sufficient unit. The husbandman took to the tilling and harvesting of crops, the women folk lend their hands to various functions like taking care of the animals; the carpenters made implements; the blacksmiths supplied the iron parts of the implements; the potters made the household utensils; the cobblers mended or made the shoes and the plough harness and the priest performed the marriage rites and other ceremonies.

There were subsidiary functions of the money-lender, the washerman, the sweeper, the cow-herd and the barber. Land was the pivot around which the whole village life revolved. The chief crops were pulses, wheat, rice, sugarcane, jute and cotton and many more. Medicinal herbs, spices were also grown and exported to a certain extent. Some new crops like tobacco, tea and coffee were also introduced. Among the fruits there were grapes, dates, plantains, apples, oranges, and jack-fruits. Production was for local consumption. Some people lived on the income derived from industries for which raw materials could be imported. The towns served as centers of distribution of agricultural products and industrial goods. The state took a large share of the produce in kind.

INDUSTRIES

There were village and cottage industries. The labour employed was the family members; the technique was conservative. There were industries of sugar, scents and spirits. Weaving and spinning of cotton were the cottage industries during that period. A small-arm making industry was also working in full swing that time. There were also goldsmiths and silversmiths. There were no factories or big enterprises. The Sultans took a hand in building up big enterprises known as the 'Karkhanas.' Craftsmen were employed under the direct supervision of officials to manufacture fashionable articles. Textile industry was the biggest industry at that time. The textiles included cotton cloth, woollen and silks. Allied industries of embroidery, gold thread work and dyeing were also there. Some quantities were exported by Bengal and Gujarat. The famous centers of cloth manufacture were Deogir and Maha Devanagari in the Deccan, Delhi in the North, Sonargaon and Dacca in Bengal.

TRADE AND COMMERCE

Inland and foreign trade flourished. As for the internal trade we had the various classes of merchants and shop-keepers. The Gujaratis of the North, the Chettis of the South and the Banjaras of Rajputana were the main traders. Bigger deals in commodities were made in 'mandis.' The Banjaras carried on the business of conveying agricultural and other products from one part of the country to another.

The native bankers used to give loans and receive deposits. The chief articles of import were silks, velvets, embroidered stuff, horses, guns, gun-powder, and some precious metals. The chief items of export were grain, cotton, precious stones, indigo, hides, opium, spices and sugar. The countries affected by India in commerce were Iraq, Persia, Egypt, East Africa, Malaya, Java, Sumatra, China, Central Asia and Afghanistan.

TAX SYSTEM

The Sultan of the Delhi Sultanate collected five categories of taxes which fall under the economic system of the empire. The taxes are Ushr, Kharaj, Khams, Jizya and Zakat. Besides, there were also other taxes. The main items of expenditure were expenses on the maintenance of the army, salaries of the civil officers and the personal expenditure of the Sultan and his palace.

ECONOMIC CONDITION IN SULTANS PERIOD

As regards private industries, the Sultans followed the policy of laissez faire. The only exception was made by Ala-ud-Din Khalji who imposed prohibition on the sale of brocade and gold cloth, finer varieties of silk of Delhi and Cambay and certain varieties of cloth. His purpose was to control the use of luxuries by the nobility, The most important industries were the textile industry, including the manufacture of cotton, woollen and silk cloth, dyeing industry, printing industry, calico printing industry etc. The other industries were sugar industry, metal work industry, paper industry, stone and brick works industries and industries such as inlay of stone work, enamelling etc.

There were minor industries like shoemaking, manufacture of liquors, brass and other metal and clay industries. In the manufacture and export of textile goods, Bengal and Gujarat were in the forefront. They had the advantage of harbour facilities and the old tradition of commercial relations with foreign countries. Mahuan tells us that ocean-going ships which carried goods to foreign countries were made in Bengal. Chittagong was a great port but Satgaon was a small port. Cambay was a great industrial city and also a great port. There is a lot of evidence regarding the abundance, variety and high quality of the textiles of Bengal Amir Khusrau was impressed by the stuffs presented by Bughra Khan, the father of Kaiqubad, who was the Governor of Bengal.

Khusrau "describes a piece of cloth the texture of which was so fine that the body was visible through it; one could fold a whole piece of this cloth inside one's nail, yet it was large enough to cover the world when unfolded". The exaggeration in the language of the poet cannot be doubted but the fact remains that Bengal produced the finest varieties of cloth. In the 14th century, Ibn Batuta found cotton fabrics of the finest texture, 15 yards in length, selling at 2 silver coins (Dinars). Mahuan found several varieties of fine cotton fabrics and silk handkerchiefs and gold-embroidered caps, He also refers to mulberry trees and silk worms. The excellence of Bengal textiles is also praised by other writers. Barbosa tells us that the high quality of Bengal textiles secured for them a good market in Malacca and Ormuz.

Varthema tells us that Cambay in Gujarat contributed about half the total textile exports of India. Barbosa says that Cambay had skilled craftsmen of many kinds who manufactured coarse and find varieties of woven white cotton fabrics, printed cotton stuffs, silk cloth, coloured velvets, satins, thick carpets, beautiful quilts, quilted articles of clothing etc. Cambay textiles found an extensive market in Western Europe, South Africa and South Asia (Burma, Malaya and Indonesia).

There were industries based on metal work. There were iron, mercury and lead mines but their output was not adequate. The industry of sword-making was well established. There were several varieties of Indian swords. Mahuan refers to the manufacture of steel guns, knives scissors, basins and cups in Bengal. Ornaments of gold and silver were often decorated with excellent inlay work and they were used by the richer classes. Barbosa tells us that there were expert goldsmiths at Cambay who did very fine work. There as also the manufacture of jewellery, coral work and ivory work.

Building industry was developed by the workers in stone, brick and wood. They were patronised by the state. It is said that Ala-ud-Din Khalji employed 70,000 such workers. Firuz Tughlaq trained 4000 slaves as skilled masons. Babar employed 2000 stone-cutters in the construction of buildings at Agra and other places. Wood-work of high quality was required for the construction of oceans going vessels, boats, doors of houses, seats and bedsteads of the rich people. There was also the paper industry but its production was not adequate and the quality of paper produced was not of a high order. In Bengal, white paper of the Chinese variety was made from the bark of a tree. Nicolo Conti refers to the use of paper in Gujarat. Sugarcane was cultivated in different parts of Northern India for the production of sugar of which there were several varieties. Soft sugar was used by the rich and unrefined sugar (Gur) was used by the poor. Bengal produced sugar not only for its own consumption but also for export. Mahuan refers to the export of sugar from Bengal.

Leather was used for saddles and bridles of horses, scabbards of swords, covers of manuscripts, shoes, water buckets and for packing of sugar for the export etc. Dressed skins of different kinds of animals were exported in larger quantities to other countries from Gujarat. Workers in leather industry formed a separate caste known as Chamars.

During the Sultante period, the volume of trade, both internal and external, carried on by Indians, was enormous. India had commercial relations with the outside world. The value of her exports was much greater than that of her imports and the balance of trade was always in her favour. That is the reason why it was generally believed that "Merchants of all countries never ceased to carry pure gold into India, and to bring back in exchange commodities of herbs and gums".

There was a large volume of internal trade. Among the important centres of trade in Gujarat, Barbosa mentions the town of Limodara and the sea port of Rander. Multan and Lahore were clearing houses for trade in the North-Western region. There were good roads which were constructed mainly for the use of the army but were also used by the traders for the transport of commercial goods. There was a road from Delhi to Daulatabad which covered a distance of 40 days' journey. Travel was often insecure and that hindered trade.

In villages and small towns, petty business was in the hands of shop-keepers, itinerant dealers, pedlars and middlemen who were professionals. Large scale business was in the hands of special groups or particular communities. The Multanis and the Banias of Gujarat were the most important business communities of Northern and Western India.

Internal trade was almost entirely in the hands of Hindu merchants while foreign trade was mostly in the hands of Muslim merchants and some in the hands of Hindus. When Ibn Batuta visited Cambay, he found foreign merchants forming the majority of the population of that city. Barbosa tells us that at Cannanore Hindu and Muslim merchants sailed in their own ships as far as Ormuz.

The Hindu Chettis of Coromandel traded with Burma and joined the colony of foreign merchants engaged in wholesale business at Malacca. Orissa had a prosperous overseas trade with South-East Asia till the 15th century. The Muslim traders had certain advantages in foreign trade. Most of the foreign countries were ruled by Muslims and they patronised the Muslim merchants. Muslim merchants were required to pay only 50% of the import duties levied on Hindu merchants. The Hindus themselves were responsible for the loss of their share in foreign trade. Foreign travel was prohibited for the Hindus and those who violtated that rule were punished. The result was that the Hindus developed a sort of aversion towards sea voyages and thus were eliminated from overseas trade. However, the Hindu merchants of Malabar and Coromandel did not care for those prohibitions and carried on foreign trade.

The Banjaras of Rajasthan played an important part in transporting agricultural and other products from one part of the country to another. Their operations were on a large scale. They employed hundreds and thousands of oxen in their carts and wagons. On those roads which were insecure, their caravans were guided and guarded by the Bhats of Rajasthan. Brokers played an important role in commercial transactions. They charged their commission from both the sellers and the purchasers. The bankers provided capital in the form loans and they also accepted deposits. Money-lenders also played their part. They lent money on interest through bonds. It appears that the rate of interest varied between 10% and 20%. Both the Hindus and Muslims did the work of lending on interest although the Shariat did not allow the Muslims to charge interest.

Foreign trade was carried on both through land routes and sea routes. Land route was interrupted for some time on account of the Mongol invasions but after their invasions were over, trade flourished in musk, furs, arms, falcons, camels and horses. Horses were imported from foreign countries in large numbers. In the time of Muhammad Tughlaq, a fixed tax of 7 Tankas per horse had to be paid on the border of Sind. Another amount had to be paid at Multan. It is mentioned in the Adi Granth that the Nawab of Sultanpur was thinking of purchasing horses in Kabul.

As regards foreign trade by sea, two routes were used on the West. Goods were carried either along the Persian Gulf and from there to Mesopotamia to the Mediterranean or by sea routes to the ports of the Red Sea and from there to the Mediterranean through Egypt. From Alexandria, Indian goods were taken by Italian merchants and they distributed them in Europe. Ormuz was the principal centre of trade by the first sea route. It was the entrepot of trade of Hind and Sind. Aden and Jiddha occupied the same position in the trade by the second route.

The ports of Malabar were the principal clearing houses for the Indian goods and Cambay occupied an important position. Goods were taken from Cambay to Ormuz and Aden and vice-versa. The principal exports were cotton and linen cloth, carpets, drugs, gems, seed pearls and carnelians. The principal imports were copper, quicksilver, vermillion, rose water, gold, silver, woollens, coloured velvets, coral, lead, alum, saffron etc. Cambay had trade relations with East Africa. Barbosa tells us that ships from Cambay visited Makdashau with cloths and spices and they brought gold, ivory and wax. Cambay cloth and beads were exported to the ports of Melinde, Mombasa and Kilwa and from there they were taken by local Muslim merchants to other places in Africa. Cambay cloth was sold at the African ports and African ivory was sold in Gujarat.

10

Rise of Islam and Sufism

The Muslims first came to India in the eighth century AD mainly as traders. They were fascinated by the socio-cultural scenario in this country and decided to make India their home. The traders who came to India from Central and West Asia carried back with them traces of Indian science and culture. As a result they became cultural ambassadors of India by disseminating this knowledge to the Islamic world and from there to Europe. The immigrant Muslims also entered into matrimonial alliances with the local people and learned to live together in harmony. There was mutual exchange of ideas and customs. The Hindus and Muslims influenced each other equally in dress, speech, manners, customs and intellectual pursuits. The Muslims also brought with them their religion, Islam which had a deep impact on Indian society and culture. Let us find out more about Prophet Muhammad and Islam in this lesson.

Prophet Muhammad preached Islam in the seventh century AD in Arabia. He was born in AD 571 in the Quraysh tribe of Arabia. He migrated to Madina from Mecca in AD 622 and this marked the beginning of the Hijira Era. According-to the Muslim belief, Quran is the message of Allah revealed to Muhammad through his archangel Gabriel. It has been translated into several languages.

The five fundamental principles of Islam are:

(1) Tauhid (belief in Allah)

(2) Namaz (prayers, five times a day)

(3) Roza (fasting in the month of Ramzan)

(4) Zakat (giving of alms)

(5) Haj (pilgrimage to Mecca).

Prophet Muhammad's sayings are preserved in what is called the Hadith or Hadees. After his death the Caliphate was established. There were four pious Caliphs.

Islam talked of equality, brotherhood, and the existence of one God. Its arrival particularly made a profound impact on the traditional pattern of Indian society. The rise of both the Bhakti and the Sufi movements contributed immensely in this regard. Both the Bhakti and the Sufi movements believed that all humans are equal, God is supreme and devotion to God is the only way to achieve salvation.

RISE OF SUFISM

Sufism is a common term used for Islamic mysticism. The Sufis were very liberal in their religious outlook. They believed in the essential unity of all religions. They preached spirituality through music and doctrines that professed union with God. Sufism originated in Iran and found a congenial atmosphere in India under the Turkish rule. Their sense of piety, tolerance, sympathy, concept of equality and friendly attitude attracted many Hindus, mostly from lower classes, to Islam. Sufi saints such as Moinuddin Chisti, Nizamuddin Auliya, Fariduddin Ganj-e-Shakar were the pioneer sufi's who are still loved, respected and honoured in India. The sufis were also influenced by the Christian and Buddhist monks regarding the establishment of their *khanqahs* and *dargahs. Khanqah* the institutions (abode of Sufis) set up by the Sufis in northern India took Islam deeper into the countryside. *Mazars* (tombs) and *Takias* (resting places of Muslim saints) also became the centres for the propagation of Islamic ideas. These were patronized both by the aristocracy and the common people. The Sufis emphasized respect for all human beings.

The Sufis were organised into religious orders or *silsilahs.* These *silsilahs* were named after their founders such as Chishti, Suhrawardi, Qadi. and Naqshbandis. According to Abul Fazl, the author of the *Ain-i-Akbari,* there were as many as fourteen *silsilahs* in India during the sixteenth century. Each order had its own *khanqah,* which served as a shelter for the Sufi saints and for destitutes, and later developed as a centre of learning. Ajmer, Nagaur and Ajodhan or Pak Pattan (now in Pakistan) developed as important centres of Sufism. These also started the tradition of *piri-muridi,* (teacher and the disciple). In order to attain a state of mystical ecstasy, the sufis listened to poetry and music (*sama*) which were originally in Persian, but later switched to Hindawi or Hindustani. They preached the unity of God and self-surrender unto Him in almost the same way as the votaries of the *Nirgun Bhakti* movement did. Music attracts everybody, irrespective of language. Slowly such music attracted the Hindus who started visiting the *dargahs* in large number. The Hindu impact on Sufism also became visible in the form of *siddhas* and yogic postures.

The rulers of Delhi, who ruled from 1206-90, were Mamluk Turks. They were followed by the Khiljis, Tughlaqs, Sayyids and Lodis, who ruled northera India from Delhi till 1526. All these rulers were called Sultans. A Sultan was supposed to rule over a territory on behalf of the Khalifa or Caliph, who was considered to be the spiritual and temporal head of the Muslims. Both the names of the Khalifa and the Sultan used to be read in the *khutha, (*Friday prayers) by the local Imams. In 1526 the Delhi Sultans were replacedby the Mughals, who initially ruled from Agra and later from Delhi till 1707.

Thereafter, the Mughal rule continued only nominally till 1857 when the dynasty ended. The Mughals did not ask for any investiture but continued to send presents to the Khalifas. They also got the *khutba* read in their own names. However, Sher Shah, a local Afghan ruler, challenged the Mughal ruler, Humayun and kept him away from the throne of Delhi for about fifteen years (1540-55). Sher Shah's reign stands out for many outstanding achievements. Among these was the construction of several roads, the most important being *Sarak-i-Azam* or Grand Trunk Road extending from Sonargaon (now in Bangladesh) to Attock (now in Pakistan) and run through Delhi and Agra a distance of 1500 *kos*. The other roads were from Agra to Burhanpur, Agra to Marwar and from Lahore to Multan. He struck beautiful coins in gold, silver and copper which were imitated by the Mughal Kings.

Mughal emperor Akbar who ruled from 1556-1605 was a great ruler in the history of India. He made a sincere effort to foster harmony among his subjects by discouraging racial, religious and cultural biases. He tried to develop friendly relations with the Hindus. To fulfil his imperialist ambitions he entered into matrimonial alliances with the Rajput rulers. His greatest contribution was the political unification of the country and the establishment of an all powerful central government with a uniform system of administration. Akbar was a great patron of art, architecture and learning. As a secular minded monarch he also started a faith called *Din-i-Illahi* which encompassed ideas from various religions. On every Thursday, scholars from different religions came to debate on religious issues raised by the emperor. This was done at the Ibadat Khana in Fateh Pur Sikri at Agra. Though illiterate Akbar patronised scholars and learned men. In his court there were nine such Navratna Mulla Do Pyaza, Hakin Humam, Abdur Rahim Khan e Khanan, Abul Tayal, Tansen, Raja Todar Mal, Raja Man Singh, Faizi and Birbal. Akbar's policy of liberalism and tolerance was continued by his successors, Jahangir and Shah Jahan. However this policy was abandoned by Aurangzeb.

Aurangzeb's short sighted policies and endless wars in different parts of the country (especially in South India) resulted in the disintegration of the Mughal empire. The rise of the Marathas in the south, the invasions of Nadir Shah and Ahmad Shah Abdali, unrest amongst the nobility in the court and the rise of the Sikhs in north- western India destroyed whatever was left of the Mughal power. Economically India was still the biggest exporter in the world and had great wealth, but it was left far behind in the process of modernisation.

CULTURAL DEVELOPMENT

It was in the field of art and architecture that the rulers of this period took a keen interest. The composite cultural characteristic of the medieval period is amply witnessed in these fields. A new style of architecture known as the Indo- Islamic style was born out of this fusion. The distinctive features of Indo-Islamic architecture were the (a) dome; (b) lofty towers or minarets; (c) arch; and (d) the vault.

The Mughal rulers were great lovers of nature. They took pleasure in spending their time in building beautiful forts and gardens. The famous Mughal gardens like the Shalimar Bagh and the Nishat Bagh are important elements of our cultural heritage. There were waterways and fountains criss-crossing these gardens and finally, there were gardens with stages or levels. The water, while cascading from one stage to another, was made to fall in small streamlets with lamps lit behind them, making the water shimmer and lend a special charm to the whole atmosphere. It could also be made to flow over a chiselled and sloping slab, so that the water flowing over it shimmered. The best example of this type of garden is the Shalimar Gardens of Lahore (now in Pakistan). The Lahore garden has three stages. But a better example can be seen in India at Pinjore Garden situated on the Chandigarh-Kalka road where we have a seven-stage garden. This impressed the British so much that they created a three-stage garden in the Vice-Regal Lodge (now the Rashtrapati Bhawan) in New Delhi, It was on these very lines that the famous Vrindavan Garden in Mysore were built in the twentieth century.

The *pietra dura* or coloured stone inlay work on marble became very popular in the days of Shah Jahan and the finest examples of this type of work are available in the Red Fort in Delhi and the Taj Mahal at Agra. Besides, the structures within the Fatehpur Sikri complex, the forts at Agra and Lahore and the Shahi mosques in Delhi and Lahore are an important part of our heritage. During this period mosques, tombs of kings and *dargahs* came to dominate the landscape.

COINAGE

Another aspect of art, which is of great importance to us, is connected with Numismatics (the study of coins) which is a major source of information for any period in history. The coins of Muslim kings are valuable in history. Their designs, calligraphy and mint marks give us plenty of interesting information on this period. From the royal titles, the name and place of minting we can find out the extent of the monarch's kingdom as well as his status. Muhammad Tughlaq's coins were minted at Delhi, Daulatabad and several other provincial capitals and had at least twenty-five different varieties. Some of the legends found on the coins are quite interesting. The warrior in the cause of God' and 'he who obeys the Sultan obeys the Compassionate', are a few examples.

RELIGIOUS CONDITIONS UNDER DELHI SULTANATE

Religious condition under the rulers of the Delhi Sultanate went through a significant change. During the initial years of their rule, all ancient religious sects in India like the Vedic religion, Hinduism, Buddhism, Jainism, Vaishnavism, Shaivism etc. existed in different forms. But with time many religion declined or were concentrated only in some parts of India. Among the Muslims, the Sunnis and the Shiahs constituted the majority. The novelties of this period were the growing popularity of Sufism among the Muslims and Bhakti movement among the Hindus.

Sufism is an old religious sect and it had penetrated into India prior to the advent of the Delhi Sultanate. Once the Muslims firmly established themselves in India, Sufism gained prominence. A large number of Sufi saints came into India and settled themselves in different parts of the country.

Sufism was influenced by the religious views prevalent among the Indians. Love towards god, non violence, practice of self discipline etc.

was common values among the Hindus, Buddhist and Jains in India. The philosophy of Sufism believes in one god and regards every individual and everything else as part of him. The Sufis were devout Muslims who moved within the Shariat and believed it as the true way to attain salvation.

The Sufi saints led a simple or rather ascetic life and believed in the renunciation of all worldly possessions and pleasures. They did not believe in image worship of any form. They regarded God as kind and benevolent and therefore they did not fear him but loved him. They regarded Desire as the primary enemy of human and therefore emphasised on giving it up. Music inspired them to remember God and therefore they engaged themselves in music and dance with ecstasy while remembering god. The Sufis believed in Guru (Master) whom they called Pir and thought that no one can approach near God without the assistance of a Guru. The Sufis were divided into different sects, most important of them being the Suravardi sect and the Chisti sect.

The influence of Suravardi sect remained limited only to Sindh, Punjab and Multan but the Chisti sect became well accepted all over India including Punjab, Rajasthan, Madhya Pradesh, Bihar, Bengal, Orissa and south India. Many Sufi saints became quite popular during the period of the Delhi Sultanate. The most important of them were Shaikh Muin-ud-din Chisti, Baba Farid-ud-din, Nasir–ud–din Mahmud, Nizam-ud-din Auliya, Khwaja Shaikh Taki-ud-din and Malik Muhammad Jaysi.

The Bhakti movement in Hinduism was a remarkable feature during the period f Delhi Sultanate. Hindu saints emphasised on Bhakti as a means to attain salvation and that resulted in the Bhakti movement. Hinduism had to face the challenge of Islam in the medieval period which gave birth to the Bhakti movement. The saints of the Bhakti movement believed in god who could be called by different names such as Lord Rama, Lord Krishna, Lord Shiva or Allah. They were against the caste system or image worship and laid stress on Bhakti as the only means to attain salvation.

The Bhakti saints believed that a devotee needed a Guru who could help and guide him to attain salvation, though that could be achieved only by the grace of God while the grace of god itself could be achieved only by one's own effort. The saints propagated these ideas among the people by means of their teachings in simple languages, poems and prayers. But the most effective way of preaching their thoughts was their personal dedicated lives to God. The saints preached their ideas not in Sanskrit but in other Indian regional languages of the people. The pioneers of the Bhakti movements were Ramanuja, Nimbakara and Madhavacharya. Bhakti movement rose to popularity through Ramananda who flourished in the fourteenth century. Other Bhakti saints like Kabir, Guru Nanak and Chaitanya contributed a lot in the expansion and popularity of Bhakti movement.

THE ARTICULATION OF POLITICAL AUTHORITY

The world is a garden, whose gardener is the state. We arrived before the Sultan. He was seated on a large gilt sofa covered with different-sized cushions, all of which were embedded with a smattering of precious stones and small pearls. We greeted him according to the custom of the country—hands crossed on our chests and heads as low as possible.

It is more challenging, however, to reconstruct the changing meaning of that authority, both to the rulers and to the subject population. All political behavior derives its meaning through the prism of culture. Equally, invocations of political symbols most effectively confer authority on rulers when they and their subjects share a common political culture.

But what happened in the cases of "conquest dynasties," as in Bengal, where the conquering class was of a culture fundamentally different from that of the subject population? How did rulers in such circumstances remain in effective control without resorting to the indefinite and prohibitively costly use of coercive force?

To raise these questions is to suggest that the political frontier in Bengal may be understood not only as a moving line of garrisons, mint towns, and architectural monuments. Also involved was the more subtle matter of accommodation, or the lack of it, between a ruling class and a subject population that, as of 1204, adhered to fundamentally different notions of legitimate political authority. The transformation of these concepts of legitimacy over time—their divergence from or convergence with one another—constitutes a political frontier far less tangible than a military picket line, but one ultimately more vital to understanding the dynamics of Bengal's premodern history.

IMPACT OF SUFISM IN INDIA

The contacts and conflicts between sufis and yogis became more frequent and meaningful. The various branches of qalandars and sufis of the Rifaiyya order, confined mainly to Turkey, Syria and Egypt, were significantly influenced by wandering yogis. Unfortunately existing literature throws little light on yogis, who are constantly referred to as "jogis". In one reference the perfect yogi is associated by Shaikh Nasirud-Din Chirag-i Dilli with the *Siddhas.* The topics discussed at the *Jamaat-khana* gatherings of Baba Farid were of great interest to visiting Siddhas whose beliefs were founded on Hatha Yoga. Supplementing these scraps of information is al-Biruni, unquestionably a profound authority on comparative religions, who notes sufi parallels in the *Yoga Sutra* of Patanjali, which he himself translated into Arabic. He also mentions similarities with Samkhya, one of the six schools of classical Hindu philosophy, and with the *Bhagavad Gita.* Patanjali's theories of the soul are defined by Al-Biruni as follows:

"The soul, being on all sides tied to ignorance, which is the cause of its being fettered, is like rice in its cover. As long as it is there, it is capable of growing and ripening in the transition stages between being born and giving birth itself. But if the cover is taken off the rice, it ceases to develop in this way, and becomes stationary. The retribution of the soul depends on the various kinds of creatures through which it wanders, upon the extent of life, whether it be long or short, and upon the particular kind of its happiness, be it scanty or ample."

He goes on to say:

"The same doctrine is professed by those sufis who teach that this world is a sleeping soul and yonder world a soul awake, and who at the same time admit that God is immanent in certain places—for example, in heaven—in the seat and the throne of God (mentioned in the Quran). But then there are others who admit that God is immanent in the whole world, in animals, trees and the inanimate world, which they call His universal appearance. To those who hold this view, the entering of the souls into various beings in the course of metempsychosis is of no consequence."

Referring to the Samkhya theory of the rewards of paradise as being of no special advantage, Al-Biruni adds:

"The sufis, too, do not consider the stay in Paradise a special gain for another reason, because there the soul delights in other things, but the Truth, that is, God, and its thoughts are diverted from the Absolute Good by things which are not the Absolute Good."

On the nature of liberation from the world and the path by which this can be achieved, Al-Biruni quotes Patanjali's text as follows:

"The concentration of thought ont he unity of God induces man to notice something besides that with which he is occupied. He who wants God, wants the good for the whole creation without a single exception for any reason whatever; but he who occupies himself exclusively with his own self, will for its benefit neither inhale, breathe, nor exhale it (svasa and prasvasa). When a man attains to this degree, his spiritual power prevails over his bodily power, and then he is gifted with the faculty of doing eight different things by which detachment is realised; for a man can only dispense with that which he is able to do, not with that which is outside his grasp."

According to Al-Biruni the sufi parallel is contained in the following theory:

"The terms of the sufi as to the knowing being and his attaining the stage of knowledge come to the same effect, for they maintain that he has two souls—an eternal one, not exposed to change and alteration, by which he knows that which is hidden, the transcendental world, and performs wonders; and another, a human soul, which is liable to being changed and being born."

Al-Biruni also quotes this passage from the *Yoga Sutra* to indicate the relation of the body to the soul.

"The bodies are the snares of the souls for the purpose of acquiring recompense. He who arrives at the stage of liberation has acquired, in his actual form of existence, the recompense for all the doing of the past. Then he ceases to labour to acquire a title to a recompense in the future. He frees himself from the snare; he can dispense with the particular form of his existence, and moves in it quite freely without being ensnared by it. He has even the faculty of moving wherever he likes, and if he likes, he might rise above the face of death. For the thick, cohesive bodies cannot oppose an obstacle to his form of existence (as, for example, a mountain could not prevent him from passing through). How, then, could his body oppose an obstacle to his soul?"

The similarities in the sufi approach is demonstrated by this story:

"A company of sufis came down (to) us, and sat at some distance from us. Then one of them rose, prayed, and on having finished his prayer, turned towards me and spoke: "Oh master, do you know here a place fit for us to die on?" Now I thought he meant sleeping, and so I pointed out to him a place. The man went there, threw himself on the back of his head, and remained motionless. Now I rose, went to him and shook him, but lo! He was already cold."

Again the likenesses between Patanjali's views and those of sufism concerning meditation of the Truth (that is, God) is reflected in the following sufi theory:

> *"...they (sufis) say: 'As long as you point to something you are not a monist; but when the Truth seizes opon the object of your pointing and annihilates it, then there is no longer an indicating person nor an object indicated."*

There are some passages in their system which show that they believe in the pantheistic union; for example, one of them, being asked what is *the Truth* (God), gave the following answer: 'How should I not know the Being which is I in essence and *Not-I* in space? If I return once more into existence, thereby I am separated from Him; and if I am neglected (that is, not born anew and sent into the world), thereby I become light and become accustomed to the *union, (sic).'*

Abu Bakr Ash-Shibli says: 'Cast off all, and you will attain to us completely. Then you will exist; but you will not report about us to others as long as your doing is like ours.

Abu Yazid Albistami once being asked how he had attained *his* stage in sufism, answered: 'I cast off my own self as a serpent casts off its skin. Then I considered my own self, and found that I was He,' *that is* God.

The sufis explain the Quranic passage '*Then we spoke: Beat Him with a part of her,'* in the following manner: 'The order to kill that which is dead in order to give life to it inidicates that the heart does not become alive by the lights of knowledge unless the body be killed by ascetic practice to such a degree that it does not any more exist as a reality, but only in a formal way, whilst your heart is a reality on which no object of the formal wolrd has any influence.'

Further they say: 'Between man and God there are a thousand stages of light and darkness. Men exert themselves to pass through darkness to light and when they have attained to the station of light, thee is no return for them.'

Regarding the sufi doctrine of love as being a total obsession with God, al-Biruni quotes interesting parallels from the *Bhagavad Gita.* The encounter of Shaikh Safiud-Din Kaziruni with a yogi, also described earlier, demonstrates the type of contacts early sufis had with yogis.

From the thirteenth century onwards Hindu mystical songs were recited at *Sama'* gatherings and many of the most talented musicians were newly converted Muslims. Shaikh Ahmad from Naharwala in Gujarat, who gave expert renditions of Hindawi *ragas,* lived during this century.

The Shaikh undoubtedly attended the most significant *Sama'* performances, as is clear from his presence when a Persian verse produced such powerful ecstasy in Shaikh Qutbud-Din Bakhtiyar Kaki that he died a few days later. Ahmad was said to have been a disciple of Faqir Madhu, the Imam of the Jami' mosque in Ajmer, who retained his Hindu name even after conversion.

The recitation of Hindawi music at *Sama'* was popular at all sufi centres, particularly those some distance from Delhi. Saiyid Gisu Daraz admitted that each language was endowed with a characteristic of its own and to him none was as effective as Hindawi for through it esoteric ideas could be so clearly expressed. Hindawi music, the Saiyid believed, was also subtle and elegant, penetrating deeply into the heart and arousing humility and gentleness. When hearing it people became more aware of their faults and therefore, it was natural, to the Saiyid that Hindawi music was becoming increasingly popular.

Most of the Hindawi songs recited at *Sama'* gatherings held during this period have been lost, but afew verses that have survived have been ascribed to Shaikh Hamid-ud-Din Nagauri and Baba Farid. What is significant, however, is the spontaneous expression of subtle mystical beliefs through verses in regional dialects. Such songs were not composed for propaganda purposes but were a natural evolution from the deep and personal involvement of these two great mystics with their environment.

Hindawi was a more convenient language in which to utter the feelings of a heart filled with divine love. In a Persian work, the *Sururus-Sudur,* Shaikh Hamid quotes a touching verse emphasizing the fact that differences in nomenclature failed to undermine the truth that Reality is One. An object could assume hundreds of different forms and be known by the same number of names but this did not alter the fact that they all emanated from One. Although earlier sufis had expressed this idea in many different ways in both Persian poetry and prose, the later use of Hindawi in further explanations of this concept was most probably a significant factor in the arousal of Hindu interest in sufism.

In another verse on the misuse of drugs and medicinal herbs. Shaikh Hamid attacks the yogi emphasis on the use of drugs and medicinal herbs, without denying their efficacy in certain circumstances. A sick man could go to China, the original source of Hindu theories of alchemy, and not being cured attribute the failure to the lack of effectiveness of *resayana* (the compounding of the *elixir vitae)* but, argued the Shaikh, a real understanding of the illness involved a belief that human effort operated only within a very limited sphere.

In Persian and Hindawi verses Shaikh Hamidud-Din emphasized that drugs were not necessarily evil, only the people who misused them were. In a Hindawi verse the Shaikh wrote that for all the claims to cure diseases it was impossible to transform a sick person into a yogi. Although the famous poet of the romantic epic, Iliyas bin Yusuf Nizami of Ganja, in Azerbayjan, died on 4 Ramazan 605/12 March 1209, his *ghazals* and *masnawis* quickly reached India and aroused the interest of those Indians who had a knowledge of Persian. Shaikh Hamidud-Din Nagauri made a free Hindi translation of one of Nizami's *ghazals* and included in the text both the Persian original and their equivalent Hindawi *dohas.*

The *Siyarul-Auliya* quotes a verse composed by Baba Farid in the Multani dialect whose precise meaning is difficult to decipher. The *Saba-Sanabil* of Mir Abdul-Wahid Bigarami contains two *dohas* by Baba Farid with a Persian translation. The Mir himself was a good poet in Hindawi and his version makes the *doha* more intelligible. Here are two verses of the baba's translated from the Hindawi.

You are yourself ignorant but you seek to make others your disciple, You give a cap as a mark of initiation, and this indicaes that you are presumptuous.

A mouse who is unable to enter into a narrow hole, Puts a heavy load over his head, although he moves in a narrow place!"

The other *doha* says:

"You shave your head but what you should do is to cut lust from the heart, By shaving the head, the path of faith is not acquired. Several thousand sheep whose wool are cut, move about in different directions, None of these is accepted in the court of the Master."

Controversy surrounds more than a hundred *slokas* ascribed to Baba Farid Ganj-i Shakar in the *Guru Granth,* compiled by the fifth Sikh Guru, Arjan, in 1604. some scholars assert they were composed by Baba Farid himself but the language indicates they were the work of his successors who may have rewritten some of Baba Farid's original *slokas* into a more intelligible Multani. Some of these *slokas* are even ascribed to Kabir. The *Janam Sakhis* includes a number of *slokas* which Guru Nanak and his successors composed to support, rather than dispute, the ideas contained in Baba Farid's *slokas.*

Others believe that the *slokas* in the *Guru Granth* were composed by Shaikh Ibrahim, a successor of Baba Farid, whom Guru Nanak visited at Ajodhan. A careful analysis of Baba Farid's *slokas* in the *Guru Granth* would tend to suggest they were not composed by one individual. Therefore it is wrong to ascribe them either to Shaikh Ibrahim or another of Baba Farid's descendants, known as Farid Sani. They represent the teachings of Baba Farid through the years from his own time to the fifteenth century and were therefore composed by a number of different descendants, all using Farid as their *nom de plume.*

The period in which the poetry of Shaikh Hamid-ud-Din Nagauri and Baba Farid was written was preceded by one in which two significant poetic traditions were established in north Indian dialects. Firstly there was the poetry of the Siddhacharyas, followers of the Buddhist Sahajiya cult which began during the eighth century. This literature continued to influence, in both style and spirit, the poetry written in local dialects until the twelfth century. Secondly this type of poetry was succeeded by that written by members of the Nath cult.

Sahajiya Buddhism was an offshoot of Tantric Buddhism, the Vajrayana or "Vehicle of the Thunderbolt", which was patronised by the Pala kings of Bengal. In northern India Vajrayana, the third vehicle, superceded Mahayana Buddhism, the second. It featured the worship of feminine deities and magico-religious practices by which superhuman powers and salvation could be attained.

The supreme deity of the Vajrayana is the *Vajra-Sattva (vajra-sunyata:* vacuity; *sattva:* quintessence), who is the nature of pure consciousness (the *vijnapti-matrata* of the Vijnana Vadin Buddhists) as associated with *sunyata* in the form of the absence of subjectivity and objectivity. The *Vajra-Sattva* is often identified with man's self and with the Ultimate Reality in the form of the Bodhicitta. The latter: "presupposes two elements in the citta, *sunyata* (the knowledge of the nature of things as pure void) and *karuna* (universal compassion)."

This is conceived as an extremely blissful state of mind produced through sexo-yogic practices. The Sahajiyas differed from the Vajrayanists because of the emphasis they laid on protesting against the formalities of life and religion. According to them truth was to be unconventionally understood through initiation in the *tattva* (secret truth) and the physical practice of Yoga. The Sahajiva recommended the transformation and sublimation of sexual impulse, rather than its annihilation. The *dohas* by Tillo-Pada and Saraha-Pada, who flourished between the eight and ninth centuries AD emphasized that Truth could be realized only through the individual. According to Saraha-Pada, the Brahmanical claims of class superiority were unfounded, the naked Jaina Ksapanaka-Yogins were frauds, the Buddhist monks were superstituous, the *Tantras* and the *Mantras* led to confusion and only Sahaja helped a mystic to gain a true understanding of the real nature of yogic discipline.

Brahmanical sacrifices, pilgrimages and penances were of no avail, what had to be done was to fix the mind to the *Niranjana* or Stainless One. The *Hevajra-tantra* says:

> *"The whole world is of the nature of Sahaja— for Sahaja is the quintessence* (svarupa) *of all; this quintessence is* nirvana *to those who possess the perfectly pure Citta."*

A Sahajiya poet compared the Sahaja stage to the flowing of nectar; according to Tillo-Pada: "Sahaja is a state where all thought—concentration is dead (that is, destroyed) and the vital sind (which is the vehicle of the defiled Citta) is also destroyed—the secret of this truth is to be intended by the self—how can it be explained (by others)" Saraha-Pada continues by saying :

> *"In Sahaja there is no duality; it is perfect like the sky. The intuition of this ultimate truth destroys all attachment and it shines through the darkness of attachment like a full moon in the night. Sahaja cannot be heard with the ears, neither can it be seen with the eyes; it is not affected by air nor burnt by fire; it is not wet in intense rain, it neither increases nor decreases, it neither exists nor does it die out with the decay of the body; the Sahaja bliss is only oneness of emotions,—it is oneness in all. Our mind and the vital wind are unsteady like the horse;—but in the Sahaja-nature both of them remain steady. When the mind thus ceases to function and all other ties are torn aside, all the differences in the nature of things vanish; and at that time there is neither the Brahman nor the Sudra. Sahaja cannot be realized in any of its particular aspects—it is an intuition of the whole, the one underlying reality pervading and permeating all diversity. As the truth of the lotus can never be found either in the stalk or in the leaves, or in the petals or in the smell of the lotus, or in the filament,—it lies rather in the totality of all these parts,—so also Sahaja is the totality which can only be realized in a perfectly non-dual state of mind. From it originate all, in it all merge again, —but it itself is free from all existence and non-existence,—it never originates at all."*

The first step in achieving the Supreme Bliss of the Sahajiya was the selection of an appropriate teacher. Sahajiya esoteric practices depended on the conception that the human body was a microcosm of the macrocosm.

The psycho-physical process of yoga should be undertaken only by a mature body.

The yogini of the Sahaja-damsel of the Sahajiyas was not a woman of normal existence but an internal force of the nature of vacuity (*sunyata*) or senselessness (*nairatma*) and great bliss residing in the different plexuses in different stages of yogic practices.

Founded on the psycho-chemical of yoga in which the old Siddha cult of the yogis specialized, the Shaivite Nath cult developed, assimilating elements from the Buddhist Sahajiya cult. The Adi Nath, the First Lord of the Naths, is the Shiva of the Hindus as is the Buddha, in the form of the *Vajra-Sattava,* of the Buddhists. The first human *guru* of the cult was Matsyendra, reported to have lived in the tenth century AD. According to legend, while swiming like a fish he overheard the esoteric doctrines of the Nath which the Lord Shiva was imparting to his spouse, Parvati. Matsyendra is therefore known by such names as Mananath or Lui-pa, meaning fish Lord in Tibetan. Matsyendra's weakness for women tended to associate him with the left-handed cults of the female deities.

These centred around Lakshinkara, a legendary princess of the mythical kingdom of Indrabhuti which was successively ruled by female issue. Lakshinkara has been compared to Eleanor of Aquitain. Gorakhnath, Matsyendra's disciple, believed to have been born from the sweat of Shiva's breast, saved his master, in whose service he had earlier lost an eye. Much mystery and legen also surround Gorakhnath's personality, but we know he wrote some treatises in Sanskrit. A number of verses in Punjabi and Hindi also attributed to him were written by successive generations of disciples using the name Gorakhnath in order to establish a spiritual link with their master.

A corpus of *dohas* with Farid as the *nom de plume* which were compiled by a number of descendants of the Baba show that their authors were also influenced by this trend. The same is true of the verses written by Guru Nanak's successors, which shall be discussed in subsequent pages. Gorakhnath's disciples were the authors of a number of treatises on magic, alchemy and left-handed occultism and Hatha-Yoga. Of the Sanskrit treatises by Gorakhnath, unlike the *Hatha-Yoga,* the *Goraksha-Sataka* has survived and has been edited and translated into English.

Other names associated with the Nath cult are "Nimnath, probably Nemi, the twenty-second Jain *tirthankara;* Parasnath, probably Parsava, the twenty-third Jain *tirthankara;* Bhutanath, "Ghost Lord," probably the

Buddha; Dayanath, "Compassionate Lord," probably a form of a *Bodhi-citta,* Nagarjunanath, the Bhuddist philosopher Nagarjuna (*c.* AD 100-200); Bharatinath, noted for his asceticism; Ratannath, a contemporary of Gorakhnath, and the subject of many miraculous tales; Dandanath, founder of a cult of staff-bearing yogis; Puranbhagat who, with his half-brother Rasula, has inspired hundreds of miraculous tales; Charpati (or Charpatinath), a *rasavada* or alchemist and poet, some of whose verses in Panjabi are extant; Guga (or Guganath) whose power over serpents was phenomenal; Manikchandra, a *bania* by caste, who left his wealth to join the Naths; Gahininath, initiated by Gorakhnath, himself initiated Nivrittinath, brother of the Maratha saint Jananadeva at Tryambaka; Dharamnath, probably the Lord Dharma of the crypto-Buddhist Dharma cult of Bengal; Jalandhari-pa: Kanu-pa; Mainamati and Gopi-Chand.

The framework of the order of the Kanphata (Split Ear Yogis) or the Naths founded by Gorakhnath serves to illustrate the latter's remarkable organizational capacity and foresight. At the time of initiation, the ear cartilages of a novice were as is still customary today split, and two enormous ear-rings were inserted in the holes. Ear splitting was believed necessary to open a mystical channel in order to assist the development of yogic powers. During the ceremony a knife was driven into the ground and vows recited over it by the initiate; these included a vow to protect the ears which, according to Hindu mysticism, were believed to contain a network of invisible *nadis* (ganglia) connecting them with the inner organs of perception. The rites also included the symbolic slaying of the neophyte, the washing of his entrails, and the hanging of his body on a tree.

The traditions venerate nine Naths and eighty-four Siddhas but this does not imply the historical authenticity of these figures. The eighty-four Siddhas represent the "totality of a revelation." The transmission of the Nath doctrine however is founded on the trinity: Shiva, Matsyendra-nath and Gorakhnath. The Naths initiated members of all castes, including those outside the Hindu caste system, such as Chandalas and sweepers, into their non-hierarchical order. Generally it would seem the Brahman caste were not attracted to the Naths. The Shaivite ascetics who haunted cemeteries, ate from skulls and even consumed corpses at the burning *ghats,* known as Aghoris or Aghora-panthis and the ascetic order of Kapalikas (wearers of skulls) are also known as yogis but are basically different to the Naths.

From the elevent century the Nath yogis began to spread throughout northern India, and from their centre at Peshawar moved to all parts of Central Asia and Iran, at the same time influencing both qalandars and sufis. Aghoris and Kapalikas were uniterested in Middle Eastern regions where there were no burning *ghats.* Some of the yogis who thronged the court of the Mongols were Buddhist Tantrics, but they were hardly distinguishable from the yogis. Many Naths might have indulged in homosexuality, orgiastic practices, necrophilia, scatology, bestiality and other sexual perversions, but there were many groups of sober Naths who disseminated the real spiritual tenets of their foundres. All Naths however were hostile to Hindu caste distinctions, particularly those practised by Brahmans and respected in the pariah and the untouchable.

The *Siddha Siddhanta Paddhati,* and some authentic works by Gorakhnath's followers formed the basis of the doctrines of the puritanical Naths and offered a common ground for the exchange of ideas with such sufis as Shaikh Hamid-ud-Din Nagauri and Baba Farid. Discussion on the conception of the Ultimate Reality enhanced the mutual respect of the Naths and the sufis.

According to Gorakhnath, Ultimate Reality could not be conceived by logical reasoning; it was a super sensuous, super intellectual, direct experience in the state of *samadhi* (trance) or a perfectly illuminated state of consciousness. Those who attained the direct transcendental experience of Reality during *samadhi,* felt united with the Absolute Truth :

> *"....Absolute Reality unveils Itself to our consciousness in its super-sensuous super-mental super-intellectual transcendent state, in which the subject-object relation vanishes and the consciousness realises itself as perfectly identified with the Absolute Reality. The Absolute Reality is thus experienced as the Absolute Consciousness, in which all time and space and all existences in time and space are merged in perfect unity, and the One Infinite Eternal Undifferentiated Changless Self-Effulgent Consciousness shines as the Ultimate Reality."*

Sat-Cit-Ananda-Murti (One who reveals Himself as Being, Consciousness and Bliss), Goraknath believed was the highest form of God, the self-manifestation of the Formless and Manifestationless One— Brahma, Shiva, parmatma, Parmeswara, the holiest names of the Nameless One.

To Gorakhnath and the Siddhas the phenomenal cosmic system was not false or illusory, nor did it have merely subjective Reality. Pure Will *(icha-matra)* inherent in the perfect transcendental nature of the Supreme Spirit was the source of the entire spatio-temporal order and of many different kinds of empirical realities. The *Siddha Siddhanta Paddhati* demonstrated the relationship between *advaita* (non-dualism) and *dvaita* (dualism) by using the analogy of water and bubbles familiar to that used by sufis in the *Wahdat al-Wujud* system. Bubbles appear at the surface of the water, then both bubbles and water appear merged with each other, the former loosing their ephemeral identity. The changing multiplicity of bubbles fails to separate them from the water. Thus :

Akulam kulam adhatte kulam cakulam icchati jala-budbuda-bat nyayat ekakarah Parah Sivah.

Akula embraces *Kula* (the *phenomenal self-expression* of Reality) and *Kula* yearns for *Akula* (the *noumenal essence* of Reality). The relation is analogous to that between water and water bubbles. In reality Para-Siva (Supreme Spirit) is absolutely one. In Nath terminology the Absolute Spirit is called Shiva and His Unique Power is Shakti. There is no difference between the two, Shiva is the father of the universe and Shakti is the mother. Creation or the origin of the cosmic system is in reality the gradual revelation of Shiva's inherent Shakti; the process of creation and dissolution has no absolute beginning or end in time. The Physical Cosmic Body is the most complicated and diversified form of free self-manifestation of the Absolute Spirit through the gradual self-revelation of His infinite and eternal Spiritual Power. The human body is the microcosm of the entire cosmic body of Shiva. The divine Shakti who in the process of cosmic self-manifestation gradually descends from the highest transcendent spiritual plane of Absolute Unity and Bliss to the lowest phenomenal material level of endless diversities and imperfections, again ascends by means of the self-conscious process and imperfections, again ascends by means of the self-conscious process of *Yoga Jnana* (knowledge) and *Bhakti* (devotion) to the transcendent spiritual plane where the divine spirit becomes perfectly and blissfully united with the supreme spirit, Shiva. Man with his developed individuality can experience Shiva, the supreme spirit, as his own true soul as well as the true soul of the universe. Yogic introspection and meditation calls for the attainment of a real understanding of the nature of the human body and of its esoteric aspects.

These consist of nine *cakras* or centres of psycho-vital forces. The supreme divine power, dormant like a coiled serpent is located in the lowest *muladhara cakra* of every human body; yogic discipline enables it to rise step by step to the higher planes of spiritual illumination, finding its culmination in the highest *cakra (sahasrara),* the plane of blissful union of Shakti and Shiva. The region below the navel is the region of Shakti, while that above it is that of Shiva. *Adhars,* according to Goraknath, are the main sources of the vital and psychical functions which have to be controlled.

Laksyas are objects on which a yogi should temporarily concentrate while summoning his psycho-vital energy with the ultimate aim of elevating it to the highest spiritual plane which can be internal, external or non-located. The processes of *asana* (posture), *dhauti* (washing), *bandha* (different kinds of motionlessness), *mudra* (gesture), *pranayama* (breathing) and other techniques of Hatha-Yoga are prescribed so as to achieve the transformation of the body in order to achieve the full control of the mind. The prerequisite of Nath discipline is the control of the *vayu* (the vital wind). This entire philosophy is called Hatha-Yoga, the union of the moon (*tha*) and the sun (*ha*).

The perfect yogi can transform his body according to his will and is therefore free of all diseases and death. Siddhas, such as the disciples of Gorakhnath and others are believed to have achieved the practical aspects of this philosophy while in the foothills of the Himalayas and came to be known as the *jivan-mukta* (lebarated while living). In fact it is the only state of true perfection in which the body is made whole throughout by control of the vital wind. Besides poetry which offered sufis an acquaintance with various aspects of the discipline of Hatha-Yoga, the most significant impact of Hatha-Yoga was the treatise, the *Amrita-Kunda.* It is believed that it was translated by Qazi Ruknuddin Samarqandi who was probably Qazi Ruknuddin Abu Hamid Muhammad bin Muhammad al-Amidi of Samarqand, the author of the *Kitab al-Irshad* who visited Lakhnauti between 1209-10 and 1216-17 and was initiated into Hatha-Yogic principles by a Siddha, called Bhojar Brahman. The work was later translated into Persian.

A further Arabic version was again prepared by a Brahman from Kamrup, apparently in collaboration with a Muslim scholar. This version was retranslated into Persian by Shaikh Muhammad Ghaus Shattari (906/1500-01-970/1562-63). Shaikh Abdul-Quddus Gangohi who had an extensive knowledge of the Arabic and Persian versions of the *Amrita-Kunda,* which were widespread before the translation by Shaikh Muhammad Ghaus, imparted its essence to one of his disciples, Shaikh Sulaiman.

Laying special emphasis on the human body as the microcosm of the macrocosm, the *Amrita-Kunda* deals at some length with importance of this belief. The work goes on to prescribe exercises by which one could achieve the Nath-Yogic goal of transubstantiation of the body into a state of *samadhi.* It main emphasis is on the discipline of the body, the senses and the mind, and it prescribes methods for the continued suppression of respiration, which involves inhaling and exhaling the breath in a specialised manner, and fixed the eye on the tip of the nose in order to effect a union between part of the vital spirit resideing in the body and that which pervades all nature. A prerequisite for yogic discipline is the control of the semen, particularly in the initial stages of ascetic exercises, and an accurate knowledge of the organs and their functions. The goal of the yogi is to transmute the physical body into a subtle body, enabling it to obtain the state of *jivan-mukti.*

The knowledge of some Indian sufis, such as Shaikh Abdul-Quddus and his Rudauli *pirs,* was not limited to understanding and practising *pranayama* or *pas-i anfas* and to some semantic similarities and dissimilarities. The Shaikh's *Rushd-Nama* which consists of his own verses and some of his *pirs* identity sufi beliefs based on the *Wahdat al-Wujud* with the philosophy and practices of Goraknath. In fact some verses with slight variations are included in Nath poetry as well as in that of Kabir and Gorakhnath. Such verses were regarded as the common property of both Muslim and Hindu mystics. Of the many verses in the *Rushd-Nama* there are six references to either "Gorakhnath," "Shri Gorakh," "Nath" and "O! Nath."

As in many Nath texts, these words at five different places throughout the work imply Ultimate Reality and Absolute Truth, while in the sixth place, the word refers to the Perfect Siddha or Perfect Man. The term *Sabad* used by Shaikh Abdul-Quddus identifies mystic contemplation with Shakti as well as Shiva and their union as the course of the existence of the three worlds. In other words the union of Shakti, the sun, and Shiva, the moon, according to the Shaikh, is the *salat-i-makus* of the sufis. The yogi equivalent is the *ulti sadhna* (regressive process) involving the "complete reversal of human behaviour, from 'respiratory behaviour' (replaced by *pranayama)* to sexual behaviour (annulled by the technique of the return of semen)". In a Persian verse Shaikh Abdul-Quddus says :

"Unless the brain comes down to the foot, None can reach the doors of God."

The Nath describes the Supreme Creator as Alakh-Nath (the

Incomprehensible or Unseeable One) or as Niranjana. Shaikh Abdul-Quddus also uses the name Alakh Niranjan in the same sense. He says that his Lord is Unseeable (Alakh Niranjan) but those who are able to comprehend Him are lost to themselves. In another verse the Shaikh identifies Naranjan with Khuda and calls Him the creator of the different worlds.

Like the Naths, Shaikh Abdul-Quddus attaches great importance to Onkar. To the Naths the word represents Para-Brahma (transcendent Brahm or the undefinable Absolute). The physical culture of the Naths is designed to make the body incorruptible and purified; Onkar is the basis of *pranayama.* In the initial stages, breath is drawn up through the left nostril, the *ira,* while the sacred Hindu syllable "Om" is repeated slowly sixteen times. The breath is then suspended in the upper part of the nose where the breath nostrils meet. The junction of the nostrils is called the *sukhmana.* Just as the breath has been drawn up by theleft nostril, so it is forced down through the right nostril to *pingala,* while the syllable is again repeated sixteen times. The highest degree of perfection is extremely difficult to achieve, but Shaikh Abdul-Quddus expects sufis to absorb themselves in Onkar through *zikr.* To him Onkar is the Absolute Oneness, is interchangeable with Niranjana and indicates the state of *sunyata* (void).

Shaikh Abdul-Quddus also explains the concept of *sahaja* according to Nath traditions. He emphasizes it in the sense of the union between Shakti and Shiva. However, the realization of *sahaja,* says the Shaikh leads to the achieving of ontological immortality or the sufi *baqa'.* A state of perfect equilibrium, it transcends perceptual knowledge with positive and negative experience. The Nath in such a state is simultaneously both the meditator and the meditation and the divinity meditated upon. The *sunya,* or *sahaja* of the Shaikh is also identical with the *sunya* and the *sahaja* of the Naths.

To both the Naths and Shaikh Abdul-Quddus, *sabad* stands for the indefinable divine word. It is the source of all words, both heard and undeard, and is precieved by only perfect mystics. Yogic exercises do help to register such mystical sounds but the most important step in the comprehension of *sabad* is to make the Truth dwell in the heart through centemplation. The Shaikh exhorts sufis to meditate on the True Name or *ism-i Azam.* In the words of Gorakh, Shaikh Abdul-Quddus warns yogis that wearing rings in their ears and rosaries of Eleocarpus ganitrus around their necks, or the recitation of *sakhi* and *sabad* (Nath poetry), fails to make one a yogi. These were only means to achieve worldly ambitions and were not true Yoga. In the same strain he warned the ulama that they were selling knowledge in return for a living, and would not achieve *Marifa*.

Muhammad was a deep mystery, believed Shaikh Abdul-Quddus and could not be approached by the mere crying of his name. In fact Ahmad (Muhammad) and Ahad (One or God) were the same and everyone in the world was misguided because of a failure to understand the true significance of the intervening *mim* (M) in the wordss Ahmad and Ahad. Although it was a Hindi version of some of Shabistari's verses from the *Gulshan-i Raz,* Shaikh Abdul-Quddus impressively expressed the same idea of the truth in relevance to Nath verses. Shabistari says:

"All these varied forms arise only from your fancy,
They are but one point resolving qucikly in a circle.
It is but one circular line from first to last
Whereon the creatures of this world are journeying;
On this road the prophets are as princes,
Guides, leaders and counsellors.
And of them our lord Muhammad is the chief,
At once the first and the last in this matter.
The One (Ahad) was made manifest in the mim of Ahmad
In this circuit the first emanation became the last
A single mim divides Ahad from Ahmad
The world is immersed in that one mim.
In him is completed the end of this road,
In him is the station of the text 'I call to God'."

Some verses ascribed to Gorakhnath in the Hindi *Gorakhbani* challenge qazis fro mechanically crying the name "Muhammad" and remind them that it was most improper for them to call themselves Muslims for they recited the *Kalima* without gaining its real meaning. A true Muslim was expected to develop spirituality in the same way as Muhammad and to die to self before the death of his earthly body. Shaikh Abdul-Quddus finds the teachings of the Naths identical to the *Wahdat al-Wujud.* According to Gorakhnath the Absolute Truth realized in the highest spiritual experience is above the concept of *bhava* (existence) and *abhava* (negation of existence), absolutely devoid of origination and destruction, and beyond the reach of all speculation and imagination. This is *Paru-Brahma,* which is without name, form, ego, causality or activity, self-manifestation or internal and external differences. This philosophy of Grakhnath and the Siddhas called the *Dwaita-dwaita-vilakshana-vada* or *Pakshapata-binirmukta-vada* is nearest to the *Wahdat al-Wujud.* The simile of the relationship between river water and bubbles applied to the Naths could also be used to explain the *Wahdat al-Wujud.*

More Hindi verses in support of the *Wahdat al-Wujud* were added by the Shaikh in the *Rushd-Nama.* He argued that steam rising from a river water from the cloud falls into a vessel it s known as water of whatever receptacle it finds itself, it if falls in the form of rain it is known as rain water. The following verses of the Quran continues the same theme:

"Everyone that is thereon will pass away;

There remaineth but the countenance of thy Lord of Migh and Glory."

"And cry not unto any other god along with Allah.

There is no God save him.

Everything will perish save His countenance.

His is the command, and unto Him ye will be brought back."

Duality according to the Shaikh Abdul-Quddus is a false concept and the idea of anything besides God is misguided. People should believe only in the Unity of Being.

The sufi theory of creation is also neatly reconciled with the corresponding Nath theory. All sufis believe in the following eplanation of creation, said to have been revealed by God to David:

"I was a Hidden Treasure and I wished to be known, so I created creation that I might be known."

This desire is identical with the concept of divine will as held by the Naths. The Nath theory of the Lord existing alone in a void is no different from Jili's theory of *al-Ama* (the dark mist and blindness).

To Shaikh Abdul-Quddus the Nath theory of cration was a replica of Ibn al-Arabi's theory which the former expressed this way:

"When God willed in respect of His Beautiful Names (attributes), which are beyond enumeration, that their essences (ayun)*—or if you wish, you may say "His essence* ('aynuhu)*"—should be seen, He caused them to be seen in a microcosmic being* (kawn jami') *which, inasmuch as it is endowed with existence, contains the whole object of vision, and through which the inmost*

consciousness (sirr) *of God becomes manifested to Him. This He did, because the vision that consists in a thing's seeing itself by means of itself is not like its vision of itself in something else that serves as a mirror for it; therefore God appears to Himself in a form given by the place in which He is seen (that is, the mirror), and He would not appear thus (objectively) without the existence of this place and His epiphany to Himself therein. God had already brought the universe into being with an existence resembling that of a fashioned soulless body, and it was like an un-polished mirror."*

All the verses by Shaikh Abdul-Quddus relating to the simile of the mirror and the polishing of the heart are based on ideas expressed by Ibn al-Arabi and Gorakhnath.

The *pas-i anfas,* founded on the yogic *pranayama* and the ontological physiology of the Naths were subjects around which the Shaikh wrote a number of eloquent verses, and his arguments were presented very forcefully. Quoting the sufi belief that those who had no human *pir* were disciples of the devil, in a Hindi verse the Shaikh said that if a blind man led another blind man, both were bound to fall into a well. A ceaseless effort was needed to find the perfect *guru* whom the Shaikh likened to a diamond mine—unless it was dug patiently and assiduously, the diamonds would never be found. The Shaikh's interest in Nath teaching was not merely theoretical. In several ways he found Nath ascetic exercises compatible with Chishti practices. Besides obligatory prayers the Shaikh would perform four hundred *rakats* of *namaz* during the day and four hundred *rakats* at night. The clothes covering his knees would be threadbare from kneeling Winter's excessive cold and frost were no obstacle to his prayng. After performing the evening *namaz* he would begin the *zikr-i jahr.*

Those who joined him would tire, but the Shaikh's absorption in the *Wahdat al-Wujud* failed to quench his enthusiasm. For years after the evening *namaz* he would perform the *namaz-i makus.* This was carried out by hanging, probably head downwards, and was generally continued the whole night. Although Chishtis believed this type of *namaz* to be a legacy from the Prophet, as pointed out earlier, Shaikh Abu Sa'id bin Abil-Khair was the first known sufi to have practised it; the first Indian sufi to perform it was Baba Farid. Shaikh Abdul-Quddus considered it to be the counterpart of the *ulti sadhna.*

Continual performance of *namaz-i makus* produced in the Shaikh a condition he called *sultan-i zikr* in which one experienced strange changes in the physical and spiritual condition including a deprivation of the senses and a lack of feeling of consciousness. Repeated appearances of the *sultan-i zikr* led to the state of *fana' al-fana.* A description of this spiritual experience, given by Shaikh Ruknuddin, would tend to indicate that *sultan-i zikr* was comparable to the Nath Siddha's, and that *fana' al-fana* was a state experienced by the *jivan-mukta.*

Sultan-i Zikr, Shaikh Ruknuddin's description contininued, would appear just before walking. During that period external senses were very weak, the inner contemplation made wakefulness and sleep appear identical. Later the state would reappear during consciousness. Initially the contemplative was quite frightened, but gradually he became accustomed to the condition. The seeker of God waited for the reappearance of this state in which he could simultaneously percieve both the entire world and identify those who were obsessed with it. Sometimes the mediator consciousness of himself as a spatial entity and was plunged into the state of *fana' al-fana.*

Shaikh Ruknuddin then compared the condition of *sulan-i zikr* with that experienced by the Prophet Muhammad when he received *wahi.* In short, he added that at the commencement of *sultan-i zikr,* the meditator felt as if he were listening to the humming of a bell whose sound then gradually became thunderous. According to Shaikh Abdul-Quddus this had special relevance to *nad* and was a privelege of only a few outstanding sufis.

The author of this remarkable Nath Hindi poetry, Shaikh Abdul-Quddus Gangohi, used Alakh as his Hindi *nom de plume.* The Shaikh was initiated into the Chishti-Sabiri order of Shaikh Ahmad Abdul-Haqq wo, like his father, wrote Hindi verses, some of which were incorporated by Shaikh Abdul-Quddus into the *Rush-Nama.* Shaikh Arif's successor was Shaikh Muhammad who was the same age as Shaikh Abdul-Quddus. In order to have a living *pir* as a guide, the latter obtained initiation from Shaikh Muhammad and also claimed to have directly obtained inspiration from the spirit of Shaikh Ahmad Abdul-Haqq.

Shaikh Abdul-Quddus came from Rudauli and was born about AD 1456. His father Shaikh Isma'il was an *'alim* but he was also a friend of Shaikh Ahmad Abdul-Haqq. From his childhood, Shaikh Abdul-Quddus was drawn to a life of ascetism and although he obtained a formal education from eminent 'ulama his absorbing interest was in the *Wahdat al-Wujud.* He decided to dedicate his life to the service of Shaikh Ahmad's *khanqah* and to live the life of a celibate. Forced by his parents to marry, the Shaikh continuously neglected his family by spending every possible moment in prayer and meditation. He seems to have written his two most significant works, the *Anwarul-Uyun* and the *Rush-Nama* at Rudauli.

In *c.* 1491 Shaikh Abdul-Quddus migrated to Shahabad, in Ambala near Delhi. On 5 Jumada I 897/5 March 1492, his son Shaikh Ruknuddin, the commentator of the *Rushd-Nama* and the author of the *Latif-i Quddusi,* was born. The reason for the Shaikh's migration, as given in the *Lataif-i Quddusi,* are emotional. The work states that Rudauli had succumbed to the infiltration of *kafirs,* Islamic practices disappeared and pork was openly sold in the bazaar.

So converned was the Shaikh that he left Rudauli for Sultan Sikandar Lodi's camp at Nakhna. One of the Shakih's servants informed Umar Khan Sarwani, the vizier of Sultan Sikandar, of the situation, and he invited him to settle in his *pargana* at Shahabad. It would appear, however, that the move was precipitated more by expedient than pious motives and that it was Umar Khan's offer of hospitality rather than the threat to Islam in Rudauli that prompted the Shaikh's migration.

The relationship between Shaikh Abdul-Quddus and Umar Khan Sarwani was long-standing. The latter had been an important Afghan chief under Sultan Bahlul and had been despatched to serve Prince Nizam Khan, who later succeeded his father as Sultan Sikandar. Umar Khan's relations with Prince Nizam deteriorated and he fled to the court of a rival, Prince Barbak Shah, the governor of Jaunpur. Not succeeding at Jaunpur, Umar Khan sought shelter with the saints of Rudauli. There Shaikh Abdul-Quddus prayed that Umar Khan's fortune might change. Soon afterwards he was reconciled with the Prince.

The Rajput invasion of Rudauli and other predominantly Muslim towns in the Sharqi kingdom were commonplace occurences. In the lifetime of Shaikh Ahmad Abdul-Haqq, Rudauli was invaded by a neighbouring Hindu chief. The Afghan wars with the Sharqi kings, whom the Rajput chiefs supported, and later Barbak's struggle to succeed Sultan Bahlul, greatly assisted the consolidation of Rajput power in that region.

After his succession, Sultan Sikandar defeated Barbak near Kanauj but in order to further strengthe his position, he restored the throne of Jaunpur to Barbak. Barbak was not however interested either in crushing the Rajput power or uprooting Husain Shah Sharqi. The region remained torn with war until Barbak was finally expelled from Jaunpur in 1493. It is little wonder therefore that Shaikh Abdul-Quddus preferred to migrate to a more peaceful region and seized the opportunity when it arose. However, he does not seem to have accepted either financial assistance or land grants. His family then faced a severe economic crisis often starving for days. But like many other outstanding sufis, the Shaikh's meditation was undisturbed by such a situation.

After settling in Shahabad, Shaikh Abdul-Quddus visited Ajodhan and Multan. He seems to have visited Delhi more than once and became friendly with Sultan Sikandar Lodi. In a letter to the Sultan, the Shaikh reminded him of his duties as a ruler. His advice was based on the traditional Perso-islamic political theories defined by Ghazali, but it marks a departure from the traditional Chishti practice of unreserved non-involvement in politics. Shaikh Abdul-Quddus wrote to Sikandar Lodi that an hour spent by rulers in the pursuit of justice was more commendable than sixty hours of prayers by others. He went on to write that religious faith and the well-being of the state depended on the Sultan; in hs absence men would devour each other. Communities needed kings just as the body needed the soul. Sultans were distinguished by the title "Shadow of God on Earth." If a monarch neglected to protect the weak, the holy, the ulama and mystics, the world would become anarchic.

The numbr of Shaikh Abdul-Quddus disciples increased and he corresponded with many who lived away from Shahabad.

Babur's victory over Dipalpur and Lahore in 1523-24 made regions around Delhi exceedingly unsafe both to Muslims and non-Muslims. According to Shaikh Ruknuddin, a large number of ulama and holy men were killed and their libraries destroyed. A lot of Punjabi families moved to safer areas and amongst the emigrants was the Shaikh who settled at Gangoh in the Saharanpur district of U.P. He returned to Shahabad again when his house and thatched *Jamaat-khana* there were burnt in an accidental fire. Meanwhile, Babur marched to panipat where the Mughal army was opposed by Ibrahim Lodi's forces.

Shaikh Abdul-Quddus and his family acoompanied the rear of the Lodi army for safety. Sultan Ibrahim had the Shaikh brought to his camp where the latter predicted his impending defeat.

The Shaikh told his disciples and family to flee to the eastern districts. Only the Shakh, his son and a Saiyid servant remained at the Afghan camp. After Ibrahim Lodi's defeat at panipat on 20 April 1526, the three were captured and taken to Delhi where they were released by Babur. Leaving Delhi the Shaikh retired to Gangoh where he remained for the rest of his life.

There is no tangible evidence that Babur met the Shaikh, however, it is likely as the Emperor always showed a great interest in sufis and holy men. Moreover a letter written by the Shaikh to Babur indicates that they were acquainted with each other. Apparently Babur had suggested the imposition of *ushr* upon the *wajah-i maash* of the ulama and the sufis. While requesting the Emperor to honour, ulama, *aima* and the weak, the Shaikh commented, that the imposition of *ushr* upon the *wajah-i maash* of these classes should not be permitted and should be considered a heinous sin; he added it was a particularly unwise act to ask for money from dervishes.

The tax should remitted so that all those people who would have fallen into such a category could live peacefully and pray for the prosperity of the Emperor and the Muslim community. The *muhtasibs* should be appointed in towns and bazaars so that the *Sharia* could be enforced. The *jama'* should be realized according to the traditions of the *Khulfa-i Rashidun,* the First Four Caliph, and their successors. Only the pious should be appointed as government officers so that revenue could be collected according to the *Sharia.* No *kafir* should be appointed to any post in the *diwan* of a Muslim capital or should hold offices such as *amirs* and *'amil.*

They should receive no financial assistance from the government, and should live in a miserable condition. Kafirs should be forced to pay regular revenue and taxes on their agricultural and commercial undertakings, their dress should differ from Muslims, their worship should be in secret and they should not openly indulge in heretical practices.

They should not draw salaries from the *Baitul-mal* but confine their activities to their traditional trades and professions. Equal treatment with Muslims was not to be given in the interests of Islam. The puritanically severe demands made by the Shaikh to Babur were matched only by those emanating from the most conservative amongst the orthodox. No doubt his attitude was prompted by the imposition of *'ushr* on the property held by the ulama and sufis, and like many he considered the Hindu officers of the *diwan* responsible for the financial difficulties of the upper class Muslims.

Guru Nanak exhibited more equanimity and resignation in the divine will than Shaikh Abdul-Quddus. It is interesting that the Shaikh objected to Hindus holding high administrative posts, at the same time failing to censure the Rajput military classes and showing no concern for Hindus charging high interest rates as long as they were involved in traditional roles. It would not be unfair to suggest that the Shaikh's views were inconsistent and extreme and the result of a sufi theorist indulging in politics in a polarized fashion. Another letter was written by Shaikh Abdul-Quddus to Prince Humayun recommending that he accord honourable status to the ulama and holy men.

Humayun paid a visit to the Shaikh's hermitage in Gangoh. On 23 Jumada II 944/27 November 1537 the Shaikh died. Shaikh Ruknuddin was, however, critical of Humayun's religious policy. The *Lataif-i Quddusi* was commenced a month before his father's death and completed after it. In it Humayun was accused of not making distinction between the *kufr* and Islam.

Shaikh Abdul-Quddus had a large number of sons who in turn had many disciples. His successor was Shaikh Ruknuddin who died in AD 1575-76. His *khalifa* was, however, Shaikh Jalal Thaneswari, who died in 1581-82. Besides the *Lataif-i Quddusi,* Shaikh Ruknuddin compiled a commentary on the *Rushd-Nama.* His most difficult problem was to justify the contents of his father's above work.

He was asked how could the poetry of the yogis and *sanniyasis* embody truths about the *Tawhid* as the moral principles of religions came from the prophets alone who were themselves divinely inspired. The Shaikh's reply was that a number of Quranic verses indicated that from the time of Adam to Muhammad more than a hundred thousand prophets were sent to guide different religious communities. Each country and nation received its own prophet. The verses in the Quran say:

> *"Lo! We have sent thee with the Truth, a bearer of glad tidings and a warner; and there is not a nation but a warner hath passed among them."*
>
> *"Whosoever goeth right, it is only for (the good of) his own soul he goeth right, and whsoever erreth, erreth only to its hurt. No laden soul can bear another's load. We never punish until We have sent a messenger."*

The prophets taught their respective communities in the local language and also received divine books in the vernacular. This was so that people might not be reproachful on the Day of Ressurrection that the prophet had not taught them in their own language. Thus the Quran says :

> *"And We never sent a messenger save with the language of his folk, that he might make (the message) clear for them. Then Allah sendeth whom He will astray, and guideth whom He will. He is the Mighty, the Wise."*

Therefore argued Shaikh Ruknuddin, it was impossible to believe that a prophet had not been sent to India and that the *Tawhid* had not been taught in Indian languages. Kafirs had distorted their prophets' message and had reverted to idol worship because of the interference of devils. The Quran states:

"And for every nation there is a messenger. And when their messenger cometh (on the Day of Judgement) it will be judged between them fairly, and they will not be wronged."

Shaikh Ruknuddin reinforced his arguments by also quoting from works on *Hadis* implying that Indian religions were founded on the *Tawhid* and must therefore contain the essence of Reality.

Turning now to other works of Shaikh Abdul-Quddus we should first mention his earliest literary attemp which was begun before his migration to Shahabad. This was a Persian poetical translation of the *Chunda'in.* The manuscript however was lost during the upheavals in Rudauli caused by the wars between Sultan Bahlul and Husain Shah Sharqi. A short treatise by the Shaikh entitled *Nurul-Huda* included an account of creation and was intended to supplement the *Rushd-Nama.* The *Qurratul-Ain* was another detailed work on the *Wahdat al-Wujud.* One of his treatises, the *Risala-i Qudsiyya,* was mentioned by Shaikh Abdul-Haqq.

The letters which Shaikh Abdul-Quddus wrote were collected by his disciple, Buddhan, the son of Rukn Siddiqi of Jaunpur, under the title the *Maktubat-i Quddusiyya.* The work contains 189 letters which deal with almost every significant sufi theme. Also included are several Hindi verses. In a letter to Qazi Abdur-Rahman Sufi of Shahabad the Shaikh wrote that the world was full of impostors and charlatans and then quoted the verse from the *Rushd-Nama* relating to the blind leading the blind, at the same time stating that it had been written by Shaikh Nur. A disciple worshipping his *pir* was better than the worshipper of the Lord, argued the Shaikh, for the latter was busy with the contemplation of his own self and therefore neglected God; one who adored his *pir,* however, worshipped God through the contemplation of His creature. A Hindi verse, *Giri Purbat Bich Base Hamaro Mit,* "Our Love Crosses Obstacles of Mountains," so strongly stimulated Shaikh Abdul-Quddus to meditate on the Omnipotence of the Lord that this prompted him to write a long letter to Bahlul Sufi explaining the subtleties contained in the *Wahdat al-Wujud.* He went on to say that *kufr* and sin alone were not obstacles to the perception of the *Wahdat al-Wujud;* faith, obedience, prayer, piety and so on, could also serve as great hindrances.

The letters of Shaikh Abdul to Shaikh Jalal Thaneswari feature very subtle explanations of the Unity of Being. They emphasize that love is the principal cause for the creation of the world. From a superficial viewpoint love appears easy, in reality, however, it reduces the lover to ashes. He supports this idea by quoting a number of Hindi verses on the subject, some of which from the *Rushd-Nama.* In another letter to Shaikh Jalal, Shaikh Abdul-Quddus quotes the verse "Had the idol worshipper been able to know the truth about the idol, they would have not been misled." He adds that one who had learnt to perceive God saw nothing but Him, however one who had learnt to see everything else but God failed to see Him at all. To the Shaikh he who saw God and not a stone idol was in fact His worshipper, whereas one who never saw God but stone was given to vanity and infidelity. He then quoted the following Pesian verse by Shaikh Bu Ali Qalandar, and used a *doha* from the *Canadian* to support it. The verse can be translated as follows:

> *"Whatever form Thous assumeth people prostrate But they don't eat any fruit from the garden of Thy love."*

FOUR CONVENTIONAL THEORIES OF ISLAMIZATION IN INDIA

Theories purporting to explain the growth of Islam in India may be reduced to four basic modes of reasoning. Each is inadequate. The first of these, which I shall call the Immigration theory, is not really a theory of conversion at all since it views Islamization in terms of the diffusion not of belief but of peoples. In this view, the bulk of India's Muslims are descended from other Muslims who had either migrated overland from the Iranian plateau or sailed across the Arabian Sea. Although some such process no doubt contributed to the Islamization of those areas of South Asia that are geographically contiguous with the Iranian plateau or the Arabian Sea, this argument cannot, for reasons to be discussed below, be used to explain mass Islamization in Bengal.

The oldest theory of Islamization in India, which I shall call the Religion of the Sword thesis, stresses the role of military force in the diffusion of Islam in India and elsewhere. Dating at least from the time of the Crusades, this idea received big boosts during the nineteenth century, the high tide of European imperial domination over Muslim peoples, and subsequently in the context of the worldwide Islamic reform movements of the late twentieth century. Its general tone is captured in the way many nineteenth-and twentieth-century Orientalists explained the rise of Islam in seventh-century Arabia, as illustrated in these lurid lines penned in 1898 by Sir William Muir :

It was the scent of war that now turned the sullen temper of the Arab tribes into eager loyalty....Warrior after warrior, column after column, whole tribes in endless succession with their women and children, issued forth to fight. And ever, at the marvelous tale of cities conquered; of rapine rich beyond compute; of maidens parted on the very field of battle "to every man a damsel or two"...fresh tribes arose and went. Onward and still onward, like swarms from the hive, or flights of locusts darkening the land, tribe after tribe issued forth and hastening northward, spread in great masses to the East and to the West.

In the end, though, after the thundering hooves have passed and the dust has settled, in attempting to explain the Arab conquests, Muir leaves us with little of substance. Rather, he simply asserts the Arabs' fondness for the "scent of war," their love of "rapine," and the promise of "a damsel or two." Muir's vision of a militant, resurgent Islam gone berserk reflected, in addition to old European associations of Islam with war and sex, colonial fears that Europe's own Muslim subjects might, in just such a locustlike manner, rise up in revolt and drive the Europeans back to Europe. Sir William, after all, was himself a senior British official in colonial India, as well as an aggressive activist for the Christian missionary movement there.

If colonial officials could imagine that the reason for the rise of Islam was its inherently militant nature, they had little difficulty explaining its extension in India in similar terms. Yet as Peter Hardy has observed, those who argued that Indian Muslims were forcibly converted have generally failed to define either *force* or *conversion,* leaving one to presume that a society can and will alter its religious identity simply because it has a sword at its neck. Precisely how this mechanism worked, either in theoretical or in practical terms, has never, however, been satisfactorily explained. Moreover, proponents of this theory seem to have confused conversion to the Islamic religion with the extension of Turko-Iranian rule in North India between 1200 and 1760, a confusion probably originating in too literal a translation of primary Persian accounts narrating the "Islamic" conquest of India. As Yohanan Friedmann has observed, in these accounts one frequently meets with such ambiguous phrases as "they submitted to Islam", or "they came under submission to Islam", in which "Islam" might mean either the religion, the Muslim state, or the "army of Islam." But a contextual reading of such passages usually favours one of the latter two interpretations, especially as these same sources often refer to Indo-Turkish armies as the *lashkar-i Islam,* or "army of Islam," and not the *lashkar-i Turkan,* or "army of Turks." In other words, it was the Indo-Muslim state, and, more explicitly, its military arm, to which people were said to have submitted, and not the Islamic faith. Nor does the theory fit the religious geography of South Asia. If Islamization had ever been a function of military or political force, one would expect that those areas exposed most intensively and over the longest period to rule by Muslim dynasties—that is, those that were most fully exposed to the "sword"—would today contain the greatest number of Muslims. Yet the opposite is the case, as those regions where the most dramatic Islamization occurred, such as eastern Bengal or western Punjab, lay on the fringes of Indo-Muslim rule, where the "sword" was weakest, and where brute force could have exerted the least influence. In such regions the first accurate census reports put the Muslim population at between 70 and 90 percent of the total, whereas in the heartland of Muslim rule in the upper Gangetic Plain—the domain of the Delhi Fort and the Taj Mahal, where Muslim regimes had ruled the most intensively and for the longest period of time—the Muslim population ranged from only 10 to 15 percent. In other words, in the subcontinent as a whole there is an *inverse* relationship between the degree of Muslim political penetration and the degree of Islamization. Even within Bengal this principle holds true. As the 1901 *Census of India* put it:

> *None of these [eastern] districts contains any of the places famous as the head-quarters of Mohammedan rulers. Dacca was the residence of the Nawab for about a hundred years, but it contains a smaller proportion of Muslims than any of the surrounding districts, except Faridpur. Malda and Murshidabad contain the old capitals, which were the center of Musalman rule for nearly four and a half centuries, and yet the Muslims form a smaller proportion of the population than they do in the adjacent districts of Dinajpur, Rajshahi, and Nadia.*

Indeed, it has even been proposed that, far from promoting the cause of Islamization, the proximity of Muslim political power in some cases actually hindered it. According to S. L. Sharma and R. N. Srivastava, Mughal persecution of the nominally converted Meo community of Rajasthan had the effect, not of strengthening the Meos' Islamic identity, but of reinforcing their resistance to Islam.

A third theory commonly advanced to explain Islamization in India is what I call the Religion of Patronage theory. This is the view that Indians of the premodern period converted to Islam in order to receive some non-religious favour from the ruling class—relief from taxes, promotion in the bureaucracy, and so forth. This theory has always found favour with Western-trained secular social scientists who see any religion as a dependent variable of some non-religious agency, in particular an assumed desire for social improvement or prestige.

Many instances in Indian history would appear to support this theory. In the early fourteenth century, Ibn Battuta reported that Indians presented themselves as new converts to the Khalaji sultans, who in turn rewarded them with robes of honour according to their rank.

According to nineteenth-century censuses, many landholding families of Upper India had declared themselves Muslims in order to escape imprisonment for nonpayment of revenue, or to keep ancestral lands in the family. The theory might even be stretched to include groups employed by Muslim rulers that assimilated much Islamic culture even if they did not formally convert. The Kayasthas and Khatris of the Gangetic Plain, the Parasnis of Maharashtra, and the Amils of Sind all cultivated Islamic culture while meeting the government's need for clerks and administrative servants, a process that Aziz Ahmad once compared with nineteenth-and twentieth-century "Westernization."

The acculturation of captured soldiers or slaves perhaps formed another dimension of this process. Severed from their families, and with no permanent sociocultural ties to their native homes, these men not surprisingly fell into the cultural orbit of their patrons.

Although this thesis might help explain the relatively low incidence of Islamization in India's political heartland, it cannot explain the massive conversions that took place along the political fringe—as in Punjab or Bengal.

Political patronage, like the influence of the sword, would have decreased rather than increased as one moved away from the centers of that patronage. What we need is some theory that can explain the phenomenon of mass Islamization on the periphery of Muslim power and not just in the heartland, and among millions of peasant cultivators and not just among urban elites. To this end a fourth theory, which I call the Religion of Social Liberation thesis, is generally pressed into service.

Created by British ethnographers and historians, elaborated by many Pakistani and Bangladeshi nationals, and subscribed to by countless journalists and historians of South Asia, especially Muslims, this theory has for long been the most widely accepted explanation of Islamization in the subcontinent.

The theory postulates a Hindu caste system that is unchanging through time and rigidly discriminatory against its own lower orders. For centuries, it is said, the latter suffered under the crushing burden of oppressive and tyrannical high-caste Hindus, especially Brahmans.

Then, when Islam "arrived" in the Indian subcontinent, carrying its liberating message of social equality as preached (in most versions of the theory) by Sufi Shaikhs, these same oppressed castes, seeking to escape the yoke of Brahmanic oppression and aware of a social equality hitherto denied them, "converted" to Islam en masse.

It can be seen that by juxtaposing what it perceives as the inherent justice of Islam and the inherent wickedness of Hindu society, the Religion of Social Liberation theory identifies motives for conversion that are, from a Muslim perspective, eminently praiseworthy.

The problem, however, is that no evidence can be found in support of the theory. Moreover, it is profoundly illogical. First, by attributing present-day values to peoples of the past, it reads history backward.

Before their contact with Muslims, India's lower castes are thought to have possessed, almost as though familiar with the writings of Jean-Jacques Rousseau or Thomas Jefferson, some innate notion of the fundamental equality of all humankind denied them by an oppressive Brahmanic tyranny. In fact, however, in thinking about Islam in relation to Indian religions, premodern Muslim intellectuals did not stress their religion's ideal of social equality as opposed to Hindu inequality, but rather Islamic monotheism as opposed to Hindu polytheism. That is, their frame of reference for comparing these two civilizations was theological, not social. In fact, the idea that Islam fosters social equality (as opposed to religious equality) seems to be a recent notion, dating only from the period of the Enlightenment, and more particularly from the legacy of the French Revolution among nineteenth-century Muslim reformers.

Second, even if Indians *did* believe in the fundamental equality of mankind, and even if Islam *had* been presented to them as an ideology of social equality—though both propositions appear to be false—there is abundant evidence that Indian communities failed, upon Islamization, to improve their status in the social hierarchy.

On the contrary, most simply carried into Muslim society the same birth-ascribed rank that they had formerly known in Hindu society. This is especially true of Bengal. As James Wise observed in 1883: "In other parts of India menial work is performed by outcast Hindus; but in Bengal any repulsive or offensive occupation devolves on the Mohammedan. The Beldar [scavenger, and remover of carcasses] is to the Mohammedan village what the Bhuinmali is to the Hindu, and it is not improbable that his ancestors belonged to this vile caste."

Finally, as with the Sword and Patronage theories, the Religion of Social Liberation theory is refuted by the facts of geography. In 1872, when the earliest reliable census was taken, the highest concentrations of Muslims were found in eastern Bengal, western Punjab, the Northwest Frontier region, and Baluchistan. What is striking about those areas is not only that they lay far from the center of Muslim political power but that their indigenous populations had not yet, at the time of their contact with Islam, been fully integrated into either the Hindu or the Buddhist social system.

In Bengal, Muslim converts were drawn mainly from Rajbansi, Pod, Chandal, Kuch, and other indigenous groups that had been only lightly exposed to Brahmanic culture, and in Punjab the same was true of the various Jat clans that eventually formed the bulk of the Muslim community.

But this is hardly surprising. The *Baudhayana-Dharmasutra*, a late Vedic text (fifth-sixth centuries B.C.) reflecting the values of self-styled "clean" castes, divided the subcontinent into three concentric circles, each one containing distinct sociocultural communities.

The first of these, Aryavarta, or the Aryan homeland, corresponded to the Upper Ganges-Jumna region of north-central India; there lived the "purest" heirs to Brahmanic tradition, people styling themselves highborn and ritually clean. The second circle contained an outer belt (Avanti, Anga-Magadha, Saurastra, Daksinapatha, Upavrt, and Sindhu-Sauvira) corresponding to Malwa, East and Central Bihar, Gujarat, the Deccan, and Sind.

These regions lay within the pale of Indo-Aryan settlement, but they were inhabited by people "of mixed origin" who did not enjoy the same degree of ritual purity as those of the first region. And the third concentric circle contained those outer regions inhabited by "unclean" tribes considered so far beyond the pale that penances were prescribed for those who visited such places.

Peoples living in this third circle included the Arattas of Punjab, the Sauviras of southern Punjab and Sind, the Pundras of North Bengal, and the Vangas of central and East Bengal.

Now, the theory of Social Liberation assumes the prior existence of a highly stratified Hindu social order presided over by an entrenched and oppressive Brahman community. If the theory were valid, then, the greatest incidence of conversion to Islam should logically have occurred in those areas where Brahmanic social order was most deeply entrenched—namely, in the core region of Aryavarta.

Conversely, Islam should have foundits fewest adherents in those areas having the least exposure to Brahmanic civilization, that is, along the periphery or beyond the pale of that civilization, in the outermost of the three concentric circles cited in the *Baudhayana-Dharmasutra*.

But it is precisely in that outer circle—the area roughly coinciding with the areas included in the original (1947) state of Pakistan, with its eastern and western wings—that the vast majority of South Asian Muslims reside. The modern, pre-Partition distribution of South Asian Muslims thus indicates an outcome precisely opposite to the one predicted by the theory—namely, the less the prior exposure to Brahmanic civilization, the greater the incidence of subsequent Islamization.

If the aboriginal peoples inhabiting India's "periphery" had never been fully absorbed in a Brahman-ordered society in the first place, the matter of their escaping an oppressive Hindu social order cannot arise logically, just as it did not arise empirically.

MUSLIM SCHOLARS AND SUFI SHEIKHS : ULAMA AND MASHAIKH

Muslim scholars and Sufi Sheikhs, though not all rich, also belonged to the upper classes because of the respect they enjoyed in society. Most of them were patronised by kings and nobles, many were actually in their employ. Some of them were very well-off.

THE ULAMA (THE MUSLIM LAW)

Ulama (plural of alim or learned) used to be well-versed in the Muslim law. As such they assisted Muslim monarchs in administering their dominions according to the Shariat. That way they also helped the Muslims in organizing their lives according to the Shariat which comprehends not only beliefs and practices, public and personal law, and rules of behaviour but even includes dress and personal appearance. Acquiring knowledge for the sake of earning money was looked down upon; hence tradition classified the Ulama into two categories, *Ulama-i-Akhirat* (the pious) and *Ulama-i-su* (the worldly). Knowledge was an extremely valuable ornament in an age when the educated were few and the Ulama were respected for their learning and ability. Naturally, there was hardly any secular approach to education.

Great emphasis was laid on theological education (*manqulat*). The most important subjects taught were Hadis, Fiqh (jurisprudence) and Tafsir (exegesis). The institutions of higher learning, called *madrasas*, were essentially schools of theology, with auxiliaries of grammar, literature and logic. 'These *madrasas* were the strongholds of orthodoxy and were subsidised by the state.' A high value is placed on Muslim orthodoxy everywhere, because it is claimed that it maintains the identity of the community as against other communities.

In actual practice it has served as a force against an integrated living, even coexistence, with other communities. In a word, the Ulama were an orthodox lot. Those who were denied the life of affluence usually took to teaching (as *mutawalli*) in some mosque or under the thatched roof of their own mud houses. Some other Ulama or *danishmands* became pious preachers and scholars. Very often they too had to work under indigent circumstances. Some outstanding scholars were appointed as teachers in *madrasas* established by the Sultans. It was the ambition of the Ulama to join government service. There were many offices which the establishment could offer to a scholar. In official hierarchy of such appointments the post of the Sadr-i-Jahan came at the top, then followed Qadis (judges), Muftis (interpreters of law) Muhtasibs (censors of public morals), Imams (who led prayers) and Khatibs (reciters of the Quran). The Sadr-i-Jahan was the chief of the judicial department. He served as the Qadi-i-Mumalik (chief judge) and recommended to the king about the appointment of junior Qadis. The Sheikh-ul-Islam was in charge of the ecclesiastical affairs of the empire. All those saints, *faqirs* and indigent scholars who enjoyed state patronage were looked after by him. Normally, only well-read scholars were appointed as Khatibs and Imams.

So also was the case with Muftis and Muhtasibs. Muslim public opinion did not approve of the appointment of less qualified persons to these posts. The Ulama received salaries pertaining to the offices they held. Most of the Ulama dabbled in politics. They wielded influence with the kings and nobles as interpreters of Muslim law. Their presence was indispensable to a ruler who was generally uneducated. During the protracted struggle between the crown and the nobility which raged throughout the Sultanate period, they aligned themselves with one or the other of political groups.

They always remained on the right side of the regime and forgot the community whom they were expected to help in times of economic distress and political oppression. In this way they encouraged political oppression on the one hand and on the other they preached the necessity of obedience and submission by the people even to an oppressor, taking shelter under the Quranic injunction: 'Obey God and obey the Prophet, and those in authority among you.' Naturally, 'an unholy alliance with them smoothed the path of king's depotism'.

They themselves did not lag behind in obsequiousness. Their collaboration with and integration into the state apparatus made them subservient to the regime, 'so much so that when Iltutmish nominated Raziya as his successor, there was not a single theologian in the Delhi Empire who could protest against this nomination on the grounds of Shariat.' The way they encouraged Sultans like Ruknuddin Firoz and Muizuddin Kaiqubad not to offer prayers or keep fasts during the month of Ramzan, and live licentious lives, shows how servile they had become and how they 'were wallowing in the dirty welters of politics.' Of course the Ulama were openly critical of one another and, for this they have been criticised by their contemporary writers like Amir Khusrau, Zia Barani, Abdul Haq Muhaddis and Abdul Qadir Badaoni. Kings like Iltutumish and Balban and prince Bughra Khan are also critical of them. But in one thing they did not fail. They kept the rulers and the ruling class on the path of Islam and virtue by informing them 'correctly' about their duty towards the non-Muslims.

Some modern secularist historians blame the Ulama for making Muslim rulers intolerant through their orthodox advice. Such writers fail to realise that it was not safe for the Ulama to cheat the Sultans by giving wrong interpretation of their holy scriptures vis-a-vis the treatment of non-Muslims. I have not come across any instance where the Ulama deliberately gave a distorted version of their scriptures in this context.

And why should they have done so' They were as much interested in seeing the Muslim state being run according to the Shariat as the Sultans. In short, they always interpreted their scriptures correctly and honestly when it came to the Hindus. So that a foreign visitor like Maulana Shamsuddin Turk, who is very critical of the Qadis of the day, condoned their faults for the reason that because of their right advice their king was prone to treating the Hindus terribly. The lifestyle of the Ulama did not come in the way of serving Islam.

Like other Muslims of the higher classes, it was normal for the Ulama to keep harems, live luxuriously and drink wine. Despite a few faults and a little criticism, therefore, the Ulama as a class were indispensable to the regime. They were advisers of the king and ran the establishment. It was from the Ulama class that the various officers of the government as well as religious institutions were chosen. It was through these people that the regime systematized the religious and social life of the Muslim community just as it organized the extension and administration of Muslim dominions in India through the nobility.

THE MASHAIKH (MUSLIM IMMIGRATION)

Equally influential, if not more, were the Sufi Mashaikh. In the early years of Muslim immigration, and more so with the establishment of Muslim rule in India, many Muslim *faqirs*, scholars and Sufi Mashaikh arrived in India. They entered Hindustan on their own or came with the invading armies. Later on, the disturbed conditions in Central Asia, consequent upon the Mongol upheaval also encouraged them to leave their homes in search of security. Many came to settle in India where peace and plenty and the protective arm of Muslim rule promised them all they wished. Sufism may be defined as Islamic mysticism.

In its early years in Central and West Asia, it was deeply influenced by Neo-Platonism, the monastic tradition of Buddhism and Christianity and the Vedantist and Yogic philosophy of Hinduism. All these were Islamized by the Sufis in such a way as to make them virtually unidentifiable. Nawbahar was a great Buddhist monastry in Balkh. The name of the city of Bokhara itself is derived from Vihar. Some Khurasan Sufis lived in caves like Buddhists. They were known as Shikafatiyah from the word Shikafat (cave). When Hindu and Buddhist thinkers and saints converted to Islam in Central and West Asia during the eighth to eleventh centuries they carried their thought and philosophy to Sufism. Ibn-al-Arabi (1165-1241) wrote in his Diwan that idol-worship, Chritian ways and Kaaba were all acceptable to him as he believed in the religion of love. The Sufism that came to India in the twelfth century with the Muslim Mashaikh did not, by and large, envisage direct communion with God without the intermedium of Islam.

Just as the soul and body are one, in Islamic sufism *Tariqah* and *Shariah* are so interrelated. Some Sufis believed in the doctrine of Wahadat-ul-Wajud, or the Unity of Being which means 'There is nothing but God, nothing in existence other than He'. This theory, propounded by Sheikh Ibn al-Arabi and akin to Hindu Vedantism, was developed later on in order to harmonise the doctrine of mysticism with the teachings of orthodox Islam. There were a number of Sufi orders or *silsila* as they are called. Abul Fazl mentions as many as fourteen. But four orders-Chishti, Suhrawardi, Qadiri and Naqshabandi-became prominent in India. Of these only the first two became more popular, for the latter two were extremely orthodox and 'legalistic in their strictness.' By the thirteenth century, northern India saw the flowering of two Sufi orders, Chishti and Suhrawardi, and we will concern ourselves with the Mashaikh of only these two orders. The founder of the Suhrawardi order was Sheikh Bahauddin Zakariya. He was born near Multan in Sind in 578 H. (1182-83 C.E.). He and his disciples played a leading part in the northwest and 'symbolically asked the Chishtis not to dispute possession (of the region) with them. Sheikh Bahauddin Zakariya (and his successors) mixed freely with the Sultans, took part in political affairs, amassed wealth and accepted government honours'.

The Chishtis established themselves at Ajmer in Rajasthan, some parts of the Punjab, Delhi, U.P. and Bihar and further east. They were probably the largest in number and represented what seems to be the most typical in the Sufi way of life. The first great Chishti Sheikh was Khwaja Muinuddin Chishti. He was born in Sijistan in eastern Persia in C.E. 1141. He came to India a little before or after the battle of Taraori or Tarain (1192) and settled down at Ajmer. There also he lies buried after his death in 1236. His mausoleum is a great centre of pilgrimage. He is known as Gharib Nawaz or Friend of the Poor and Nabi-ul-Hind or Prophet of India. Sheikh Saiyyad Muhammad Gesu Daraz (he of the long locks) said that if people were unable to make the pilgrimage to Mecca, a visit once in their lives to the mausoleum of Muinuddin Chishti would convey the same merit.

Sheikh Muinuddin is very famous today. But he was not known as such to his contemporaries. The three contemporary chronicler-Hasan Nizami, Fakhr-i-Mudabbir and Minhaj do not refer to him at all. Early mystic records, the *Favaid-ul-Fuad* and *Khair-ul-Majalis* do not give any information about him. Barani makes no reference to him. Isami tells us only this much that Muhammad bin Tughlaq had once visited his grave. In all probability his fame spread from the time of emperor Akbar (1556-1605 C.E.) who held his memory in great reverence and often paid visit to his dargah in *Ajmer*. However, the legend and fame of Muinuddin rests, as of all other Sheikhs, on the magic-like miracles (*karamah*) he is supposed to have performed. It is difficult to say when the stories of the miracles of Sufis be and to be told but once this process had begun, it could not be stopped. It became a criterion by which Sufis were judged, and the common reason why people believed in them. They credited them with supernatural powers and feared and respected them. P.M. Currie quotes Muhammad Habib to say that most of the mystic records and Diwans are forgeries, 'but regard for public opinion has prevented them (Indian scholars) from making a public declaration that these are forgeries.' However, stories of miracles apart, 'he (Muinuddin Chishti) was Saiyid by descent. He did not depart in any way from Sunna, the Ulama could not fault him, and he performed the hajj.'

Sheikh Muinuddin Chishti had a number of disciples two of whom, Sheikh Hamid and Qutbuddin, had earned reverence of great and small. Sheikh Hamiduddin Nagauri lived with his wife as a villager. Sheikh Qutbuddin Bakhtiyar Kaki came to Delhi in the reign of Iltutmish and lived in a *khanqah* outside the city. He was very fond of *sama* (devotional music). Once he was so overtaken by *wajd* (ecstasy) that he collapsed and breathed his last. One of his principal disciples was Sheikh Fariduddin Ganj-i-Shakar (1175-1265) popularly called Sheikh Farid.

Sheikh Farid lived in extreme poverty bordering on starvation. He trained a large number of disciples, established many *khanqahs* and raised the prestige of the Chishti order. The greatest disciple of Sheikh Farid was Hazrat Nizamuddin Auliya (1236-1325). He was born at Badaun.

In 1258 he settled at Ghayaspur near Delhi where his shrine exists and a railway station is named after him. The Sheikh had a large circle of disciples who hailed from all sections of society, rich and poor, noble and plebian. In his life of almost a century, Nizamuddin Auliya witnessed the reigns of seven Sultans, but he did not attend the darbar of any one of them. He was popularly known as *Mahbub-i-Ilahi* (Beloved of God). His popularity was due to his saintly virtues and service to humanity. His disciples included Amir Khusrau, Ziyauddin Barani and the renowned Sheikh Nasiruddin Chiragh-i-Delhi whom he appointed as his successor (Khalifa). Professor Muhammad Habib rightly calls Nasiruddin the last great saint of the Chishti *Silsilah* to have enjoyed an all India status. This was the best period in India for Sufism in general and the Chishti *Silsilah* in particular. To this famous line of Sufis belongs Sheikh Salim Chishti, a contemporary of emperor Akbar, for whom the latter built a mausoleum in Fatehpur Sikri.

Many of the Sufi Mashaikh lived in poverty. Sheikh Hamiduddin (d. 1276 C.E.) lived in a small mud house in the city of Nagaur in Rajasthan.

He eked out his meagre subsistence by cultivating a single *bigha* of land. His wife spent her time in cooking and spinning like a peasant woman. He was a strict vegetarian. He refused to accept government gift of land and money from the muqta of Nagaur and Sultan of Delhi. 'Sheikh Muinuddin and Sheikh Qutbuddin Bakhtiyar never owned houses of their own. Sheikh Farid Ganj-i-Shakar built a small *kachcha* house only when his family had considerably increased'. For many years during his early life Sheikh Nizamuddin Auliya had to wander from one quarter of the city to another in search of a house'. Generally starvation conditions prevailed in the houses of the Chishti saints'. Very often these saints did not possess sufficient clothes to cover their bodies.'

This is one side of the coin. The other is that Sheikh Muinuddin's sons owned land, which may have been granted to them directly or accepted by the Sheikh for their sake. Sheikh Fariduddin was destitute to the end of his days, but gifts were received and distributed at his *khanqah*. The *khanqah* of Nizamuddin Auliya, probably after he received money from Sultan Nasiruddin Khusrau, 'became an institution in which money, food and goods circulated freely'. However, the Sheikhs who lived in affluence were deemed to possess no less merit than those who elected to remain destitute.

The Sufi Mashaikh are also reported to have shunned the company of the nobles and nearness to the court. But that too was not always so. On the contrary, the attractions of staying near the throne were compulsive. Sidi Maula was a disciple of Sheikh Farid at Ajodhan.' He aspired for name and fame and shifted to Delhi. Once in the capital, Sidi Maula hurled himself headlong in the politics of the court and, after many vicissitudes paid with his life. But Sidi was not alone in this pursuit. As K.A. Nizami has pointed out, 'Even Chisht the cradle-land of the *silsilah* looked to Delhi for guidance in spiritual matters.' The Mashaikh mostly lived in cities and towns where they were popular with kings and people and enjoyed the respectability of upper class elite. Sheikh Qutbuddin Bakhtiyar Kaki was much admired by the people of Delhi headed by Sultan Iltutmish himself. Muinuddin Chishti was very much liked by the Muslims of Ajmer but he was suspected of dabbling in politics which prompted Prithviraj III to ask Ramdeva to expel him from Ajmer. Sheikh Nizamuddin Auliya used to hold his own *darbar* which was often more awe-inspiring than even the court of kings. The Sheikh was so popular with the people that Sultan Alauddin Khalji began to entertain suspicions about his influence and authority in Muslim society. With a view to ascertain the real intentions of the Sheikh, and to find out to what extent he was interested in seeking political power, the Sultan sent him a note seeking his advice and guidance on certain political problems. The Sheikh immediately surmised Alauddin's motives in sending the letter, and replied that he had nothing to do with politics and so could render no advice on political matters: he kept busy with seeking God's grace for Muslim monarchs (*duagoee*). Only after this was the Sultan's mind set at rest. But to many he was popularly known as Sultan Nizamuddin and his resting place as Dargah Sultanji Saheb.

Alauddin greatly respected Nizamuddin Auliya for his supernatural powers and knack for correct predictions. But his son Sultan Qutbuddin Mubarak Khalji disliked him because of his political leanings. He even declared a reward of a thousand *tankahs* for one who would cut off Nizamuddin's head. Once when they chanced to meet, the Sultan refused to acknowledge the salutations of the saint and even called Sheikh Ruknuddin from Multan to eclipse Nizamuddin's popularity.

After Qutbuddin's death, Sultan Nasiruddin Khusrau ascended the throne at Delhi, but his authority was challenged by Ghazi Tughlaq. Khusrau Shah, to gain the support of the Sheikhs sent two or three lakhs of *tankahs* to each of them and five lakh *tankahs* to Nizamuddin Auliya. When Ghazi Tughlaq ascended the throne as Sultan Ghiyasuddin Tughlaq (1320 C.E.) he asked Nizamuddin to render the account of the amount he had received.

The latter sent a reply, 'seemingly insolent', that the money belonged to the *Bait-ul-mal* (Public Treasury) and therefore he had given it to the poor. The Sultan took umbrage at the Sheikh's answer. The relations between the two were sore also because of the Sultan's dislike of sama in which Nizamuddin freely indulged. In this scenario, Nizamuddin Auliya began to support Ghiyasuddin's son, Muhammad Tughlaq, who aspired for the throne. When Ghiyasuddin Tughlaq went on an expedition to Bengal, Nizamuddin Auliya prophesied that the Sultan would never come back from there. When the news of his return was received in Delhi, a worried Prince Muhammad rushed to Nizamuddin with the tiding at which the Sheikh uttered the famous words, 'Delhi is still far off (*hanuz Delhi dur ast*)'. Nizamuddin Auliya was thus immersed in Delhi court politics, at least towards the end of his life (1320-25). But he was a Sufi. He had many disciples who were regular visitors to his *khanqah*. Such an one was Amir Khusrau.

Abul Hasan, popularly known as Amir Khusrau, was the most

favoured disciple of Nizamuddin Auliya. He was a historian, a musician, a poet, a literaturer, a Sufi Sheikh, and a full-fledged protege of Delhi Sultans. His first patron was Prince Muhammad, son of Sultan Ghiyasuddin Balban.

Thereafter for about forty years (1285-1325) he served a continuous succession of monarchs-Muizuddin Kaiqubad, Jalaluddin Khalji, Alauddin Khalji and Mubarak Shah Khalji-and his shrewdness was successful in keeping them all pleased. 'The Sultan (Kaiqubad) flattered him by calling him 'the seal of authors' and promised to give him a big reward which would free him from all worldly cares ever afterwards. His genius, if not character, helped him spend 'the whole of his life in spinning yarn' (or writing many untruths).

Soon after, when Kaiqubad was murdered by Jalaluddin Khalji, he composed a new *masnavi, Miftah-ul-Futuh* in praise of his new patron. Six years later Jalauddin was murdered by his nephew and son-in-law Alauddin Khalji who marched into Delhi with the late king's head held aloft on the point of a spear and, writes Dr. Wahid Mirza, our poet Khusrau 'was one of the first to offer his congratulations to the murderer whose hands were still red with the blood of his king, his uncle and his benefactor? The poet changed with changing time and turned with shifting wind.' No wonder, even Ghiyasuddin Tughlaq, who was hostile to Khusrau's *pir-o-murshid,* Nizamuddin Auliya, receives fulsome praise in Khusrau's *Tughlaq Nama.*

Amir Khusrau was very shrewd. When he found the reign of Qutbuddin Mubarak Khalji nothing to boast about, he wrote *Nuh Sipehr,* praising all things Indian, including the beauty of Indian women. In *Nuh Sipehr* he also wrote: 'They have four books in that language (Sanskrit), which they are constantly in the habit of repeating. Their name is *Bed* (Vedas). They contain stories of their gods, but little advantage can be derived from their perusal.' This betrays the one-track mind of Muslim elite in general. This weakness was shared by almost all Sufi Mashaikh, debunking the belief that Sufi Mashaikh treated Hindus and Muslims on terms of equality or helped bring the two communities nearer to one another.

They were keen on maintaining only orthodox Muslim rule and showed a general disregard for others. Since it was believed that Muhammad bin Tughlaq was not orthodox, Sheikh Nasiruddin Chiragh obtained a promise from Firoz Tughlaq before supporting the latter's claim to the throne, to the effect that he would rule according to the

Shariat. In 1409, when Raja Ganesh (Kans of Muslim chroniclers) obtained the throne of Bengal and sought to establish his authority by keeping the prominent Ulama and Sufis under control, Sheikh Nurul Haqq (Qutbul Alam) wrote to Sultan Ibrahim Sharqi of Jaunpur to come and save the Muslims of Bengal.

Sultan Ibrabim responded to the call and Raja Ganesh, finding himself too weak to meet the challenge, came to the Sheikh and begged for his intercession, promising to agree to any conditions. Sheikh Nurul Haqq said he would intercede for him if he accepted Islam. The Raja retired in favour of his son Jadu, who ascended the throne as Sultan Jalaluddin Shah. Sheikh Nurul Haqq induced Sultan Ibrahim, much against his will, to withdraw his armies. Sheikh Abdul Quddus combined spirituality with dogmatism. 'His letters to Sultan Sikandar Lodi and Babur (1526-30) show that he was as anxious to maintain Muslim rule as any wordly Muslim, that he had no scruples in using the language of a courtier in asking the rulers' to establish the Shariah' 'Akbar's attempt at secularizing the state' had exasperated the divines, and Mulla Shah Ahmad and Sheikh Farid Bukhari exhorted court dignitaries to alter the state of things in the very beginning of Jehangir's reign, 'otherwise it would be difficult to accomplish anything later on.' There are many other such instance.

It is understandable if disgruntled nobles and courtiers invited foreigners to 'rescue Islam,' but the Sufi Mashaikh by such actions compromised their image as 'Indians first' and respecters of all people as equals. They were as opposed to 'national integration' as any orthodox Muslim.

Similarly, many modern scholars have shown that some Sufi Mashaikh too resorted to aggressive and violent means in fighting infidelity. Even Sheikh Muinuddin Chishti's 'picture of tolerance is replaced by a portrait of him as a warrior for Islam.' Since we have studied this problem in detail elsewhere, we would not like to repeat the cases of aggressive proselytization of Sufi Mashaikh mentioned therein. However, one shocking instance of forcible conversion not mentioned in my book referred to above, may be given here. Saiyyad Jalaluddin Bukhari Makhdum-i-Jahanian of Sind (d.1384) fell very seriously ill. Nawahun, the *darogha* of Uchch, called on him to enquire about his health. As a matter of courtesy and to raise his sinking spirits, Nahawun said: 'May God restore your health' your holiness is the last of the saints as the Prophet Muhammad was the last of the prophets.'

Sayyid Jalaluddin Bukhari even on death-bed construed it as an expression of faith in Islam and demanded a formal declaration of conversion from him. Nawahun firmly declined to make any such declaration. Thereupon he was charged with apostasy. He fled to the court of Firoz Shah Tughlaq in search of asylum and redress. When Sayyid Jalaluddin Bukhari expired, his younger brother Sadruddin Raju Qattal, rushed to Delhi in order to persuade Firoz Shah to execute Nawahun. Though some scholars of the capital did not agree with the viewpoint of Raju Qattal, the latter prevailed upon Firoz Shah in obtaining his permission for Nawahun's execution as a renegade.

Poor or rich, the Sufi Mashaikh lived as householders. Except Nizamuddin Auliya and Nasiruddin Chiragh, all Sufi Sheikhs married, and had large families. Since the word saint is associated with celibacy in people's minds of most religions, it would be pertinent to state that 'marriage is enjoined on every Muslim, and celibacy is frequently condemned by Muhammad. 'It is related in the Traditions that Muhammad said: When the servant of God marries, he perfects half his religion'? Consequently in Islam, even the ascetic orders are rather married than single.' Sheikh Muinuddin Chishti took two wives-Ummatullah and Asmatullah, and had three sons and one daughter. He had married in his old age 'only to realise that his spiritual powers had greatly suffered on that account.'

Sheikh Qutbuddin Bakhtiyar Kaki Ushi also married twice, late in life. He divorced one of his wives, soon after marriage, as her presence upset his programme of prayers. He had four sons.

Sheikh Farid had a number of wives and a large family. Sheikh Nasiruddin Chiragh is reported to have stated that Sheikh Farid had a number of wives (*harem bisyar bud*). He had at least four wives and eight children. Sheikh Hamiduddin had led a very voluptuous life in his early years, but when he joined the circle of Sheikh Muinuddin Chishti, he adopted the life of a mystic in all sincerity. He had a number of children. Sheikh Qutbuddin Husain Kirmani, uncle of the author of *Siyar-ul-Auliya*, used to put on the garments of the finest Chinese silks and Kamkhawab and always used to have pan in his mouth. Sheikh Nizamuddin Auliya also relished betel.

All this was normal life and all these were normal pleasures. But Sufi Mashaikh, known by many names like Wali, Shah, Qalandar, Murshid, Marabout, Sheikh, Faqir and Darwesh, indulged in all kinds of pleasures and luxuries. The case of Sidi Maula was exceptional. He had ready at hand brand new *tankahs* under every coverlet to spend. So many people dined at his *khanqah* that, if Barani is to be believed, 'two thousand *man* of flour (*maida*), two to three hundred *man* of sugar and a hundred to two hundred man of vegetables used to be consumed in his kitchen every day.'

But others were equally non-poor and generous. 'We know that Sheikh Farid was destitute to the end of his days, but we also know that gifts were received and distributed. It could be said generally of every *khanqah* that even in the bad days a person' was sure to get some sort of a meal and, with luck, a share of money' in every *khanqah* ideals of austerity fought against satisfaction of physical needs,' so that there was no dearth of money and parasites because of the well-to-do admirers of the Sheikh.

Sama or devotional music was a common feature of the *khanqah*. During *sama*, the Sheikhs and Qalandars placed strong insistence on the practice of *Nazar-ilal murd* or gazing at good looking boys. One reason why Ghiyasuddin Tughlaq could not see eye to eye with Nizamuddin Auliya was the latter's fondness for *sama* and his ecstatic fits. The Sultan was free from unnatural lust (*lawatat*) and did not allow 'handsome beardless boys' from coming near him. In the *khanqahs* were also used drugs of the hashish family, and even drinking was common. Love affairs of sufis were of common occurrence. Ahmad Yadgar mentions the case of a *faqir* who fell for the newly wed bride of the son of Tatar Khan. He relates another story about the love of a *darwesh* and a woman. Love between a Hindu girl and a *darwesh* created flutter and tension.

The Sheikhs used to marry in high families and possessed a clout which sometimes became a problem for Sultans. A sixteenth century Suhrawardi writer says that Sheikh Sadruddin Arif had married a divorced wife of Prince Muhammad, the eldest son of Balban. The circumstances of this marriage are given as follows: The prince divorced his wife, whom he passionately loved, in a fit of fury. When he recovered his normal state of mind, he felt deeply pained for what he had done. Legally he could not take her back into his *harem* unless she was married to someone else and then divorced by him. A man of genuine piety was searched to restore the broken relationship. Sheikh Arif, the most outstanding saint of the town, promised to marry the princess and divorce her the next day. But, after the marriage, he refused to divorce her on the ground that the princess herself was not prepared to be divorced. This incident led to bitterness between the saint and the prince.

The latter even thought of taking action against the Sheikh, but a Mongol invasion cut short the thread of his life. Sheikh Salim Chishti had great influence with emperor Akbar, much more than Sadruddin Arif had in the time of Balban. And both Badaoni and Father Monserrate make unflattering comments about Sheikh Salim. The Sufi Mashaikh lived a full-fledged life, different from saints of other religions. But among Indian Muslims their memory has always been cherished with utmost reverence.

It is said that saint-worship among Muslims is a practice unique to India. *Dargahs* of Sufis, real or figurative, are found all over the country and Muslims flock to them in large numbers. It is a legacy of medieval times. One reason for this can be that most Indian Muslims are converted Hindus, who, when their places of worship were converted into (*khanqahs* and later) *dargahs,* did not give up visiting them. For instance, at the most holy *dargah* of Sheikh Muinuddin Chishti, the Sandal Khana mosque is believed to have been built on the site of a Dev temple. The other is that stories of miracles of saints give a hope and a chance to people to obtain fulfilment of their desires. Hence besides Muslims, a few Hindus also resort to such shrines.

THE INTERACTION OF ISLAM AND HINDUISM

AN Aspect of the cultural life of Islamic India that demands special consideration is the nature of the interaction of faith and practice that took place between Islam and Hinduism.

There are, however, a variety of factors involved that make the study of this interaction exceedingly complex and prevent any very assured conclusions being attained. One is simply the lack of evidence, for the religious movements of medieval India have left few records.

Then there is the uncertainty at times whether a pattern of behavior and belief in both religions has a common origin in one, or if it grew up independently in both cultures. The intricate question of the relation of Hindu and Islamic mystical movements is an example of this difficulty.

Finally, since one is confronted not just with the problem of identifying Islamic influence on Hinduism but also Hindu influences on Islam, it is clear that the process of interaction may be complicated by a double movement. Original Hindu influences, for example, may have passed over into Islam; the movement or process that resulted from this may then in turn influence Hinduism, causing a rather different phenomenon. Mysticism again provides a possible illustration.

The most obvious result of the religious impact of Islam on Hinduism is, of course, the existence of a large Muslim population in India. The view that Islam propagated itself in India through the sword cannot be maintained; aside from other evidence, the very distribution of the Muslim population does not support it. If the spread of Islam had been due to the might of the Muslim kings, one would expect the largest proportion of Muslims in those areas which were the centers of Muslim political power. This, however, is not the case.

The percentage of Muslims is low around Delhi, Lucknow, Ahmadabad, Ahmadnagar, and Bijapur, the principal seats of Muslim political power. Even in the case of Mysore, where Sultan Tipu is said to have forced conversion to Islam, the ineffectiveness of royal proselytism may be measured by the fact that Muslims are scarcely 5 percent of the total population of the state.

On the other hand, Islam was never a political power in Malabar, yet today Muslims form nearly 30 percent of its total population. In the two areas in which the concentration of Muslims is heaviest—modern East and West Pakistan—there is fairly clear evidence that conversion was the work of Sufis, mystics who migrated to India throughout the period of the sultanate.

In the western area the process was facilitated in the thirteenth century by the thousands of Muslim theologians, saints, and missionaries who fled to India to escape the Mongol terror. The names and careers of some of these are well known.

Thus Pir Shams Tabriz came to Multan; Khwaja Qutb-ud-din Bakhtiyar went to Delhi; and Syed Jalal settled in Uch, the great fortress south of Multan. The influence of such men, and of many others, can be traced through the families of their spiritual descendants.

In Bengal, the Muslim missionaries found the greatest response to their message among the outcastes and the depressed classes, of which there were large numbers in Bengal. To them, the creed of Islam, with its emphasis on equality, must have come as a liberating force.

Then too, the acceptance of the religion of the conquerors would have been a powerful attraction, since it would undoubtedly carry with it possibilities of advancement they had never known before. Another factor in the large number of conversions is the somewhat peculiar religious history of Bengal. From the eighth to the twelfth century the Pala dynasty had supported Buddhism. Then in the twelfth century the Sena dynasty, which had its roots in South India, began to encourage Hindu orthodoxy.

The result was probably a good deal of religious unrest and uncertainty, which made it possible for Islam to find an opening for its work of proselytization.

When the Islamic missionaries arrived they found in several instances that the conquering armies had destroyed both the temples of revived Hinduism and the monasteries of the older Buddhism; in their place—often on the same sites—they built new shrines. Moreover, they very frequently transferred ancient Hindu and Buddhist stories of miracles to Muslim saints, fusing the old religion into the new on a level that could be accepted by the masses.

By the end of the fourteenth century Islam had permeated all parts of India, and the process was fully under way which led to the conversion of a large section of the Indian population to Islam, and resulted in far-reaching cultural and spiritual changes outside the Muslim society.

The developments in the cultural sphere—development of regional languages, the rise of Hindustani, and the evolution of Indo-Muslim music and architecture—have been outlined in the preceding chapter; here an attempt will be made to examine those religious movements which seem to owe something to the interaction of Hinduism and Islam.

The process of interaction is undeniably obscure, and knowledge of many vital links is lacking, but what is certain is that the period was of great importance for the development of the religious and cultural traditions of modern India. The fifteenth century, it has been observed, "was marked by an extraordinary outburst of devotional poetry inspired by these religious movements, and this stands out as one of the great formative periods in the history of northern India, a period in which on the one hand the modern languages were firmly established as vehicles of literary expression, and on the other the faith of the people was permeated by new ideas."

The religious schools and movements which arose in the fifteenth and sixteenth centuries are generally characterized as variants of bhakti, or devotional religion, and the influence of Islam has been seen as a determining factor. This understanding of the movements is, however, an oversimplification of a very complex phenomenon.

It is important to remember, first of all, that many of the elements associated with the religious movements at the end of the sultanate had already been dominant in Hinduism itself for many centuries. This is especially true of those areas of South India where Muslim influence had not been strong.

It is also quite possible that the Islamic mystics, the Sufis, had been directly or indirectly influenced by Hindu thought and institutions before the conquest of India. Hinduism in the fifteenth century, then, was receiving in an elaborated form what it had already given to Islam.

But of even greater importance in examining the religious movements of the fourteenth and fifteenth centuries is an awareness of two very different attitudes which Hindu religious leaders had toward Islam. One group accepted what was congenial to it in the new spiritual system; the other group adopted a few elements from the spiritual structure of the dominant race in order to strengthen Hinduism and make it better able to withstand Islam.

Both reacted to Islam, but one was sympathetic while the other was hostile. The two trends are similar to the growth of the tolerant, cosmopolitan Brahmo Samaj and the militant Arya Samaj, when Hinduism was confronted with Christianity in the nineteenth century.

Kabir, Guru Nanak, Dadu, and other founders of syncretic sects are included in the first group, while the movement in Bengal, associated with Chaitanya, mirrors the latter tendency.

RELIGIOUS LEADERS

One of the earliest of the religious leaders, and probably the most influential, was Kabir. His dates are uncertain, some scholars giving his birth date as 1398, and some as late as 1440, but it is generally agreed that he flourished in the middle of the fifteenth century.

There has also been much controversy concerning his religious origins, but it is quite certain that he was born into a Muslim family. The names of Kabir and Kamal, his son, are both Islamic. According to the popular *Tazkirah-i-Auliya-i-Hind* (Lives of Muslim Saints), he was a disciple of the Muslim Sufi, Shaikh Taqi.

A further indication of his Muslim origin is that his grave at Maghar has always been in the keeping of Muslims. But Kabir was above all a religious radical who denounced with equal zest the narrowness of Islamic and Hindu sectarianism.

According to one tradition he was a disciple of Ramananda, the great mystic who is credited with the spread of bhakti doctrines in North India. That Ramananda himself was influenced by Islam is not certain, but his willingness to admit men of all castes, including Islam, as his disciples, suggests the possibility of this.

The right conclusion seems to be that Kabir was a Muslim Sufi who, having come under Ramananda's influence, accepted some Hindu ideas and tried to reconcile Hinduism and Islam. However it was the Hindus, and particularly those of the lower classes, to whom his message appealed.

With many of his works not available for study, and serious doubts existing about the genuineness of others, it is difficult to assess Kabir properly, but there is no difference of opinion about the general tenor of his writings. He often uses Hindu religious nomenclature, and is equally at home in Hindu and Muslim religious thought, but there is no doubt that one of the most salient features of his teachings is denunciation of polytheism, idolatry, and caste.

But he is equally unsparing in his condemnation of Muslim formalism, and he made no distinction between what was sane and holy in the teachings of Hinduism and Islam. He was a true seeker after God, and did his best to break the barriers that separated Hindus from Muslims. What has appealed to the millions of his followers through the ages, however, is his passionate conviction that he had found the pathway to God, a pathway accessible to the lowest as well as the highest. That he has in the course of time become a saint of the Hindus rather than of the Muslims is a reflection of the temper of Hinduism, which finds it easier than Islam to bring new sects and doctrines within its spiritual hegemony.

The second great religious leader whose work shows undoubted Islamic influence is Guru Nanak (1469–1539). The Sikh religion, of which Nanak was the founder, is noted for its militant opposition to Islam, but this is largely a product of historical circumstances in the seventeenth century.

Nanak's own aim was to unite both Hindu and Muslim through an appeal to what he considered the great central truths of both. He acknowledged Kabir as his spiritual teacher, and their teachings are very similar.

His debt to Islam is shown in his rigorous insistence on the will and majesty of God, while the underlying structure of his thought, with its tendency to postulate a unity that comprehends all things, suggests his Hindu inheritance. Accompanied by two companions, one a Muslim and the other a Hindu, he wandered throughout North India and, according to some accounts, to Arabia, preaching his simple gospel. The followers he gained became, in the course of a century, a separate religious community, but the Sikh scriptures, of which Nanak's sayings provide the core, are a reminder of the attempt to bridge the gap between Hinduism and Islam.

Dadu (1544–1603) was the third of the religious leaders through whose teachings Islamic ideas found wide currency among non-Muslims. While he does not belong chronologically in a survey of the early interaction of Hinduism and Islam, since he lived into the seventeenth century, his membership in a Kabir sect makes a brief consideration of his career useful.

Furthermore, his biography shows the same process at work that is seen in the accounts of the life of Kabir. Dadu is stated by his later followers to have been the son of a Nagar Brahman, but recent researches have shown that he was born in a family of Muslim cotton-carders. This is borne out by his own works and the fact that all the members of his family have Muslim names: his father's name was Lodi, his mother's, Basiran; his sons were Garib and Miskin and his grandson, Faqir.

His teacher was Shaikh Budhan, a Muslim saint of the Qadri order. The early Hindu followers of Dadu were not disturbed by the knowledge that he was a Muslim by birth, but later ones were. The legend of his Brahmanical origin made its first appearance in a commentary on the *Bhaktamala,* written as late as 1800.

It is said that until recent times documents existed at the monasteries of the followers of Dadu which suggested that he had been a Muslim, but that these were destroyed by the keepers who were unwilling to admit that his origins were not Hindu.

The metamorphosis which the life story and teachings of Kabir and Dadu have undergone is not merely the work of those who were anxious to secure for their heroes high lineage and a link with Hinduism; it is symptomatic of the general movement of separation that became common in both Islam and Hinduism in later centuies.

As the Muslims grew more orthodox, they turned away from men such as Kabir and Dadu, while the Hindus accepted them as saints, but forgot their Islamic origins. In order to conform to the requirements of the Hindu bhakti tradition, they have undergone a transformation that at times necessitates a falsification of history. Two poet-saints who are clearly in the Hindu Bhakti tradition but show traces of Islamic influence are Namadeva and Tukaram, the great religious figures of the Maratha country. Namadeva, who lived in the late fourteenth or early fifteenth century, used a number of Persian and Arabic words, suggesting that even at this early time the influence of Islam was felt by a man, in a remote area of the country, whose only concern seems to have been with religion. The writings of Tukaram (1598–1649), the greatest of the Marathi poets, contain many obvious references to Islam, such as the following:

First among the great names is Allah, never forget to respect it.
Allah is verily one, the prophet is verily one.
There Thou art one, there Thou art one, There Thou art one, O friend.
There is neither I nor thou.

In general the attitude of the Marathas to Muslim saints was one of respect, the most vivid example of this being the great faith Shivaji's grandfather had in Shah Sharif of Ahmadnagar.

In honour of the saint he gave his sons the names of Shahji and Sharifji. While a full study of the religious and social ferment of Maharashtra in the fifteenth and sixteenth centuries has yet to be made; it seems certain that the new religious life did not take the form of a Hindu revivalism that emphasized the separation of the Hindus from Islam.

Antagonism toward Muslims came later, and, as was the case with the Sikhs, had definite antecedents in particular historical events.

The creative spiritual and literary movement provided the basis on which the Maratha nation could be built, and its emergence as the great antagonist of Muslim power in India was based on political, not religious, factors.

The evidence from the songs of Namadeva and Tukaram strongly suggests that they were not reacting in any hostile fashion to Islam. For this reaction one must look to Chaitanya and the Vaishnavite movement in Bengal.

Chaitanya (1485–1533) of Bengal represents an aspect of the Bhakti movement that is very different from that seen in the lives and teachings of Kabir and his successors. Chaitanya's concern, unlike that of Kabir, was not with bringing people to an understanding of a God beyond all creeds and formulations; it was to exalt the superiority of Krishna over all other deities.

It was, in other words, a revivalist, not a syncretic, movement, a return to a worship of Vishnu under one of his most appealing forms, the loving ecstatic Krishna. The attitude of Bengal Vaishnavites toward Islam was the antithesis of the attitude advocated by Kabir and Nanak. Conscious of the appeal being made by Islam, they did not try to reform Hinduism by adopting any of the attractive features of the rival faith. Instead, they emphasized precisely those features, such as devotion to Krishna, which were most antipathetic to the Islamic spirit. Another difference between Chaitanya's movement and that of Kabir is the attitude toward caste.

While it is true that Chaitanya made disciples from all classes, one does not find the same note of condemnation of caste as one does in Kabir. According to some students of the period, this indicates the essential difference between the two aspects of Bhakti in the fifteenth and sixteenth centuries: only where Hinduism was directly influenced by Islam was there evidence of concern for social inequities.

Because of the interest that is attached to such great names as that of Kabir, there is a tendency to think of the movement of interaction between the two faiths as mainly from Islam to Hinduism.

This was not true, however, for Muslim society was deeply influenced by its contacts with Hinduism. Some contacts had been made even before Islamic rule was established in India; for example the probable Hindu element in certain forms of Islamic mysticism, and the intellectual interchanges that had taken place after the conquest of Sind in the seventh and eighth centuries. During the sultanate, changes of a quite different order were apparent.

One of these concerns the lives of converts to Islam. Here the important point to keep in mind is that when one sees Hindu practices followed by Indian Muslims, it is not a case of Hindu influence, but simply of incomplete change from the old way of life.

Indian Muslims did not start with orthodox Islam, but began by accepting a few basic features, and only in the course of time, particularly during the last two centuries, have they become more orthodox.

The process is less complete in the lower classes, or those groups which, like the Khojas, adopted a somewhat composite form of religion. More than religious beliefs, Indian Islam retained certain characteristic features of Hindu society which, if not religious in themselves, certainly had been given religious sanction. One of these was the place given to caste, with converts clinging to some memory of their former status in a hierarchical society, while what may be called Muslim castes developed as Indian Muslims classified themselves as Sayyid, Shaikh, Mughal, or Pathan.

This structure was never very rigid; as Bernier commented, anyone who put on a white turban called himself a Mughal. An old saying makes the same point: "Last year I was a Julaha (weaver); this year a Shaikh; and next year if the harvest be good, I shall be a Sayyid." And in the mosque the Islamic ideals of brotherhood and equality remained triumphant.

Bibliography

Adikaram, E. W.: *Early History of Buddhism in Ceylon,* D. S. Puswella, Migoda, 1946.

Amin Qazvini, *Badshah Nama,* Ms. Raza Library, Rampur.

Bagchi, P. C.: *Studies in Dharmashastra,* University of Calcutta Press, Calcutta, 1939.

Borchert, Bruno: *Mysticism: Its History and Challenge,* Samuel Wiser, York Beach, 1994.

Bowle, John: *The Imperial Achievement: The Rise and Transformation of the British Empire,* Little, Brown, 1974.

Brooks, E.: *The Original Analects: Sayings of Confucius and His Successors.* Columbia University Press, New York, 1988.

Chandra, Satish : *History of Medieval India,* New Delhi: Orient Longman, 2007.

Chaudhary, M.: *Partition and the Curse of Rehabilitation,* Calcutta, Bengal Rehabilitation Organization, 1964.

Coomeraswamy, Ananda K.: *Buddha and the Gospel of Buddhism,* MacMillan, London, 1928.

Dalton, Dennis : *Gandhi's Power : Nonviolence in Action,* New Delhi, OUP, 2001.

Das, Kamal Kishore: *Economic History of Moghul India: An Annotated Bibliography, 1526-1875.* Calcutta: Santiniketan, 1991.

Doniger, W.: *The Rig Veda: An Anthology,* Penguin, New York, 1981.

Duboi, Abbe: *Hindu Manners, Customs and Ceremonies,* Fifth Indian Impression, CUP, 1985.

Edwardes, Michael: *Battles of the Indian Mutiny,* London; B. T. Batsford Ltd., 1963.

Fay, Peter Ward: *The Opium War, 1840-42,* University of North Carolina Press, 1975.

Frauwallner, E..: *History of Indian Philosophy,* Motilal, Delhi, 1973.

Goradia, Nayana: *Lord Curzon: The Last of the British Moghuls,* New Delhi,

Oxford University Press, 1993.

Gurcharn Singh Sandhu: *A Military History of Medieval India*, Vision Books, Delhi, 2003.

Gurumurthy, S. : *Hindu Heritage, Assimilative, Not Divisive*, Vigil, Madras 1993.

Heimann, Betty: *Facets of Indian Thought*, Geroge Allen & Unwin, London, 1964.

Hirschman, Edwin: *White Mutiny: The Ilbert Bill Crisis in India and the Genesis of the Indian National Congress*, New Delhi, Heritage, 1980.

Hopkirk, Peter: *The Great Game: The Struggle for Empire in Central Asia*, Kodansha, 1992.

Husain, A. M.: *The Rise and Fall of Muhammad bin Tughluq*. London, 1938.

Ikram, S.M. : *Muslim Civilization in India*, New York:Columbia University Press, 1964.

Ira Mervin Lapidus, *Muslim Cities in the Later Middle Ages*, Cambridge, Mass, 1967.

Jonathan Bloom: *The Art and Architecture of Islam, 1250-1800*, Pelican History of Art. New Haven, 1994.

Kalika Prasad Tiwari: *Foundations of Indian Culture*, Pointer Publishers, Delhi, 2001.

Kaviraj, G.: *Aspects of Indian Thought*, University of Burdwan, Calcutta, 1966.

Knipe, M.: *Hinduism: Experiments in the Sacred*, Harper, San Francisco, 1991.

Kosambi, D. D. : *The Culture and Civilisation of Ancient India in Historical Outline*, London, Routledge and Kegan Paul, 1956.

Lai, K.S., *History of the Khaljis*, Asia Publishing House, Bombay, 1967.

MacIver R.M. : *Society, An Introductory Analysis*, Rinehart and Company, New York 1949.

Moin, Zaidi, A. : *Evolution of Muslim Political Thought in India*, New Delhi: S. Chand, 1975.

Neale, Walter C.: *Economic Change in Rural India: Land Tenure and Reform in the United Provinces, 1800-1955*, New Haven, 1962.

Oddie, G.A. : *Hindu and Christian in South-East India*, London, Curzon Press, 1991.

Okada, Amina: *Indian Miniatures of the Mughal Court*, New York, Harry N. Abrahms, Inc. Publishers, 1992.

Peter S.: *The Early Islamic Architecture of the East African Coast*, British Institute of History and Archaeology in East Africa, Nairobi, 1966.

Poole: Stanley. *Medieval India under Mohammedan Rule, A.D. 712-1764*. New York, 1903; Calcutta, 1951.

Qureshi, I. H.: *The Administration of the Sultanate of Delhi.* Lahore, 1944.

Richards, J. F. : *The Mughal Empire*, New York: Cambridge University Press, 1993.

Satyamurthy, T.V.: *Region, Religion, Caste, Gender and Culture in Contemporary India*, Delhi, OUP, 1996.

Sharma, Sri Ram, *The Religious Policy of the Mughal Emperors*, Asia Publishing House, Bombay, 1962.

Singh Sandhu: *A Military History of Medieval India*, Vision Books, Delhi, 2003.

Smith, V.A., *Akbar the Great Mogul,* Delhi, 1962.

Stephen Carr.: *Archaeology and Monumental Remains of Delhi*, Calcutta, 1876.

Thevenot : *Indian Travels of Thevenot and Careri*, New Delhi, 1949.

Trimingham, J.: *Sufi Orders in Islam*, Oxford University Press, New York, 1998.

Tughlaq, Firoz Shah , *Fatuhat-i-Firoz Shahi,* Aligarh, 1943.

Visvantha, K.: *Essentials of Hinduism,* Narosa Pub. House, New Delhi, 1989.

Vivian, W. : *Mine Managers Reports 1855-57*, Unpublished UCNW Archives, Bangor, 1856.

Yadav, Kripal Chandra : *India's Unequal Citizens : A Study of Other Backward Classes,* Manohar, New Delhi, 1994.

Zaidi, A. Moin: *Evolution of Muslim Political Thought in India,* New Delhi: S. Chand, 1975.

Index

❑❑❑

www.ingramcontent.com/pod-product-compliance
Ingram Content Group UK Ltd.
Pitfield, Milton Keynes, MK11 3LW, UK
UKHW042018290726
14061UKWH00001BB/69

9 789395 034371